Khadi and Village Industries in North-East India

About the Editor

Dr. Ram Krishna Mandal completed his graduation with honours in Economics from Balurghat College, Balurghat (West Bengal) and did his M. A. in Economics with Distinction, M.Phil. and Ph.D. in Economics, BLIS and B.Ed. from the North Bengal University, Darjeeling (West Bengal). Dr. Mandal has to his credit 55 published research papers in National and International Journals.

Dr. Mandal has to his credit 12 (Twelve) books on various economic issues, some are particularly on North-East India. He has three UGC sponsored research projects in his credit. He is also a Post Doctoral Research Awardee UGC Fellow. Presently he is an Associate Professor in Economics in Dera Natung Govt. College, Itanagar, Arunachal Pradesh.

Khadi and Village Industries in North-East India

Challenges and Opportunities

Edited by

RAM KRISHNA MANDAL

CONCEPT PUBLISHING COMPANY PVT. LTD.

New Delhi - 1100059

ISBN-13 : 978-81-8069-880-4

First Published 2013

Published and Printed by

Concept Publishing Company Pvt. Ltd.
A/15-16, Commerical Block, Mohan Garden
New Delhi - 110059 (India)
T : 25351460, 25351794, F : 091-11-25357109
E : publishing@conceptpub.com, W : www.conceptpub.com
Editorial Office : H-13, Bali Nagar, New Delhi-110015, India

Cataloging in Publication Data--*Courtesy:* D.K. Agencies (P) Ltd. <docinfo@dkagencies.com>

Khadi and village industries in North-East India : challenges and opportunities / edited by Ram Krishna Mandal.
p. cm.
Includes bibliographical references and index.
ISBN 9788180698804

1. Cottage industries—India, Northeastern—Congresses. 2. Rural industries Government policy—India, Northeastern—Congresses. 3. Small business—India, Northeastern—Congresses. 4. Entrepreneurship—India, Northeastern—Congresses. 5. Rural development—India, Northeastern—Congresses. 6. India. Khadi and Village Industries Commission—Congresses. I. Mandal, Ramkrishna, 1966-

DDC 338.6309541 23

Dedicated to

Archana Mandal (Wife),

Miss Anusree Krishna Mandal (Daughter) and

Master Avinandan Krishna Mandal (Son)

Preface

Economic development of any region is an outcome of purposeful human activity. Both the developed and the underdeveloped world look at the industrialization process as an important key to economic development. Most of the social scientists agree that man stands at the centre of economic activity and he assumes various roles in the development process, namely, as an organizer of human and material resources, worker, consumer and exchange agent. Out of these multiple role, his role as the organizer of human and material resources is the most important and basic one.

All the states of the North-East region are a homeland of a large number of tribes. The development of villages has become the need of the hour, especially the hill villages in North-East India. Basic necessities of life of these people are much lower than that of the people living in the town or city. The tribal hill village, particularly in the North-East is quite different from other villages in the country. They have some uniqueness in their structure, socially, culturally, and economically. Social life here is organized along definite ritual and secular principles, such as those of caste, kinship, economy, politics, and religion. The economic system of these communities revolves around their social structure.

The main principle of Gandhian approach is to set up a system of village self-sufficiency. In this regard, the hypothesis of M.K. Gandhi was establishment of 'gram swaraj' in the country side which means the complete independence of the Indian villages. The ultimate goal of Gandhian planning was to make Indian villages fully independent. Mahatma Gandhi often used to say that the real India was to be found in the villages, not in the cities and towns. In his hypothesis of gram swaraj M.K. Gandhi explained that every village should produce all needed crops, food and non-food items. Each village should possibly produce its own goods such as cloth, shoes and leather products and similarly a village should have essential amenities, such as schools, hospitals, entertainment facilities and playground. Gandhiji's assumption was that India lives in villages and majority of its population depends on agriculture and its allied occupations. In case of gram swaraj is established, India would get naturally an economic freedom and would stand as a prosperous and independent country in the world.

The present volume is a collection of twenty papers contributed to the seminar by eminent scholars, academicians, policy makers, bureaucrats and thinkers. The publication of this book would not have been possible unless the seminar has been organized. In organizing the seminar we have received supports and cooperation from different persons and institutions that we thankfully acknowledge. At the very outset, I express my deep gratitude to Chief Guest, Prof. Tamo Mibang, Director,Arunachal Institute of Tribal Studies, Rajiv Gandhi University, Rono Hills, Itanagar, Arunachal Pradesh, Guest of Honour, Prof. Amitava Mitra, Department of Economics, Rajiv Gandhi University, Rono Hills, Itanagar, Arunachal Pradesh and also Guest of Honour, Dr. Tejum Padu, Joint Director, Higher and Technical Education, Government of Arunachal Pradesh, Itanagar, Arunachal Pradesh who kindly inaugurated the seminar and delivered their valuable inaugural speech. Chief Guest, Prof. Tamo Mibang, Director, Arunachal Institute of Tribal Studies, Rajiv Gandhi University, Rono Hills, Itanagar, Arunachal Pradesh deserves a special thank for his kind presence and gracing the participants through his keynote address on the seminar. I feel obliged to our Principal, Mr. Tomar Ete and Vice-Principal, Mr. Tageng Tamuk, for their constant cooperation, encouragement and guidance in organizing the seminar. I would be falling in my duty if I do not extend my gratitude to our Ex-Principal, Mrs. Uma Dutta for generating in me an interest to organize a seminar in the college.

In the valedictory function, I am also thankful to the Chief Guest Prof. J.S. Panwar, Professor and Head, Postgraduate Department of Business Management, Sardar Patel University, Gujarat and the Guest of Honour Dr. Yogesh C. Joshi, Associate Professor of Economics, Postgraduate Department of Business Management, Sardar Patel University, Gujarat for the distribution of certificates to the participants. We are very much encouraged by the wide response from the scholars from the different parts of India and abroad. I express a deep sense of gratitude to all the contributors in the volume.

I owe the debt of gratitude to the chair persons, Prof. J. S. Panwar, Professor and Director, Postgraduate Department of Business Management, Sardar Patel University, Vallabh Vidyanagar, Anand District, Gujarat, Dr. R.P. Bhattacharje, Deputy Director, North-Eastern Regional Institute of Science and Technology, Nirjuli, Itanagar, Arunachal Pradesh, Dr. P.C. Dutta, Associate Professor and Head, Department of Statistics, S.S. College, Hailakandi, Assam and Dr. Yogesh C. Joshi, Associate Professor of Economics, PG Department of Business Management, Sardar Patel University, Vallabh Vidyanagar, Anand District, Gujarat who has presided the first, second, third and fourth technical sessions respectively very efficiently.

I am very much thankful to Mrs. Madhuparna Bhattacharjee, Associate Professor of Geography, Dera Natung Govt. College, Itanagar who has constantly discharged her duty as a rapporteur in the seminar. I also express my gratitude to my colleague, Dr. A.I. Singh, Associate Professor of Economics who constantly helped me in organizing this seminar. I extend my sincere thanks to all my colleagues and also to all my dear students especially of B.A. second and third year honours who have shared with me all the troubles and pains in organizing the seminar and made it successful.

I am also sincerely grateful to The Director, Indian Council of Social Science Research (ICSSR), New Delhi for providing the financial assistance to hold the seminar. I am also taking the opportunity to thank profusely to **Concept Publishing Company (P) Ltd.** for publication of this book.

Lastly, I owe my apology to my wife, Mrs. Archana Mandal and my children Miss Anusree Krishna Mandal and Master Avinandan Krishna Mandal who have to bear the loss of my company during the work of the seminar and this book.

Ram Krishna Mandal

Contents

Section-III
Empirical Study

Section-IV
Entrepreneurial Development

Introduction

North-East Region (NER) was popularly known as the Land of 'seven sisters' consisting of the States of Arunachal Pradesh, Assam, Manipur, Meghalaya, Mizoram, Nagaland and Tripura. In 1971, following the North-Eastern Reorganization Act, 1971, the state of Assam was constitutionally recognized and Meghalaya, Manipur and Tripura became full-fledged states. But Mizoram and the erstwhile NEFA (present Arunachal Pradesh) were made Union Territories. In 1987, these two Union Territories were elevated to the status of states. These states are comparatively small in area and also in population. It was felt necessary to involve interstate cooperation in sharing of costs of building basic infrastructure for the development of the region. Consequently, in 1971 another important Act was passed to establish in 1972 the North-Eastern Council (NEC) as an advisory body for formulating regional development plans with these seven states as members. Recently, the State of Sikkim also has come under the umbrella of this region owing to its proximity to the area and somewhat similar type of developmental and other problems. For the purpose of development activities, Sikkim has also come under the purview of the North-Eastern Council, which is a Regional Planning Body, by an Act of Parliament, in December, 2002 as per the NEC Reorganization Act. This Act provided for the inclusion of Sikkim as a member of the NEC. Presently for development purposes, the NER consists of eight states i.e., Arunachal Pradesh, Assam, Manipur, Meghalaya, Mizoram, Nagaland, Tripura, and Sikkim.

All the States of this region, except Assam are mostly hilly. Assam is also having hilly regions, but it is comparatively less than the plain areas of the state. The states of this region are very much unique in their own ways. There is a wide variation in the altitude ranging from 300 to 5000 metres. The NER of India occupies a strategic geo-political situation due to its international boundaries with Bangladesh, Bhutan, China, Myanmar and Nepal. No doubt, these states constitute a homogeneous natural region of the hills, plains, valleys, flora and fauna and other related geographical features. Though the NER reflects some ecological and cultural adaptive contrasts between the hills and the plains, there are also significant elements of continuity in the biological, cultural and social factors between these segments. Also, as per available records, we find a lot of independence and interactions between the hills and the plains in this region. The North-Eastern mosaic is a replica of the Indian mosaic but with the prominence of some other special ingredients. There are nearly 150 ethnic groups and sub-groups. All the known anthropological offshoots, e.g., Negroids, Mongoloids, Austro-Asiatic, Tibeto-Burmans, and the equally important Caucasians are here in the North-Eastern part of India with Assam having more than 20 major ethnic groups.

The total Geographical Area (notional area) of the NER including Sikkim is 2,63,179 sq. km. accounting for 7.9 per cent of the total land space of the country. These eight states of NER together have a total population of 3,88,57,769 as per 2001 Census and constitute about 3.8 per cent of the total population of the country (NEDFi, quarterly data bank, 2005). The state of Assam, though, is the second largest in area, but it is the homeland of the highest number of persons i.e., 68.60 per cent of the population of this region with an equally highest density of 340 persons per sq. km. The State of Arunachal Pradesh is though the largest, but there is only 2.28 per cent of population of this region with a density of 13 persons per sq. km. which is the lowest in this region. NER of India with its absolute pristine virginal territory remains completely unexplored. The valley is beautified with lush green vegetation, grandiose mountains and feral rivers. North-east India is also abode of exceptional range of flora and fauna and the brilliant tribal life. North-east Indian tribes are perhaps some of the most mysterious and yet most studied and observed band in the country, with host of things to offer in a slice of everyday life.

"India lives in villages". Because, 72.18 per cent of its population is living in rural areas and only 27.82 per cent lives in urban areas. This is also very true in context of the NER as it is seen that 84.34 per cent of people of this region is living in the rural areas only and 15.66 per cent of people is living in urban areas. One of the bases of Indian economic growth has been the transformation of the hill-forest regions for the use of the mineral resources therein, and the utilization of the hydropower and irrigation potential. These developments have increased power availability, irrigated water to increase agricultural productivity and the development of an industrial base. The benefits of these developments, however, have been largely concentrated among Indians in the plains, including workers who have secured employment. The inhabitants of the hill-forest regions, the indigenous people (or Scheduled Tribes as they are legally termed) on the other hand, have had to bear the brunt of involuntary displacement and destruction of their traditional livelihoods through mines, dams, etc. (Nathan, Dev, 2009). States viz. Arunachal Pradesh, Meghalaya, Mizoram and Nagaland are tribal dominated states. So far North-East region is concerned, it is a new approach. The region has been neglected even by the centre so long and is lagging behind on all fronts, so far any type of modern resources are concerned. And to talk about the tribal population in the NER and the Impact of Globalization on Tribal Women of North-East, is completely a new concept.

The impact of globalization on socio-economic life of tribals of North-East cannot be ruled out. If a part of change occurs, evolution and revolution on the totality of life are likely to take place. The impact on traditional lifestyle of tribals is unavoidable but there is need to prevent loss of indigenous knowledge systems besides ethnicity. When we think of the social problems faced by women, it is true that the women of North-East are deprived of several privileges as enjoyed by their counterparts in advanced states. Education may be one of the major factors for the women of North-East not making much progress in life, especially to fight for the legitimate rights. But much more important is the grip the man exercises over the society through the age old social taboos, forcing the women to play a subdued role in the development process. The women are subjugated to various myths and beliefs and the lack of ignorance about their rights have made their life restricted to doing household duties and raising their family.

After the opening of the NER some decade past people have been witnessing significant socio-economic and political development and having the influence of new scored high in respect of well-being of women in the region. Socially advanced Meitei dominated Manipur has ranked top followed by tribal dominated Nagaland and Mizoram. Other states except Assam with lack of social and infrastructural development has brought tribal people at the lower standard with existing socio-economic backwardness particularly among the Scheduled Tribes. In-migration has been a major factor of demographic change. This affects the social behaviour, economic condition, employment and even political atmosphere. This migration has affected very badly the tribal life in North-East region.

Handloom, handicraft, cottage industries, woollen product, brass metal, cane and bamboo, village industries, agriculture based industries is the field where tribal women are engaged at home along with their household work. The products are limited if proper infrastructures are provided they may increase the production, they will be benefited in the competition with globalization. They gain and add to the knowledge of the world community. Not much impact has been on the surface since there is no easy communication and contact from outside. However, globalization during the modern period of history of the world was attempted at the initiative of the member countries of the Non-aligned Movement in 1975 when they initiated a move in the General Assembly of the United Nations Organization. At their initiative, the programme was adopted by the U.N. General Assembly which included (i) opening Northern markets to Southern industrial exports, (ii) improving terms of trade for tropical agricultural products and minerals, (iii) better access to international finance, and (iv) creating more normal condition for technology transfer. Simultaneously, the developed industrial countries made a countermove against this programme by taking advantage of stiff rise in oil price and debt trap to impose current pattern of globalization consisting of five monopolies: (a) technological monopoly, (b) control of worldwide financial markets, (c) monopoly access to planet's natural resources, (d) media and communication monopoly, (e) monopoly of weapons of mass destruction.

In 1991, the industrialized countries fostered their own model of globalization which has become a new mantra for integration of national economics with the world economy. It is being carried out through removal of barriers on the way of flow of trade, capital, technologies and labour across national frontiers with a view to export led growth. The process of globalization started in Indian Economy in 1991 when India joined the World Trade Organization. Since then, about a decade and half have passed and appraisal of the impact of globalization must be evaluated now to formulate strategic move for the future course of action. Linkage multiplicity, interconnections between the different states, societies, which opens the door for economic, cultural goods, technology, labour etc. may be termed as globalization. This affects greatly the integration in several manners on the national eoncomy, multinational production corporations' foreign direct investments, consumption, production etc.

Coming to the question of globalization in the context of NER, we find that the region is lagging behind on all fronts so far as the technology aided articulations of its resources are concerned. The issue is further complicated by the fact that the study of the tribal women in the NER is a new concept arising out of the worldwide emphasis over empowerment of women. The declaration of General Assembly of the UNO on the "elimination of discrimination against women" has still to go a long way for empowerment of women. However, we cannot sit idle since women's full services and talents are needed alongside those of men for the full and complete development of a country, the welfare of the world and the cause of peace. Thinking on this line, the Research Centre for the Himalayan and Tribal Regions has ventured under the sponsorship of the North-Eastern Council, Shillong to organize the present national seminar to assess and evaluate the attitudinal, structural and functional impacts of Globalization on Women.

In this context it is to be noted that social change is possible only by empowering and educating women. Nehru once said, "to awaken the people, it is women who is meant to be awakened, once she is on the move, the family moves, village moves and the nation moves". Swami Vivekananda also once said, "there is no change for the welfare of the world unless the condition of women is improved. It is not possible for a bird to fly on one wing." Likewise no nation can flourish keeping half of its population in negligence and ignorance, as women constitute half of its human capital. A modern society cannot bring all-round development without utilizing the talent of its women. Tribal women have developed their own interesting design of weaving, knitting, carpet making, wood carving, cane and bamboo work etc., which is locally marketed, and some of them have outside market also, with local materials and skill. On the other side, globalization may help women with opening of socio-cultural, political and economic awareness in the region. Women share equal responsibility with man in this tradition bound subsistence economy in all the states in North-East Region. With development and change in the world on all front of life like economy, culture, political, trade, industry, education to the women movement have been noticed for the rights and welfare which indicate all-round development and awakening. It may be the distance impact of the world family or globalization. To cope up with the global change, tribal women require infrastructural facilities, mobility, new mechanized training, and socio-economic open contact. For that, they require support of the financial institutions, governments' and NGOs' involvement, skill training etc. They can take major share in the development of Khadhi and Village Industries.

The NER is considered as an undifferentiated unit for all practical purposes. For purposes of policy, the most of the socio-economic characteristics of Assam, including poverty ratios have been assigned to the remaining states in NER (GoI, 1993). Even in understanding of development problems and potentials, the region is treated as a homogeneous unit while selecting the sample. It is evident from India's Human Development Report, 1999 in which all the seven states have been clubbed together into a NER category and data collected from Assam have been made the basis to draw inference on NER as a whole. In fund allocation, the states are not considered separately. Each Central Department/Ministry (except those exempted) is required to earmark at least 10 per cent of Gross Budget support for the Region. Evidently, there have been no serious efforts to understand the region from its heterogeneous reality. Besides, very little data is available across states making the task of interventions equally difficult. The region is bountifully endowed with biodiversity, hydro-power potential, oil and gas, coal, limestone and forest wealth. It is ideally suited to produce a whole range of plantation crops, spices, fruits and vegetables, flowers and herbs, much of which could be processed and exported to the rest of the country and worldwide. Markets must be developed and problems of transportation, power, infrastructure, finance and services overcome. Its natural beauty, serenity and rich flora and fauna invite trekking and tourism. In terms of potentials the following are the strength of this region:

Tea: North-east produces more than 50 per cent of tea in the country. Tea being an agricultural plantation crop and a major revenue generator, it plays a vital role in improving the socio-economic condition of the States of North-Eastern Region of India. Assam is the largest producer of tea in India.

Bamboo: Bamboos play an important role in the rural economy. Bamboos are a subfamily of grasses that include over 1,200 species worldwide.18 genera and 130 species are so far known from India. The region has abundant bamboo resources. The heavy rainfall and temperate climate has assured an abundance of bamboo and cane in the region over the ages. Out of 136 species of bamboos found in India, 63 species in 22 genera are found in North-east India, spread over an area of 30,500 sq.km.

Tourism: The North-Eastern Region of India with its large untapped potential for development of Tourism, still remains in the backward of development insofar as the tourism sector is concerned. The natural wealth of the region should have changed its own face with significant social and economic development. Each of the eight constituent states of the region has too enormous a potential for development of tourism industry.

Handloom and Handicraft: In the North-East States, KVIC took initiative to put foothold of its presence and established its field officials in the entire region. KVI occupy a unique position in the rural economy of this region and collaborative approach has been initiated. Spices Board of India and Khadi and Village Industries Commission have jointly extended financial and technical support for setting up of spices making units in Assam and Arunachal Pradesh .The Central Leather Research Institute (CLRI) under its

Leather Technology Mission has extended support for setting up leather products manufacturing projects in Manipur and Nagaland. From time immemorial handloom industry has been playing a vital role in the economy of the north-east region. The traditional skill of handloom weaving was not only a status symbol for the women-folk but it was also an indispensable aspect of the socio-economic life of the people in this region. The NER has a rich and fairly ancient tradition of handloom weaving. On a conservative estimate there are about 1.3 million handlooms and nearly 1.4 million weavers in the entire region. The total production of handlooms in the NE region is valued around Rs.1,145 million on an annual basis.

We, all know that the vision of Gandhiji was to achieve self-dependent, self-reliant society through the promotion of Khadi and Village Industries. Before Independence, the development of Khadi and Village Industries was entirely a non-governmental movement under his guidance. Though after independence, the Government of India took the responsibility to bring its development within its framework.

We gained our independence on the principles of Mahatma. But there is still a way to achieve the level of what Gandhiji had thought of. The principles of Gandhiji are equally important today and for future generations to come as it was in the past. KVI sector is getting marginalized and more marginalized as the day goes. India lives in villages, but rural people are swarming in the urban areas to get employment. This important sector can play a vital role in restoring the lost glory of the time tested self-employment model aiming the distribution of wealth employing local resources and promote local talent in order to achieve self-sufficiency.

The village industries and traditional unorganized industries constitute an important segment of the economies of the North-East States where 40 per cent people are living under BPL and more than 80 per cent in the rural belt making agriculture as the main occupation. Today the developing economies, particularly the states of North-East Region are facing the acute problem of unemployment. Formal sector is not sufficient to fulfil this objective that is why; informal sector is given more weightage to create employment through village industries. The People of the North-East States have a rich tradition of craftsmanship and are very adept at crafts such as weaving, woodcarving, carpet weaving, cane and bamboo works, smithy works, etc. Khadi and Village Industries (KVI), therefore, offers enormous prospects for increasing the opportunities for income and employment generation in this region.

Village self-sufficiency: The main principle of Gandhian approach is to set up a system of village self-sufficiency. In this regard, the hypothesis of M.K. Gandhi was establishment of 'Gram Swaraj' in the country side which means the complete independence of the Indian villages. The ultimate goal of Gandhian planning was to make Indian villages fully independent. Mahatma Gandhi often used to say that the real India was to be found in the villages, not in the cities and towns. In his hypothesis of Gram Swaraj M.K. Gandhi explained that every village should produce all needed crops, food and non-food items. Each village should possibly produce its own goods such as cloth, shoes and leather products and similarly a village should have essential amenities, such as schools, hospitals, entertainment facilities and playground. Gandhiji's assumption was that India lives in villages and majority of its population depends on agriculture and its allied occupations. In case of Gram Swaraj is established, India would get naturally an economic freedom and would stand as a prosperous and independent country in the world.

Achievement of Self-employment: We have to generate mass employment at the same time; the produced goods should have sustained market. The investment part should also be affordable. Cloth may be one such commodity which can be bought by all the people irrespective of their economical standard so it has market both sustainable and permanent. Take for example Khadi, though it has great potential to generate employment facilities in the rural areas. Without development of Kadhi and Village Industries it is not possible to generate the employment and side by side to develop the region as well as to develop the quality of tribal people in the region. Keeping in mind of the above phenomenon of development, a National Seminar on the topic, 'The Role of Khadi and Village Industries in Socio-Economic Development of North-East States' sponsored by Indian Council of Social Science Research, New Delhi was organized by the Department of Economics, Dera Natung Govt. College, Itanagar on November 20, 2009. The present volume is a collection of **twenty** papers contributed to the seminar by eminent scholars, academicians, policy-makers, bureaucrats and thinkers.

In the inaugural speech, the Chief Guest, Prof. Tamo Mibang, Director, Arunachal Institute of Tribal Studies, Rajiv Gandhi University, Arunachal Pradesh exhorted in the august gathering that the economic development in North-East Region was not encouraging in comparison to other parts of India. Hence, its policy towards all development needs to be looked into by examining the ground realities and bounties of its natural resources. The clear-cut policy in this regard also would reduce the social tension, he emphasized. The development of Kadhi and Village Industries is very crucial for all-round development of Arunachal Pradesh and the participation of local people is the need of the hour for self-employment, he said. He highlighted the constitutional rights, impact of migration, role of education, ethno-medicine and ethno-technology of the country's scattered tribal groups. He dwelt on the problems of assimilation and marginalization of tribals and pointed out the close relationship of the tribal people with forests. The professor called for committed implementation of sustainable developmental schemes to benefit the tribal people. In the process of industrial development, the importance of cottage industries should not be ignored. To set up heavy industry is not so much possible in different places of this State as its major portions are not easily accessible. But to set up small scale industries in the State is not so much difficult. That is why; top priority must be given to those small scale industries like Khadi and Village Industries which need light machine tools and other equipments in order to produce qualitative products because today, a State's progress is measured by the quality of goods it produces. To strengthen the economy of the State, the Government should provide larger scope to the private sector. At the same time, a number of changes in policy should be introduced with regard to industrial licensing to the non-tribal, removal of Inner Line, technology upgradation, fiscal policy, removal of controls and restrictions, rationalizing and simplifying the system of fiscal and administrative regulation and improving law and order problems so as to encourage for free flow of goods, capital, technology and labour from other States to this State. All these changes will be directed towards creating an uninhabited climate for private sector so that private sector investment can get a big boost to modernize the economy approaching towards global economy. He highlighted that in an age in which mechanical inventions are the prime factor in economic progress, it is difficult to realize that in certain lines, hand-made goods are unsurpassed in excellence by the products of modern machinery. The efforts taken by both Central and State Governments must be made to reach the beneficiaries. The implementing agencies and machineries must take it as a venture with all commitment and positive attitude towards Khadi and Village Industries in the North-East States. The feedback as well as follow-up is very much needed to revive and sustain this sector in the global context.

In the Guest of Honour Speech, Prof. Amitava Mitra, Professor and Head, Department of Economics, Rajiv Gandhi University, Rono Hills, Itanagar, Arunachal Pradesh lamented that progress in health, education and connectivity has not strengthened the state's economy and the state still remains a mere consumer of goods and services. Underscoring the need for interdistrict equality in terms of human development indicators particularly with reference to Kurung Kumey and East Kameng which are the most backward districts in the state. Prof. Mitra said that the backward districts need to be given special attention, particularly in the health and education sectors.

The Special Guest of Honour, Dr. Tejum Padu, Joint Director, Higher and Technical Education, Government of Arunachal Pradesh, Itanagar called Arunachal Pradesh a storehouse of traditional designs in terms of weaving and yarn spinning, not to mention that the people are gifted with natural craftsmanship skills. The Khadhi and Village Industries in the state need to be promoted to boost rural economy and self-employment, Dr. Padu said on the developmental front, he called for committed and dedicated implementation of schemes with target oriented and time bound projects, depending on their feasibility. The khadi cloths have to be incorporated in our life but now it needs some modifications, incorporations of our design in fit. KVI is to be expanded in Arunachal Pradesh in a major way. We have few stall of KVI products here and there in the North-East States. We have not seen major inputs into the development of Khadi in Arunachal Pradesh, we need to make it.

The volume is divided into four sections. The First Section "Present Scenario" focuses on the present position of Khadi and Village Industries in India in general and in North-East States in particular and thereby its issues and policies related to the employment and overall socio-economic development of people. It consists of six articles.

The first article entitled, "Present Scenario of KVI" written by **Mr. Ashok Kumar Saran** highlights elaborately about the network of KVI in the country. Being a Director of KVI, he put forth the practical scenario of KVI in the country in general and in the north-east in practical. He pointed out about the functions of partner agencies in urban and rural areas, its physical performances, New Programmes and Schemes, Quantum and Nature of Financial Assistance, Levels of Funding of Margin Money, Bank Finance, Entrepreneurship Development Programme and Scheme for Enhancing Productivity and Competitiveness of Khadi Industries and Artisans, Rural Industrial Consultancy Service, Rural Industry Service Centre, Marketing and Its Major Achievements Under Marketing. There are also 5,000 Registered Institutions (NGOs) working at the grass roots level for generating employment and helping artisans to uplift their social and economic status.

The second article entitled "Khadi and Village Industries: Strategies for Competing with the Organized Sector" written jointly by **Prof J.S Panwar** and **Dr. Yogesh C. Joshi** focuses on twenty per cent increase of SSI products which is a significant increase since the previous decade. Export of SSI products has also increased because of Government support and application of Innovations in KVIC. Citing the case of Tribhuvan Das Foundation which is a cooperative society of milk producers, the paper emphasizes relevant cooperative movement of KVI sector of North-East Region. Finally, the paper concludes that strategic planning is required for the development of KVIC which should not be uniform for the entire nation but it should be either state specific or region specific.

Next, **Mr. Debabrata Maji** in his paper "An Approach through Pragmatic Model for the Development of KVI Sector in Arunachal Pradesh" demonstrates that Gandhiji launched the Khadi programme in the country in 1919 and the importance of Khadi was realized even after independence in 1947. Subsequently, Khadi and Village Industries Commission is a statutory body established by an act of Parliament in April 1957 for the development of Khadi and Village Industries in India with social objectives of providing employment, economic and creating self-reliance amongst the poor and building up of a strong rural community spirit. The Government of India dissolved the Commission of KVI in October, 2004 and constituted an Expert Committee for revamping KVI due to decline in employment in the Khadi Sector.

The fourth paper "Role of Small-scale and Village Industries in Economic Development of Nepal" written by **Dr. Udaya Raj Regmi** and **Dr. Arjun Kumar Baral** aims at analyzing the role of Small-scale and Village Industries in economic development of Nepal. The performance of these industries has been observed in terms of number of industries, employment generation, production, investment, sources of output growth, total factor productivity, technical efficiency, technological progress and contribution to exports. Divisia Tornquist approximation and production frontier models have been applied to estimate the sources of output growth and total factor productivity of the small and village industries.

The next joint paper entitled "KVI and Its Role in the Socio-Economic Development of Assam" written by **Ms. Mousumi Borah** and **Ms. Sangeeta Kakoty** aims at analyzing the role of KVI in the Socio-Economic development of the state of Assam. Various KVI programmes have been implemented in Assam through its Zonal office located in Guwahati, the State KVI Boards, registered institutions, cooperative societies and entrepreneurs. The rural industries like pottery, beekeeping, processing of cereals and pulses, fibre, fruit and vegetable processing industries, soap, activities like carpentry and blacksmithy are generally being set up in the backward areas of the state. The programmes of Khadi and Village Industries Commission for rural industrialization aims to augment the earning of artisans, weavers, spinners and individual entrepreneurs along with output and high quality KVI products from this state.

The last paper entiled, "Socio-Economic Development of North-Eastern States: Role of Khadi and Village Industries" by **Dr. R.P. Bhattacharje** tries to postulate that the North-Eastern Region is sensitive geographically due to natural isolation amidst rugged terrain. It recently became more sensitive internationally after the claim of China over Arunachal Pradesh on the eve of recent visit of His Holiness Dalai Lama. Despite being rich in natural resources with fertile land, rich forest and mineral deposits, development of the region has lagged behind from the rest of the country due to historical reasons. For proper socio-economic development, it is essential to remove infrastructure bottlenecks, human resource development, health care, provision of basic minimum services, creating conducive environment for private investment, control illegal immigration etc.

The Second Section "Challenges and Opportunities" focuses on the challenges for development of Khadi and Village Industries in north-east states. This section discusses the growing unemployment problem which can be solved only with the development of Khadi and Village Industries. This Section consists of five articles.

The first paper entitled "Problems of Khadi and Village Industries in Arunachal Pradesh" presented by **Mr. Sukamal Deb,** emphasizes on a success story of Mrs. Mechi, who began with a steel fabrication unit with a very passive mind towards this initiative. This case study actually was to highlight the negative mindset approach towards the self-employment opportunities in the state of Arunachal Pradesh. The paper also highlights on cost chart, devising own wages system from general to particular to specificity of the area concerned. The drawback of the system was specified with the lack of reach out system of implementation, lack of coordination amongst the line departments and the need of convergence with PRIs and grass roots institutions.

The next article, "Khadi and Village Industries in Arunachal Pradesh" jointly written by **Ms. Sarita Srivastav** and **Mr. Manas Kumar Jana** highlights the present scenario of village and small-scale industries. This sector has not only continued to play a vital role in fulfilment of socio-economic objectives but also offers an excellent opportunity for industrial self-employment. A number of policy measures have been taken to promote entrepreneurship in the State. The Government is focusing on entrepreneurship development through institutional support from organisations like Khadi and Village Industries Commission (KVIC), District Industries

Centres (DIC), Development Commissioner (Handlooms), Development Commissioner (Handicrafts), Small Industries Development Organisation (SIDO), etc. Attempt has been made for the entrepreneurship development *vis-a-vis* fulfilling the condition of sustainable development.

The third paper, "Development of Khadi and Village Industries in Manipur: Issues and Challenges" presented by **Dr. Jayanti Ningombam** and **Dr. Victoria Ayekpam** emphasizes that Manipur, a small state in the North-Eastern corner of India needs the industrialization and entrepreneurship development especially in the rural and hilly areas through Khadi and Village Industries. Despite massive development efforts taken by both Central and State Governments through various schemes and programmes, the pace of economic and industrial development of the state is very poor. As a result, the number of educated unemployed youth of the state has crossed 4,60,143 as in January 2005 of which 1,18,121 were female unemployed youth.

The fourth paper was presented by **Ms. Swapnali Baruah,** Research Scholar and **Dr. B. D. Nayak**. In their paper, "Prospects and Scenario of Khadi and Village Industries in North-East India with special Reference to Assam", they try to explain that with the celebration of 62nd year of Independence, India has been practicing Five Year Plans giving importance to the development of rural industries through the development of Khadi and Village Industries (KVI). In the country as a whole we have 15,431 sales outlets, out of which 7,050 are owned by the KVIC. Products of these industries are sold at the international level through various exhibitions. But development of KVI in North-East India is almost negligible than that of the rest of India.

Lastly, **Dr. Ram Krishna Mandal**, in his paper, "Handicraft and Cottage Industry in Arunachal Pradesh: Challenges and Opportunities" illustrates that the main principle of Gandhian approach is to set up a system of village self-sufficiency. This sector has not only continued to play a vital role in fulfilment of socio-economic objectives but also offers an excellent opportunity for industrial self-employment. The tribal communities in Arunachal Pradesh are extremely self-reliant; they constructed their own inter-village path, build their own cane bridge, devised their own indigenous equipments to husk or grind rice and millets, weaving their own cloths, ornaments and jewels, hats, cooking vessels, weapons. This shows the exceptional similarities of Gandhian concept of self-reliance in the tribal communities of the state.

The Third Section "Empirical Study" focuses on the case study of different places in the north-east region. This section tries to find out the existing problems, its solutions, employment scenario. This Section contains four articles.

The first article, "Traditional Handicrafts of Assam: Challenges and Opportunities — A Case Study of Bamboo and Cane Crafts" written by **Dr. Manoj Kumar Paul** points out that North-Eastern Region (NER) is a land of beautiful handicrafts with a wide range in variety of crafts. The people of the region have a tradition of artistic craftsmanship. Crafts such as weaving, painting, pottery, basketry, woodcarving, bamboo and cane crafts, smithy work, etc. are widely practiced in NER as the tradition of their art of living and culture. These crafts can reduce the dependence of rural people on agriculture as their exclusive source of livelihood by providing gainful subsidiary employment. In spite of its vast natural resources, Assam is industrially backward.

The next joint paper presenters were **Dr. Paritosh Chandra Dutta** and **Mr. Arabinda Kherkatary**. The paper "Problems and Prospects of Khadi and Village Industries in Assam of NER – An Empirical Study" voices that every effort towards the development of the country must begin with the development of villages. The economic upliftment of the people of Assam especially in rural areas is possible only through the development of the Khadi and Village Industries (KVI) in these areas. The development of KVI is required not only for the mobilisation of local resources but also for creating adequate employment opportunities. These industries provide part-time and full-time employment to a large section of people.

The third article, "The Role of Human and Social Capital in Forming Financial Capital – An Empirical Study with Special Reference to KVIC, Assam" written by **Dr. Chimun Kumar Nath** postulates that the present researcher argues that initial legitimacy is transferred to the organization from the founding team. Moreover, the present researcher suggests that which features of the founding team's biography are used to determine an organization's legitimacy will depend primarily on the industry status of the founding team. Why do some organizational founders receive resources when others do not? To answer this question, the present researcher develop a framework that teases apart the relationships between three facets of the founder's prior experience—namely, industry status, entrepreneurially relevant demographic features, and social capital—and its organization's ability to gain legitimacy and thus resources.

The next paper entitled, "Present Scenario of KVI in Sonitpur District of Assam: A Brief Study of Tezpur Sub-Division" was presented by **Mr. Dulal Biswas** and **Mr. Biman Kumar Nath.** They highlighted that a good number of rural areas necessarily reveal the importance of Khadi and Village Industries in the Sonitpur district situated in North bank of Brahmaputra valley of Assam. These industries have developed local initiatives, self-reliance and also helped in utilizing the available manpower in rural areas for processing locally available raw materials. The paper was an attempt to monitor the present status of Khadi and Village Industries in Sonitpur district of Assam.

The Fourth Section, "Entrepreneurial Activities" deals with performance of small enterprises, entrepreneurial efficiency, entrepreneurial problems and entrepreneurial development. This section consists of five articles.

The first article entitled, "Performance of Micro and Small Enterprises with Special Reference to North-Eastern Region" written by **Dr. J. U. Ahmed** seek to explain that Micro and Small Enterprises (MSE) are considered to be one of the principal driving forces in economic development of any country. The importance of this sector is well recognized worldover from its significant contribution in gratifying various socio-economic objectives, such as higher growth of employment, output, promotion of exports and fostering entrepreneurship. Micro, Small and Medium Enterprises (MSMEs) including Khadi and Village Industries/rural enterprises constitute an important segment of Indian economy in terms of their contribution to country's industrial production, exports, employment and creation of an entrepreneurial base.

The next paper was presented by **Dr. Deepali Mandal**. In her paper, "Entrepreneurial Development for KVI: An Urgent Issue in

North-East States with Special Reference to Arunachal Pradesh", she shows that after Independence, the Government of India set up the All India Khadi and Village Industries Board in 1953. This Board, aimed to function in close cooperation with the State Governments and the Akhil Bharat Sarva Seva Sangh plagued with procedural handicaps. It was then decided in 1955 to replace this Board by a statutory body. Accordingly, the Khadi and Village Industries Commission (KVIC) came into being in 1957. The State Khadi and Village Industries Boards have come into existence in response to advice of the All India Khadi and Village Industries Board which was required by the Government Resolution of January 14, 1953 to work "in close cooperation with the State Government".

Mr. O. Deepakkumar Singh and **Dr. Rajmani Singh** in their joint paper, "A Study on Entrepreneurial Problems of Village Industries in Manipur", they wants to find out that rural Industrialization is a forward step towards industrialization and it seeks to utilize local resources (raw material and men) to maximum possible extent. It may provide them not only to face the artificial congestion in those areas in future but also to mitigate their needs and requirements. The growth and development of small scale industries particularly in the rural areas depends upon the infrastructural facilities available to them. The present trends of economic development of Manipur is becoming more worsening due to the problems of unemployment, lack of basic infrastructural development and law and order situation.

The next article, "Women Entrepreneurship in Small and Cottage Industry of Nepal: A Means of Poverty Alleviation" presented by **Dr. Ved Raj Acharya** shows a general picture of women entrepreneurship in Nepal. He also added that Women entrepreneurship in a systemic way is the recent development trend in the country and the number of women involved in this sector is still negligible. But the number of women who are coming out from the door of the house is increasing. The economic contribution of women in GDP is also seemed favourable.

Lastly, **Mr. S. Suresh Kumar** and **Prof. M Muralidhar** in their joint paper, "Entrepreneurial Efficiency for Production of Bio-Diesel in Rural Energy Needs" voices that sustainable alternate renewable source of energy needs biodiesel which seems to be one of the good options for alternative source of energy in future. Arunachal Pradesh being hilly terrain, having vast wasted and barren lands has scope for cultivation of plants which provides bio-diesel. It will not only meet the rural energy needs of this region but also improve the economic development of particular region. Besides contributing to the clean environment it also provides freedom to rural areas to access power and agricultural purposes. Cultivation and consumption of biodiesel derived from oil bearing trees prevent soil erosion and global warming.

REFERENCES

Arunachal Times, Vol. 19, No. 251, February 20, 2008, Itanagar, Arunachal Pradesh.

Arunachal Times, Vol. 17, No. 98, September 13, 2005, Itanagar, Arunachal Pradesh.

Behera, M.C. (2004): *Globalisation and Development Dilemma: Reflections from North-East India*, Mittal Publications, New Delhi.

Bhattacharje, P.R. (2002): "The Problem of Ensuring Financial Efficiency in the North-Eastern States", *Dialogue*, Vol. 4 (1), July-September.

Datta Ray and Baishya, P., (1998): *Sociological Constraints to Industrial Development in North-East India*, Concept Publishing Company (P) Ltd., New Delhi.

Ganguly, J.B. (1998): "Status of and Sociological Constraint on Industrial Development in North-east India", in Datta Ray and Baishya P., (eds): *Sociological Constraints to Industrial Development in North-East India*, Concept Publishing Company (P) Ltd., New Delhi.

Government of India: Census Reports, 1961, 1981, 1991 and 2001.

Haksar, P.N. (1984): "Problem of Building a Diverse Society", in *North-East Region, Problems and Prospects of Development*, Abbi, B.L., (ed), Centre for Research in Rural and Industrial Development, Chandigarh.

Kulshrestha, U.C. (2003): *Economic Development and Planning*, Educational Publishers, Agra.

Kundu, A. (2004): *Infrastructure, Financing and Emerging Pattern of Urbanization: Vision 2020, India Vision 2020*, Planning Commission, New Delhi.

Kundu, A. (2006): "Social Development Report", Oxford Univ. Press, New Delhi.

Mandal, R.K. (2005), "Trend of Diversification of Arunachal Economy with Special Reference to Agriculture: A Strategy for Sustainable Development" Resarun: Journal of the Directorate of Research, Vol.29, Itanagar.

Mandal, R.K. (2008): "Position of Women in Tribal Society of Arunachal Pradesh with Special Reference to Galo Women" in Pandey, B.B.(ed): *Impact of Globalisation on the Himalayan Tribes of India*, Himalayan Publishers, New Delhi, Itanagar.

Mandal, R.K. (2005): "Arunachal Pradesh Emerging as Power House" *Journal of Global Economy*, Vol. 1, No. 4.

Megu, K.(2007): *Development Issues in North-East Region*, Mittal Publications, New Delhi.

Nathan, Dev (2009): "Social Security, Compensation and Reconstruction of Livelihoods", *EPW*,Vol.XLIV, No. 30, July 25-31, Mumbai.

NEDFi, quarterly data bank, 2005.

Pandey, B.B.(2008): *Impact of Globalisation on the Himalayan Tribes of India*, Himalayan Publishers, New Delhi, Itanagar.

Pandey, G.S.: *Buddhism and Khamtis*, San Park Press Pvt. Ltd., Ashok Vihar I, Delhi.

Prasad, P. (1995): *Urban Slums: Health, Education and Development*, Delta Publications, New Delhi.

Rao, N.A. and *et al.* (2004): "Urbanization Trends in Andhra Pradesh: A Region-wise Study", *Asian Economic Review*, 46(1).

Sen, A.(2002): "Globalisation, Inequality and Global Protest", Development, 45, June, pp.11-16.

Shukla Commission, (1997): "Transforming North-East, Tackling backlogs in Basic Minimum Services and Infrastructural Needs", High Level Commission Report to the Prime Minister, *Planning Commission*, New Delhi.

Singha, Komol (2009):*Village Development in North-East India,* Concept Publishing Company (P) Ltd., New Delhi.

Sinha A.C.(1994): "North-Eastern Frontier of India: Structural Imperatives and Aspects of Change", Indus Publishing Company, New Delhi.
UNDP (1993: Human Development Report).

List of Contributors

Mr. Ashok Kumar Saran, Director of Khadi and Village Industries, Government of India, Vivek Bihar, P.O. : R.K. Mission- 791 113, Itanagar, Arunachal Pradesh.

Dr. Arjun Kumar Baral, Associate Professor, Department of Economics, Tribhuvan University, Birat Nagar, Nepal.

Mr. A. Kherkatary, Assistant Professor, Department of Economics, S. S. College, Hailakandi-788151, Assam.

Dr. B. D. Nayak, Asstt. Professor and Head, Department of H.S.S., NERIST, Nirjuli, Arunachal Pradesh.

Mr. Biman Kr. Nath, C/o Shri Prabhat Ch. Nath, Bhalukekhowa, P.O.: Pithakhowa, Dist.: Sonitpur - 784153, Assam.

Dr. Chimun Kumar Nath, Associate Professor, Department of Commerce, Dibrugarh University, Dibrugarh-786004, Assam.

Dr. Deepali Mandal, Principal, GLM College, Banmankhi, Purnea, Bihar.

Mr. Debabrata Maji, Department of Mechanical Engineering, North-Eastern Regional Institute of Science and Technology, Nirjuli, Itanagar, Arunachal Pradesh.

Mr. Dulal Biswas, R.S., C/o Hill Queen Studio,'C'- Sector, Itanagar-791111, Arunachal Pradesh.

Prof. J.S. Panwar, Professor and Director, Postgraduate Department of Business Management, Sardar Patel University, Vallabh Vidyanagar- 388 120, Dist. Anand, Gujarat.

Dr. Jayanti Ningombam, Associate Professor, Department of Accounting, D.M.College of Commerce, Imphal-795001.

Dr. J. U. Ahmed, Associate Professor of Finance, Department of Management, North-Eastern Hill University, Tura Campus, Chandmari-794002, Meghalaya, India.

Prof. M. Muralidhar, Head and Professor (Centre for Appropriate Technology and Rural Development), Deptt. of Mechanical Engineering, NERIST, Nirjuli, Arunachal Pradesh, India.

Dr. Manoj Kumar Paul, Associate Professor, Department of Economics, Radhamadhab College, Silchar, Assam, India, Pin- 788006.

Ms. Mousumi Borah, Assistant Professor, Department of Economics, Arya Vidyapeeth College, Guwahati-781 016, Assam .

Mr. Manas Kumar Jana, Associate Professor, Department of Commerce, J.N. College, Pasighat, Arunachal Pradesh.

Mr. O. Deepakkumar Singh, Research Scholar, Department of Commerce, Manipur University, Manipur.

Dr. Paritosh Chandra Dutta, Associate Professor and HoD, Department of Statistics, S. S. College, Hailakandi-788151, Assam.

Dr. R.P. Bhattacharje, Deputy Registrar, NERIST, Nirjuli, Itanagar, Arunachal Pradesh.

Dr. Rajmani Singh, Associate Professor, Department of Commerce, Manipur University, Manipur.

Dr. Ram Krishna Mandal, Associate Professor, Department of Economics, Dera Natung Government College, Itanagar, Arunachal Pradesh.

Mr. Sukamal Deb, Deputy Director, Khadi and Village Industry Board, Chandan Nagar, Itanagar, Arunachal Pradesh.

Ms. Sangeeta Kakoty, Assistant Professor, Department of History, Arya Vidyapeeth College, Guwahati-781 016, Assam.

Ms. Sarita Srivastav, R.S., R G U, Rono Hills, Itanagar, Arunachal Pradesh.

Ms. Swapnali Baruah, Research Scholar, Department of H.S.S., NERIST, Nirjuli, Arunachal Pradesh.

Mr. S Suresh Kumar, Head of Department (Automobile Engineering), Rajiv Gandhi Govt. Polytechnic. Itanagar, Arunachal Pradesh.

Dr. Udaya Raj Regmi, Associate Professor, Faculty of Management, Tribhuvan University, Birat Nagar, Nepal.

Dr. Victoria Ayekpam, Assistant Professor, Department of Accounting, D. M. College of Commerce, Imphal-795001.

Dr. Ved Raj Acharya, Associate Professor, Department of Economics, M.M.A.M.Campus, Tribhuvan University, Birat Nagar, Nepal.

Dr. Yogesh C. Joshi, Reader in Economics, PG Department of Business Management, Sardar Patel University, Vallabh Vidyanagar- 388 120, Dist. Anand, Gujarat.

SECTION - I
Present Scenario

1

Present Scenario of KVI

ASHOK KUMAR SARAN

KVIC Network

KVIC has its central office at Mumbai. It has 34 State/Divisional Offices all-over the country to look after the developmental activities specially at rural areas. To further decentralize its work KVIC set up 6 zonal offices at New Delhi (NZ), Bhopal (CZ), Kolkata (EZ), Guwahati (NEZ), Bangalore (SZ) and Mumbai (WZ) and delegated the powers to these offices. To impart qualitative training, KVIC is running 15 departmental, 24 non-departmental training centres. To help the units who are under the umbrella of KVIC, it is running 12 departmental Sales outlets. To facilitate quality production of Khadi, KVIC is providing Cotton and Poly Silvers to the Khadi institutions through its 6 departmental Control Silver Plants.

Partner Agencies

There are large numbers of Government and Non-Governmental agencies working with KVIC in the development and implementation of various Khadi and Village Industries programmes. 33 States and Union Territories of Khadi and Village Industries Board under the administrative control of the State Governments and UT are implementing the KVIC's programme. There are also 5000 Registered Institutions (NGOs) working at the grass roots level for generating employment and helping artisans to uplift their social and economic status. To market the products of these artisans and institutions there are more than 7,000 sales outlets all-over the country. 27 Public Sector Banks with a network of more than 50,000 branches besides Regional Banks and Co-operative Banks spread all-over the rural areas in the country are also financially helping the units sponsored by the KVIC and its agencies.

Definitions of Khadi, Village Industries and Rural Area

Khadi

'Khadi' means a cloth woven on handlooms in India from cotton, silk or woollen yarn handspun in India or from a mixture of any two or all of such yarns.

Village Industries

'Village industry' means any Industry located in a rural area which produces any goods or renders any service with or without the use of power in which the fixed capital invested per head of artisan or a worker does not exceed one lakh rupees in plain areas and one lakh fifty thousand rupees in hilly areas or such other sum as may be by notification in the Official Gazette, be specified from time to time by the Central Government.

Rural Area

Any area classified as village as per the revenue records of the State/Union Territory, irrespective of population. It will also include any area even if classified as town, provided its population does not exceed 20,000 persons.

Physical Performance at a Glance

(Rs. in Crores)

Year	*Production*			*Sales*		
	Khadi	*V.I.*	*Total*	*Khadi*	*V.I.*	*Total*
2007-08	543.39	16,134.32	16,677.71	724.39	20,819.09	21,543.48
2008-09	585.25	16,753.62	17,338.87	799.60	21,948.59	22,748.19

(Persons in lakhs and Rs.in Crores)

Year	*Employment*			*Earnings*		
	Khadi	*V.I.*	*Total*	*Khadi*	*V.I.*	*Total*
2007-08	9.16	90.11	99.27	329.47	7,822.38	8,151.85
2008-09	9.50	94.41	103.91	373.95	8,000.12	8,374.07

The 11th Plan Approach

Keeping in view the unemployment scenario, creation of seven crore new employment has been emphasized in the XIth Plan, the share of KVI sector would be around 45.34 lakhs additional employment, which makes the expected employment by the terminal year of XIth plan at 144.61 lakhs.

In spite of the slow down in the overall growth of the economy during first 2years of XIth five year plan, KVI sector has registered progress of 11.42 per cent in production and 14.13 per cent in sales, 8.15 per cent in employment and 11.67 per cent in earnings of artisans.

New Programmes and Schemes

Prime Ministers Employment Generation Programme (PMEGP)

Ministry of Micro, Small and Medium Enterprises, Govt of India has announced a new credit linked subsidy programme called Prime Minister's Employment Generation Programme (PMEGP) on 15th August, 2008, for generation of employment opportunities through establishment of micro enterprises in rural as well as urban areas, KVIC is the nodal agency for implementation of the scheme at the national level. The scheme will be implemented by KVIC/ KVIBs in rural areas and by District Industries Centres in Urban and other rural areas.

During the current financial year 2009-10, funds provided by Government of India under PMEGP schemes will be fully utilized for establishment of 61,697 units targeted for the year across the country. This will provide new employment opportunities to more than 6.16 lakh persons.

Under this scheme during 11th plan period a record number of 3,73,750 micro projects will be established in India and Rs. 4,485 crores of Margin Money will be disbursed by KVIC through a network of more than 20,000 Bank branches.

Under PMEGP during the period mentioned above a record credit of Rs. 15,000 crores will be made available to the first generation entrepreneurs and 37.37 lakhs new employment opportunities will be created in India.

(i) *Quantum and Nature of Financial Assistance:* The maximum cost of the project/unit admissible under manufacturing sector is

Rs.25 lakh and the maximum cost of the project/unit admissible under business/service sector is Rs. 10 lakh.

(ii) *Levels of funding of Margin Money:*

Categories of beneficiaries under PMEGP	*Beneficiary's Contribution (of project cost)*	*Rate of Subsidy (of project cost)*	
Area (Location of project/unit)		*Urban*	*Rural*
General Category	10%	15%	25%
Special (including SC/ST/ OBC/Minorities/ Women, Ex-servicemen, Physically handicapped, NER, Hill and Border areas etc.	05%	25%	35%

(iii) *Bank Finance:* The Bank will sanction 90% of the project cost in case of General category of beneficiary/institution and 955 in case of special category of the beneficiary/institution, and disburse full amount suitably for setting up of the project. Normal rate of interest is charged on the Loan.

Bank will finance capital expenditure in the form of Term Loan and Working Capital in the form of Cash Credit. Project can also be financed by the Bank in the form of Composite Loan consisting of Capital Expenditure and Working Capital. The amount of bank credit will be ranging between 60-75 per cent of the total project cost after deducting 15-35 per cent of margin money (subsidy) and owner's contribution of 10 per cent from beneficiaries belonging to general category and 5 per cent from beneficiaries belonging to special categories.

(iv) *Modalities of the operation of the scheme:* Project proposals will be invited from potential beneficiaries at district level through press, advertisement, radio and other multi-media by KVIC, KVIBs and DICs at periodical intervals depending on the target allotted to that particular district. The scheme will also be advertised/publicized through the Panchayati Raj Institutions which will also assist in identification of beneficiaries.

(v) *Entrepreneurship Development Programme (EDP):* The objective of EDP is to provide orientation and awareness pertaining to various managerial and operational functions like finance, production, marketing, enterprise management, banking formalities, book-keeping, etc. The duration for EDP under REGP was only 3 days, whereas, under PMRY it was 10 days. During various meetings, discussions and recommendations of Department Related Parliamentary Standing Committee for Industry (DRPSCI) it was felt that 3 days were not adequate for providing this input effectively and, hence 2 to 3 weeks period has been provided under PMEGP which will include interaction with successful rural entrepreneur, banks as well as orientation through field visits.

(vi) *Negative List:* The following list of activities will not be permitted under PMEGP for setting up of micro enterprises/projects/units.

- Any industry/business connected with Meat (slaughtered), i.e. processing, canning and/or serving items made of it as food, production/manufacturing or sale of intoxicant items like Beedi/Pan/Cigar/Cigarette etc., any Hotel or Dhaba or sales outlets serving liquor, preparation/producing tobacco as raw materials, tapping of toddy for sale.
- Any industry/business connected with cultivation of crops/plantation like Tea, Coffee, Rubber etc. Sericulture (Cocoon rearing), Horticulture, Floriculture, Animal husbandry like Pisciculture, Piggery, Poultry, harvester machines etc.
- Manufacturing of Polythene carry bags of less than 20 microns thickness and manufacture of carry bags or containers made of recycled plastic for storing, carrying, dispensing or packaging of food stuff and any other item which causes environmental problems.
- Industries such as processing of Pashmina Wool and such other products like hand spinning and weaving, taking advantage of Khadi Programme under the purview of Certification rules and availing sales rebate.
- Rural Transport (Except Auto Rickshaw in Andaman and Nicobar Islands, House boat, Shikara and Tourist Boats in J&K and Cycle rickshaw).

Scheme for Enhancing Productivity and Competitiveness of Khadi Industries and Artisans

The scheme was introduced in 2008. It aims to make Khadi Industry more productive as well as competitive and also strengthen its potential for creation of qualitative and sustainable employment.

The scheme provides financial support of 42 lakhs per Institution with Government subsidy of Rs. 34.45 lakhs. For North-East and SC/ST institutions the Government subsidy in the scheme is Rs. 37.90 lakhs. It is expected to cover 200 institutions by 2011-12 and about 60,000 artisans will be benefited with improved Khadi infrastructure and enhanced wages. In 2009-10, 23 such projects will be sanctioned involving grant of Rs. 8 crore. KVIC has already accorded approval for 12 projects.

Workshed Scheme for Khadi Artisans

Artisan's welfare has always remained a high priority for the Government. KVIC introduced workshed scheme during 2008-09, to provide sufficient space and congenial environment to artisans smooth and fatigue free working to facilitate enhanced production and increased earning. During XIth plan, 38,000 artisans will be covered under the scheme. In 2008-09, KVIC extended benefit to 11,076 artisans as against the target of 10,000 artisans. 6000 artisan's workshed have been sanctioned during 2009-10 as per the approved budget of KVIC.

Scheme for Strenghtening of Infrastructure of Existing Weak Khadi Institutions and Assistance for Marketing Infrastructure

The Scheme has been formulated to extend need based support to weak/sick institutions which have potential to attain normalcy and for creation of marketing infrastructure in identified outlets. During XIth plan, 100 weak Khadi institutions and 30 identified marketing outlets are to be assisted. KVIC has targeted to support 30 weak institutions and 10 potential sales outlets under the scheme during 2009-10.

Scheme of Fund for Regeneration of Traditional Industries (SFURTI)

To uplift the Socio-Economic condition of Artisans, Spinners and Weavers, a Cluster Development Programme under SFURTI (scheme of Fund for Registration of Traditional Industries) has been introduced.

The objective is to make traditional industries more productive, competitive, and innovative, create employment opportunities for rural artisans and facilitate their sustainable development.

The Central Government approved total outlay of Rs. 75.12 crore for development of 79 KVI clusters (29 clusters of Khadi and 50 clusters of Village Industries). Around Rs. 123.50 lakhs (I.A. Rs. 17.25 lakhs + N.A. Rs. 106.25 lakhs) fund outlay is provided for Khadi cluster, Rs. 88.50 lakhs (I.A. Rs. 8.50 lakhs+N.A. Rs. 80 lakhs) fund outlay provided for a Village Industries Cluster.

The grant support is provided for : Replacement of Charkhas and Looms: establishment of Common Facility centre with Machineries, Quality Control Laboratory, Design Development, packaging etc., Product Development and Design Intervention, Market Promotion and capacity building Measures.

Each cluster is supporting minimum of 500 artisans. For North-East Region, the minimum criteria are 250 artisans per cluster.

Khadi Clusters involve production of Khadi readymade, bed sheets etc. Village Industries cluster involve production of wooden beads, wooden handicrafts, tribal jewellery, phulkari work, cane and bamboo, honey and value added products and food products.

The category-wise geographical progresses of SFURTI Clusters are as follows:

SC/ST Clusters-14, clusters in NER-13, clusters in disturbed areas-03, clusters Naxal prone areas-03, clusters in Remote areas-02, Clusters in Minority Districts-12.

Due to SFURTI interventions, 27,262 artisans families are benefited; around 9,000 Charkhas and 950 Looms are distributed to the artisans; 63 Common Facility Centres were created; 3,500 tool kits are distributed to the Village Industries artisans; around 20,000 artisans upgraded their skills through the training programmes conducted at cluster level. An average increase in production and sales reported 27 per cent and 31 per cent in Khadi Clusters and 46 per cent, and 47 per cent increase in Production and Sales in Village Industry Clusters. The increased earnings of Spinners-60 per cent, Weavers-61 per cent and Artisans-34% due to SFURTI interventions. The SFURTI clusters also received patronage from most of the State Governments. Some of the State Governments allotted land for establishment of CFC in the clusters under SFURTI.

Rural Industrial Consultancy Service (RICS)

To make PMEGP/REGP scheme more effective and accessible to the new entrepreneurs, KVIC has launched Rural Industrial Consultancy Services (RICS) under which first generation entrepreneurs are provided services, such as project formulation, co-ordination with banks, technical back-up, marketing support, etc. Such incentives will help new entrepreneurs to set-up projects, which will be more viable and better manageable.

Rural Industry Service Centre (RISC)

A Rural Industries Service Centre Scheme was launched during 10th plan in order to provide common facility services to KVI units, in a cluster based manner.

It is the common facility unit, which aims to provide infrastructural support and necessary services to the local units to upgrade their production capacity, skills and market promotion and backward forward linkage to Khadi and V.I. activities in a cluster, services like raw material support, skill upgradation, training, quality control, testing facilities, design and product development in order to strengthen the rural clusters.

260 numbers of projects were launched up to 2000-09 under Rural Industry Service Centre.

Operationalisation and Programme Implementation

- For the purpose of establishing Rural Industry Service Centre (RISC), it may be ensured that the number of artisans/Village Industries units shall not be less than 5 REGP units and 25 individual artisans and 25 REGP units and 125 individuals for projects up to Rs. 5 lakhs and up to Rs. 25 lakhs respectively.
- The implementing agency/organization should have its own land where the Rural Industry Service Centre (RISC) will be established.
- The period of setting of project should not be more than 6 months from the date of release of final instalment of sanctioned funds.

Product Development, Design Intervention and Packaging (PRODIP)

This scheme was introduced to allow institutions to engage professional designer for better designing of Khadi apparels. The Scheme also facilitates village industries products to improve the packaging to attract the customers. Under the scheme, as many as 556 projects were sanctioned; so far 531 projects were established in the country. National Institute of Design and National Institute of Fashion Technology (NIFT) are collaborators of KVIC for these ventures.

Marketing

KVIC has been extending best of marketing support and export opportunities to khadi institutions, PMEGP/REGP units, to help venture their products and service.

Major Achievements Under Marketing

- KVIC has been organizing domestic exhibition of different types like National Level, State Level, Zonal Level and District Level. In the last two years 246 exhibitions have been organized. During 2009-10, 21 Domestic exhibition of National and State Level have been planned for effective implementation.
- KVIC has also been participating in International exhibition for exploring export opportunities. A target of Rs. 1,000 crore worth of export has been earmarked during 11th Plan.
- Participated in IIFT-2009, New Delhi with the best and exclusive products of KVIC.
- Renovation and modernization of KVI sales outlets under Public Private Partnership (PPP mode) are being encouraged. Renovation of an institutional sales outlet under PPP mode has achieved significant sale growth.
- Some good outlets including Khadi Gramodyog Bhavan, New Delhi have obtained ISO 9000-2000 for their best managerial practices.
- NEZ is being highly focused in all sorts of marketing exposures including exhibition. Necessary grant assistance is being given to NEZ institutions/units/other backward areas like Andaman and Nicobar, Jammu and Kashmir etc.

- Government supply under Rate Contract (RC) and non-RC are being executed.

Export Promotion Council (EPC)

KVIC has geared up all efforts to accelerate the export opportunities of KVI sector. Deemed Export Promotion Council (EPC) status has been accorded to KVIC by the Ministry of Commerce, Government of India, in order to streamline export of KVI products. About 839 KVI institutions/REGP units have taken the membership of EPC during 2008-09.

The enrolment of more members would further strengthen the supply chain of the export of various items in the international market. A target of Rs. 1,000 crore worth of exports has been fixed for 11th Five Year Plan and presumably this will become a major boost to the PMEGP/REGP entrepreneurs.

Science and Technology

KVIC has close liaison with premier Academic and Research Organizations like IITs, IISc, NITs,NIFT, NID etc. for technological support in the areas of development of efficient processes, products, tools/equipments, etc.

- During last 3years 75 test labs have been set up for testing Khadi and Village Industries Products in the country.
- 52 KVI institutions/REGP units have obtained ISO 9001-2001 certificate under ISO certification Scheme of KVIC.
- 8 New Technical Interfaces have been initiated in addition to existing 12 interfaces with National Level institutes like IITs and NITs.
- KVIC in collaboration with IIT Delhi has established MGIRI—an autonomous body which has started functioning.
- 145 R&D projects have been completed by the technical interfaces and Mahatma Gandhi Institute of Rural Industrialization, Wardha.
- Some of the following technologies to reduce human drudgery and improve productivity and quality of production of Khadi and Village Industries have been developed:
  (a) Soft and stiff finish technology for Khadi
  (b) Development of hank dyeing and mercerizing machine
  (c) Technology for wrinkle free Khadi

(d) Bio manure testing kit
(e) Soap and detergent testing kit
(f) Energy efficient Potters Kiln
(g) 14 technologies have already disseminated to the field for adoption.

New Initiatives

1. Asian Development bank after field study of the KVI sector by M/s. Price Water House Coopers sanctioned an amount of US$ 150 million for the Khadi Reform and Development Programme. The intervention shall cover Khadi Mark Development; Raw material procurement and Production; Artisans, Earnings and Empowerment; Skill Development Through Quality training facilities; Market linked pricing and introduction of Benefit Chart; reforms at khadi institution Level; etc.
2. The National Institute of Rural Industrialization, Nashik would be imparting advanced training for upgrading the technology and skill development training through tailor made courses to rural youth. This will help the rural masses to produce or service with a quality output.
3. Artisan Insurance Scheme 'Janashree Bima Yojana' for Khadi artisans provided insurance cover against death and disability. 2,76,858 artisans have been covered under the scheme during 2008-09. Through the scheme deaths claims of Rs. 209.85 lakhs and educational scholarships of Rs. 488.17 lakhs have been settled in favour of Khadi artisans.
4. Artisans Welfare trusts have been set up in all states, which maintain artisan welfares fund providing security to the savings of Khadi artisans. 21 state Level Trusts including the State Govt. run Board in Kerela have been established. 1618 institutions have joined the Trust. The total deposit as on 31.03.2009 with the Trusts was Rs. 49.78 crores. These Trusts released around Rs. 20.00 crore to the artisans to meet their needs.
5. KVIC has decided to promote production of Khadi using naturally coloured cotton developed by University of Agricultural Sciences, Dharwad, Karnataka. The use of

naturally coloured cotton will help in saving water, extensively used in dyeing industries, and also save consumers from the adverse effects of synthetic chemical dyes.

6. KVIC is researching to develop solar charkha. Gandhigram Urja Sanstha—an NGO of Amaravati, Maharashtra is working on the project in collaboration with MGIRI, Wardha.
7. Concept of 'Honey Hut' has been successfully introduced for promoting Honey added products in Showrooms, Malls and prestigious Exhibition like IIFT, New Delhi.
8. E-CHARKHA one of the major achievement of KVIC is development of one, two and eight-spindle NMC E-CHARKHA, in collaboration with flexitron organization, Bangalore, where the spinner while plying the charkha, rotates an armature/dynamo which in turn charges a battery. It allows the spinner to light her dwelling place, listen to transistor and recharge cell phone.

Abbreviations Used in the Article

1. **KVIC** – Khadi and Village Industries Commission
2. **KVIB** – Khadi and Village Industries Board
3. **U.T.** – Union Territories
4. **DIC** – District Industry Centre
5. **IA** – Implementing Agency
6. **NA** – Nodal Agency
7. **PMEGP** – Prime Minister's Employment Generation Programme
8. **SFURTI** – Scheme of Fund for Regeneration of Traditional Industries
9. **RICS** – Rural Industry Consultancy Service
10. **RISC** – Rural Industry Service Centre
11. **PRODIP** – Product Development, Design Intervention and Packaging
12. **NZ** – North Zone
13. **SZ** – South Zone
14. **EZ** – East Zone
15. **WZ** – West Zone
16. **CZ** – Central Zone
17. **NEZ** – North East Zone

18. **EPC** – Export Promotion Council
19. **PMRY** – Prime Minister's Rojgar Yojana
20. **REGP** – Rural Employment Generation Programme
21. **MGIRI** – Mahatma Gandhi Institute of Rural Industrialization
22. **IIT** – Indian Institute of Technology
23. **IIS** – Indian Institute of Science
24. **NIT** – National Institute of Technology
25. **NIFT** – National Institute of Fashion Technology
26. **NID** – National Institute of Design
27. **IITF** – India International Trade Fair
28. **NMC** – New Model Charkha
29. **E–Charkha** – Electronic Charkha
30. **NER** – North East Region
31. **VI** – Village Industries
32. **RC** – Rate Contract.

2

Khadi and Village Industries: Strategies for Competing with the Organized Sector

YOGESH C. JOSHI AND J.S. PANWAR

Introduction

KVIC industries are basically a part of unorganized rural industries producing variety of consumer goods and handicraft items. Many such items are very skill specific but in the absence of organized marketing efforts fetch a non-remunerative price for the producers. As Taori (1990), and Taori and Singh (1991) have observed, the KVIC industries are under pressure to market their produce for they find it difficult to match their resources with the organized sector, especially in terms of distribution, promotion and marketing spending. Village industries are of utmost importance for the north-eastern states of India as they have a predominant rural population and lack industrial development.

The geography and natural resource endowment of the region is also conducive to development of KVI in the region. The local people have a tradition and culture of producing a variety of handicraft items, handlooms, carpets, paintings, bamboo products, wood carvings and other traditional products using locally available resources and skills. The village and tiny industries if promoted properly have a great potential to contribute to the economy of this region. By promoting productivity and employment these industries may help improve the income and living standard of the people in the rural area.

The growth and progress of KVI is hampered due to many reasons peculiar to industry and environment in which they operate. The problems like small scale of operations leading to a low marketable surplus, non-business approach, lack of training and knowledge of market, lack of transportation infrastructure, non-availability of finance, poor marketing practices and overall coordination have proved a bane for sustained growth of Khadi and Village Industries. KVIs producing consumer goods like edible oils, soaps, fruit juices, ketchup, jams, apparels, furniture and like find it increasingly difficult to compete with the firms from organized sector because they don't have that kind of a distribution network and promotional budget.

Quoting a KVI Manager Taori (1991) States in a Research Paper: "With the onslaught of the modern expensive techniques of advertisements, jingles on TV which covers more than 80 per cent of the population with novel noises of sales campaign and packaging, the KVI and tiny sector have a difficult time for surviving. A 30 second super "A" TV ad has a tariff tag of Rs. 2 lakhs. How can small entrepreneur of KVI and tiny sector survive in competition with big business houses and big companies whatever his product may stand on merit?"

With a brief revisit to hierarchy of effects, it can be said that at the first stage one must inform the potential consumers about the availability of the goods for which various types of promotion mix elements such as advertising, personal selling are used. Advertisement makes attempt to create a measure of stability by moderating random pairing of buyers and sellers (Braithwaite, 1928). Advertising hence is associated with the maintenance of competition rather than with the establishment of monopoly. Advertising has the basic function of increasing demand and nothing to do with supply whereas monopoly is concerned with absolute and single control over the supply (Alderson, 1965).

The manufacturing firms (both consumer and industrial goods) apart from other activities, allocate some resources for promotion of its produce. The firms registered with KVIC have limited budget for the abovesaid activity and it is not possible on their part to follow the same style of promotion adopted by MNCs and big players. Other components of promotion mix such as sales promotion, public relations again need dedicated effort of the firms to manage the perception of people. Hence, the importance of promotion mix for the rural industries and need to sharpen focus by including promotion mix of rural industries for the managers of KVIs.

Recent Macro Economic Developments

The past couple of years have seen drastic changes in economic scenario in the global economy. The crude oil prices soared to a life time high internationally. The increase in the price of imported crude was passed on into the domestic market. Further, the rise in the price of other commodities, in particular metals and ores from the latter half of 2006-07 to the second half of 2008-09 had its undesirable effect on the cost side of the industry in the country. Another important component of the cost, namely interest costs, also increased due to higher interest rates regimes. Obvious implication of liberalization has been an increased, trade orientation of Indian manufacturing resulting greater integration of the Indian economy with rest of the world. Hence global economic recession lead to the shrinkage in demand for exports and hence sharply dented the performance of industries with high export intensity. The growth in exports from India declined from 28.9 per cent (in US dollar terms) in 2007-08 to 3.6 per cent in 2008- 09 (*Economic Survey*, 2008-09, Government of India).

The impact of the export slowdown has been particularly pronounced in sectors like textiles, leather and fur products and transport equipment. The MSME sector has been contributing significantly to the manufacturing output, employment and exports. Between 2003-04 and 2007-08, the MSME sector registered average annual growth in the number of units and employment of around 4.1 per cent and 4.0 per cent respectively. The Micro and Small Enterprises (MSEs) provide employment to an estimated 31.2 million persons in the rural and urban areas of the country. During 2003-07, the MSE sector registered continuous growth in the number of enterprises, production, employment and exports. It is estimated that there are about 128.44 lakh MSEs in the country as on March 31, 2007, accounting for about 39 per cent of the gross value of output in the manufacturing sector (*Economic Survey*, 2007-08, Government of India).

Since the transmission of global shocks came predominantly through the financing channel, the private corporate sector has also been affected adversely. However, it is understood that MSMEs that undertook manufacturing as subcontracts or as suppliers/

ancillaries to larger units and those predominantly in export-oriented sectors stand affected due to the slowdown. Although it is desirable to assess impact on performance of the MSMEs in the wake of recent developments, limitations of data may not allow us doing so. The micro and small enterprises have been showing excellent growth of production by more than 10 per cent in the economy as indicated in Table 2.1.

Table 2.1: Performance of Micro and Small Enterprises

Year	*Number of units (in lakh)*			*Production (Rs. Crore) (at 2001-02 prices)*	*Employ-ment (in lakh)*	*Exports (Rs. Crore)*
	Regis-tered	*Unregis-tered*	*Total*			
2002-03	16.03	93.46	109.49 (4.1)	3,06,771 (8.7)	263.68 (4.5)	86,013 (20.7)
2003-04	17.12	96.83	113.95 (4.1)	3,36,344 (9.6)	275.30 (4.4)	97,644 (13.5)
2004-05	18.24	100.35	118.59 (4.1)	3,72,938 (10.9)	287.55 (4.5)	1,24,417 (27.4)
2005-06	19.30	104.12	123.42 (4.1)	4,18,884 (12.3)	299.85 (4.3)	1,50,242 (20.8)
2006-07	20.32	108.12	128.44 (4.1)	4,71,663 (12.6)	312.52 (4.2)	N.A.

Source: Office of the Development Commissioner (MSME), Economic Survey, 2008-09.

Estimates based on definitions prior to enactment of MSED Act, 2006.

Note: Figures in parenthesis indicate percentage growth over previous year.

The employment growth in the sector has also been impressive and consistently over 4 per cent. As indicated by the Table most impressive aspect has been the growth in exports which is more than 20 per cent since 2002-03. Thus, it is evident that the micro and small enterprises have started focusing on export market and are earning increased export earnings during last some years now. And hence it is evident that there is need for strategically orienting the micro and small enterprises including Khadi and Village Industries to improve the lot of rural economy. This will also lead to increased inclusive growth in the country.

Recent Initiatives by the Government

During 2008-09, The Prime Minister's Employment Generation Programme (PMEGP) has been launched by merging the Rural Employment Generation Programme and Prime Minister's Rozgar Yojana. It is aimed at generating employment in rural and urban areas by setting up new self-employment ventures/projects/micro enterprises, bring together dispersed traditional artisans and unemployed youth and give them self-employment opportunities. It provides continuous and sustainable employment to traditional and prospective artisans and unemployed youth to prevent rural-urban migration and increase their wage earning capacity. The Khadi and Village Industries Commission (KVIC) is the national nodal agency to look after and implement this programme. At the state level, the scheme is being implemented through State KVIC Directorates, State Khadi and Village Industries Boards (KVIBs) and District Industries Centres (DICs) and Banks.

The upper limit of the project cost that can be set up in the manufacturing sector and the business/services sector is Rs. 25 lakhs and Rs.10 lakhs respectively. The subsidy for setting up micro enterprises is 15 per cent and 25 per cent respectively in urban areas and 25 per cent and 35 per cent respectively in rural areas for general category and special category. Under the scheme, Rs. 4,735 crore, in addition to Rs. 250 crore towards forward and backward linkages, has been earmarked to generate around 37.38 lakh employment opportunities during four years (*Economic Survey*, 2008-09, Government of India).

The Government of India has provided renewed emphasis for micro and small enterprises during 2008-09. It has under the National Manufacturing Competitiveness Programme (NMCP), focused on five components. These include quality management systems and quality technology tools, building awareness on intellectual property rights, support for entrepreneurial and managerial development through incubators, setting up of new mini tool rooms and marketing assistance/support to MSEs. The Credit

Guarantee Scheme has been modified with reduction in one-time guarantee fee and annual service fee to 1 per cent and 0.5 per cent respectively for loans up to Rs. 5 lakh, increase in loan limit from Rs. 50 lakh to Rs. 1 crore with a guarantee cover of 50 per cent, increase in guarantee cover from 80 per cent to 85 per cent for loans up to Rs. 5 lakh and reduction in lock-in-period for preferring claims from 24 to 18 months. To provide handholding assistance to potential first generation entrepreneurs through lead agencies or Udyami Mitra, the Rajiv Gandhi Udyami Mitra Yojana has been launched, offering guidance and help to them in completing the formalities for establishment of enterprises. In order to support the Khadi sector, two new schemes have been launched. Under Workshed Scheme for Khadi artisans, it has been targeted to provide 38,000 worksheds to khadi spinners/artisans. The 'Scheme for Enhancing Productivity and Competitiveness of Khadi Industries and Artisans' aims at increasing productivity of khadi artisans through 200 selected khadi institutions by assisting them with quality raw material, capacity building, value addition and marketing linkages. A scheme to rejuvenate, modernize and technologically upgrade spinners and tiny household sector in coir production has been launched. Under the scheme, outdated ratts/looms would be replaced and worksheds would be provided. Financial aid has been tied up from the Asian Development Bank amounting to US$ 150 million over a period of three years for implementing a comprehensive Khadi Reform Programme. Under this, the khadi sector would be revitalized with increased incomes, employment, sustainability and artisans' welfare and KVIC would be enabled to reduce dependence on government grants. Initially, programme will be initiated in 300 khadi institutions.

Rural Industries

With a view to ascertaining the types of industrial units which required special support, it was considered necessary to develop an appropriate classificatory definition for Small Scale Industries(SSI) spelt out under the Industries Act (Development and Regulation Act, 1951) (SIDBI Report, 2000). The classification is available as per the ownership pattern, dispersal and spread of industrial units and sector-wise distribution of service establishments.

The National Sample Survey Organisation defines the entire industrial sector in terms of organised and unorganised segments, as well as in terms of industrial units run by households and non-households. As per the recent definition, Government of India has lowered down the upper investment limit from 30 million to 10 million. There are different segment of SSI. For the present study, any industry marketing of rural produce in rural or urban areas will be taken. As per the definition that has been used for the present study, village industry means any industry located in rural area or township (the population of which does not exceed twenty thousand or such other figures as the Central Government may specify from time to time) which produces any goods or renders any services with or without use of power and in which the fixed capital investment per head of an artisan or a worker does not exceed fifty thousand rupees (in plant and machinery and land and building). Village is further classified as a village under revenue records (Source: http://www.kvic.org.in).

The Office of the Commissioner for Khadi and Village Industries (OCKVI) which is the new name of KVIC (KVIC and OCKVI have been used interchangeably) has broadly re-grouped various village industries under seven heads for the purpose of implementation of its programmes. OCKVI tries for the promotion, organisation and implementation of programmes for the development of Khadi and other village industries in the rural areas in coordination with other agencies engaged in rural development. In other words, OCKVI acts as a nodal agency or a regulatory body for all Khadi and Rural Industries of India. A new unit has to get it registered with OCKVI for obtaining a certificate and get all benefits it deserves as rural industries. OCKVI has its own share of glowing history fraught with problems and resulting failures. At present too, it has witnessed lot of many problems in the form of lack of understanding of the market and the recent developments in the field. For this, new research studies and exploration of the world may be needed.

Promotional Literature in Context of Rural Industries

There are many unanswered questions in the field of marketing which needs immediate attention. Rural marketing as a field is being explained by some pioneering conceptual work (Jha, 1988; Vaswani *et al.*, 2004).

Rural Buyer Seller Matrix

Buyer \ Seller (Producer)	Rural	Urban
Rural	I **RS-RB** Intra-Rural	II **US-RB** Consumer Goods/Services
Urban	III **RS-UB** Farm & Non-Farm products	IV **US-UB** Intra-Urban

Fig. 2.1: Rural Buyer Seller (Producer) Matrix

Some studies like that of Chadha and Sahu (2003) describe the plight of rural industries, specifically that of the agro industries (NIC classification, 2004). This study focuses on the local industries which have ventured into rural marketing with a hope of surviving and carving out their own space by fighting out with the national and multinational biggies. Ram Murthy *et al.* (1991) while discussing the problems of small scale industries have identified marketing as one of the dominant problems among a host of other problems. It has been found from their study that out of the 44 firms have identified marketing as the area of concern out of total 88 firms taken for study.

In this context, the study of Reddy and Rao (1995) has specifically cited the significance of the advertising and promotion for the successful marketing of products of rural industries. The promotion mix in turn includes four ingredients such as advertising, publicity, personal selling and all forms of sales promotion (Ramaswamy, 1990). He has further emphasised upon personal selling as the best means of oral and face to face communication and presentation with the prospect for the purpose of making sales. Designing rural promotion strategy is a new area insofar academic research is concerned. Because many companies are in this field and no one claims to have the required understanding of the market, practitioners are more or less groping in an unknown terrain.

As per Taori (1990), there are several needs of the rural and small industries. He opines that advertising of the products of the organisation is a must for the successful marketing of the same.

Pande (1990) has identified the absence of advertising as one of the problems in marketing of the small and cottage industries of India. He states that due to lack of awareness among people about the positive aspects of the product, they will be reluctant to buy it. Hence advertising of a product is necessary to launch a new product as well as to keep a hold on the market. Pande (1990) further states that due to shortage of capital and resources, small scale units cannot afford the heavy cost of advertising as against the other private concerns who spend heavily and many times more on salesmanship as the need of the hour for khadi and village industries products. Ramaswamy (1990) has emphasised upon a single important component of advertising. There are not enough research studies (academic) which focus on the promotion strategies adopted by the local brands which have a main base in the rural areas. Researchers Natarajan (1992) and Rajadhyaksha (1992) have also showed the importance of different components of promotion mix. In following section case studies have been discussed for the purpose of understanding the best practices for KVI.

Case: Tribhuvandas Foundation, Anand, Gujarat

The Tribhuvandas Foundation, Anand, Gujarat is promoted by Anand-Kheda district Cooperative Milk Producers Union and Amul-Kheda district Milk Producers Cooperative Union. The foundation covers the Charutar region of central Gujarat. Late Shri Tribhuvandas K. Patel, who was the first Chairman of AMUL and Dr. V. Kurien set up the Tribhuvandas Foundation. This was founded in 1980 under the Public Trust Act, 1950. It started its functioning from the village Hadgud, Anand. The aim was to provide primary health care and education to the villagers of Kheda and Anand Districts, who were contributing milk to the Amul Dairy. At the end of 2008-09, a population of 16,22,847 from 562 villages from Dairy Co-operative societies of Kheda and Anand Districts were covered.

The foundation is working for the benefit of the people of member societies. It has motivated women to learn handicraft based production activities. The aim is to provide them with productive employment and earn incomes to supplement their household incomes. During the year 2008-09, a total of 56 women artisans from 17 villages sold handicrafts worth Rs. 6, 06,844 (Rupees Six lakh six thousand eight hundred forty four only).

The handicraft department of the foundation takes care of the customers' needs in deciding the items to be produced at the handicraft centre. It arranges to manufacture bed sheets, pillow covers, cushion covers, file folders and aprons and other items through women in villages. This offers them opportunity to be engaged in productive activity and generate income for the family, utilising their leisure time during the day. These items are sold at the Handicraft centre at Anand. In all 65 women have worked at or through our handicraft centre of the foundation during 2008-09. The centre provides for training of the interested women who wish to learn stitching and tailoring from the villages. The sourcing of raw material, distribution to workers, designing, technical assistance and marketing of the finished products is being handled by the personnel at the headquarters. Hence, the foundation is improving the skills of the rural women and enhancing their abilities to earn regular income independently sitting at home and utilising leisure time.

The acceptance of the foundation among women in villages is due to trust it generates among the population due to its involvement in uplifting the lot of villagers owing to being engaged in some key areas affecting human life. Thus, the foundation provides maternal and child health care. They are provided in the following table -2.

Table 2.2: Maternal and Child Health Care

Details/Taluka	*Anand*	*Kapadwanj*	*Balasinor*	*Kheda*	*Tarapur*	*Total*
No. of villages covered	126	104	127	106	99	562
No. of population covered	564024	210536	261739	291491	295057	1622847
Patients and other individuals covered by VHWs and FWs	160069	96844	108424	125705	182083	673125

Contd...

Details/Taluka	*Anand*	*Kapadwanj*	*Balasinor*	*Kheda*	*Tarapur*	*Total*
No. of pregnant women who were provided care at home	10271	3118	4449	5284	4943	28065
No. of infants and children treated at the sub-centres	148	44	26	-	20	238
No. of patients treated at OPD	7723	6712	14442	7069	2642	38588

Besides, it also provides awareness regarding health and hygiene, prevention from Cancer, immunisation, vaccination, family welfare, referral services, training and guidance for students, Balwadi for child education as well as production and distribution of safe delivery kits to the population of the villages. The village health workers are chosen with the help of the Dairy Co-operative Societies of the village, from the same village. The medical officer, the group leader and field workers of the sub-centre call those under their supervision, to one of the 13 training centres of Kheda and Anand districts. Such training enables the village health workers to carry out health care from door, in groups, and at the Dairy Co-operative Societies centre, with confidence.

Tribhuvadas Foundation gets its income from internal sources and also receives grants and donation from private donors. The foundation has a surplus fund as on 31-3-2006 of Rs. 8,17,823 in income and expenditure account. It has increased to Rs. 22,04,022 as on 31-3-2009.

Case: Rural Non-Farm Development Agency, Government of Rajasthan

The Rural Non-Farm Sector (RNFS) holds the key to faster economic development of the country. It has potential and promise for generating employment and increased income in the rural areas. Hence, not only Rajasthan but other states and also NABARD have identified financing, development and promotion of RNFS as one of its thrust areas.

Rajasthan is the first State in the country to have announced the Rural Non-Farm Development Policy for promoting the non-farm sector as an alternate strategy for generating additional avenues of employment particularly in rural areas. Looking to the maximum potential, three sub-sectors—leather, wool and minor-mineral have been taken up for focused development under the State Industrial Policy, 1998 which has now been expanded to include Handloom, Khadi and Village Industry also.

Leather Sub-sector

Keeping in view the large natural resource base of hides and skins produced in the State, RUDA has taken up integrated package by providing all backward and forward linkages in selected areas like Mangrol (Baran), Manpur-Machedi (Jaipur), Beawar (Ajmer) and Nagaur; so as to develop them as areas of excellence.

Wool Sub-sector

Rajasthan produces around 40 per cent of the country's raw wool and this sector supports nearly 30 lakh persons. It is aimed that greater value addition may be given to raw wool through promoting scientific methods of shearing, sorting, grading and other services. Sheep rearers have been organised into producers associations. Product diversification of woollen products is being done in association with NIFT (National Institute of Fashion Technology, New Delhi) and RCWPDS (Rajasthan Carpet and Woollen Products Development Society, Jaipur). To augment the skill base of carpet industry, RUDA is supporting it by providing training of artisans. The traditional Namda industry in Tonk district has given special assistance in product development and design upgradation.

Minor Mineral Sub-sector

The strategy for the development of this sector aims at improving the skills of the workers engaged in the mineral processing industry. Also additional employment is being generated through programmes which impart skills in diamond cutting and polishing; gangsaw training; promotion of stone etching through design and market led inputs. A major intervention has been started for design upgradation for potters in Dausa and Sawai Madhopur. The red sandstone cluster in Manpur and Shahpura has become a hub of economic activity and income levels of the artisan groups have increased manifold.

Handicrafts

The exports of handicrafts from Rajasthan in 2003-04 stood at Rs. 1,800 crores as against 1,200 crores in the previous year, with a growth rate of 33 per cent. Every district has its distinctive handicrafts and over 7 lakh craft persons are employed in this activity. The new policy must focus on revival of traditional dying crafts, heritage promotion and craft based livelihood for combating drought as well as expanding export earnings from this sector.

Handloom

The Handloom Sector has an edge over the powerloom and mill sectors, in its ability to produce goods commercially in small volumes, rapid switchover to new designs and creation of aesthetically appealing designs which cannot be woven on powerlooms. According to the last survey completed in the year 1995-96, there are 66,000 active weaver families in Rajasthan and about 700 weavers' cooperative societies. The principal goal of the State Government's efforts in the Handloom Sector would be to extend the coverage of weavers and to provide them with enhanced earnings. The main plank of the development strategy for the handloom sector would be a focused approach in respect of identified high value products and clusters. Handloom products which are no longer competitive must be phased out and greater attention given to commercially viable products meant both for the domestic and foreign markets.

Khadi and Village Industry

Rajasthan is the biggest producer of woollen Khadi in the country and ranks third in the overall Khadi production. Under Village Industries, the State's total production is of the order of Rs. 270 crore. Through these twin activities, the sector provides regular or subsidiary employment to an estimated 4.25 lakh people.

The strategy for this Sector would have to be increasingly market-oriented. Steps will be needed to ensure commercial viability of the activities which have so far been run on 'no profit no loss' basis. The Khadi and Village Industries Board (KVIB) will have to both upscale its operations and function on the lines of a Development Finance Institution. It is essential, therefore, to strengthen the Board's managerial, technical and marketing capabilities. Special emphasis will have to be given to human resource development, which would include designing of new policy for personnel, their training and orientation as well as placement. The Khadi and Village Industries institutions must be strengthened by the Board through support in the field of management, design and credit. Training to institution personnel will be imparted to reorient their outlook. The Khadi Institutions will be made more market and product conscious.

Along with RUDA, these bodies must closely network the Khadi and Village Industries Sector with National Institute of Fashion Technology, National Institute of Design, Wool Development Board, Jodhpur and Wool Research Association, Pune. Linkages would also be established with the private sector for marketing and export of khadi products. RUDA has organised design programmes for Khadi samities of Bikaner through NIFT and more such workshops must be organised. Product and project profiles in simple language must be arranged through professional agencies and distributed at the District/Block levels. Appropriate entrepreneurship development programmes for entrepreneurs engaged in village industries must be designed and organised at the block level. The Khadi Sector is facing the crisis of declining number of quality weavers. A promotional package will be devised by the Board for ensuring medical benefits and development of community assets for this set of weavers. The spinners and weavers will be encouraged to adopt the Self-help Group Scheme of NABARD. Exchange visits of artisans, institutions and Board employees must be sponsored by the Rajasthan Khadi and Village Industries Board to other States to learn from their experience. Experts from successful institutions will be asked to visit the State to share their experience.

RUDA: The Exclusive Agency

Government of Rajasthan established the Rural Non-Farm Development Agency (RUDA) in November 1995 as an exclusive agency to promote the rural micro-enterprises in the State. Its primary mandate is:

- Create alternative avenues of employment
- Generate incremental incomes

RUDA is perhaps the only agency of its kind, promoting rural micro-enterprises on sub-sectoral basis. Initially, 3 sub-sectors viz. Leather, Wool and Minor-Minerals (Stone, Ceramics and Pottery) had been identified. During the Tenth Five Year Plan three new sub-sectors namely Handicraft, Khadi and Village Industries and Handloom have been added. RUDA works through a cluster based approach. It adopts a truly integrated strategy to promote the sector and all its interventions are based on the felt needs of the producers. Among others, RUDA's package of interventions include:

- sub-sectoral analysis
- capacity audit of artisan clusters
- identifying operational constraints
- organizing artisans
- micro-finance for SHGs and CIGs
- micro-enterprise development
- skill development training
- technology dissemination
- design support
- product development
- credit facilitation

Important Interventions of RUDA

Cluster Development

A cluster is generally defined as a geographically bounded concentration of similar, related or complementary businesses with shared infrastructure, markets and services and faced with common opportunities and threats.

Importance of Clusters

Micro-enterprises in rural areas face competition from each other as well as from the organised sector. Development of clusters helps in deriving benefits of economies of scale in procurement of raw materials, production and post-production operations.

The Cluster Philosophy includes:

- Focused assistance.
- Demand based assistance.
- Flexible instruments of assistance to meet specific needs of cluster.
- Close monitoring to spur continuous development and innovation.
- The Cluster Development Action Plan is finalised with the help of the SHG and the NGO covering credit/refinance requirement year-wise for three years and promotional intervention suggested during each year.
- The groups are thereafter federated into associations and cooperatives to empower them with negotiation and marketing capacities.

Technology Dissemination

- Through C.L.R.I. for improving vegetable tanned process in the leather clusters, C.F.T.I. (Central Footwear Technology Institute) for development of western footwear, C.G.C.R.I. (Central Glass and Ceramics Research Institute) for developing lead free Blue pottery and C.S.W.R.I. for improving processing of raw wool etc.
- Improving traditional looms through Development Alternatives and the Weaver Service Centre.
- Technical improvement of traditional "mojaris" under an UNDP-NLDP (National Leather Development Programme) assisted Operation Mojari Project.

Market Facilitation

In congruence with its facilitation of forward linkages, RUDA has developed an innovative programme of marketing facilitation. This includes facilitating artisans to directly reach the markets, linking them with exporters and buyers and virtual stores to help them understand the demands of consumers and innovate and adopt accordingly.

Strategies for Khadi and Village Industries

Diversified export markets should be focused for promotion of produce from KVI so that dependence on few countries can be avoided. This will allow KVI to be safeguarded from international demand fluctuations.

REFERENCES

Aaditya Mattoo, Deepak Mishra and Ashish Narain, The World Bank Oped Special to The Times of India, April 26, 2007, From "Competing at Home to Competing Abroad: A Case Study of India's Horticulture", by A. Mattoo, D. Mishra and A. Narain, Oxford University Press and World Bank, 2007.

Anon. (2009) Status of Agriculture (Base Year 1999-2000) Area, Production, Productivity of different crops (2000-05) Area, Production, Productivity of different crops (2006-10) Area, Production, Productivity of different horticulture crops (2000-05) Area, Production, Productivity of different horticulture crops (2006-10).

Anon. (2009) A development profile of Arunachal Pradesh, Department of Planning, Government of Arunachal Pradesh, Itanagar.

Anon. (2009) Importance and Scope of Horticulture - Ag. Technologies (Horticulture).

Alderson (1965) Dynamic Marketing Behaviour : A Functionalist Theory of marketing, Homewood, IL; Richard D. Irwin.

Border and Area Development Programme in Arunachal Pradesh.

Chandrakant Puri (July 7-12, 2003) At 17th Asia-Pacific Social Work Conference on Evaluation of the role of NGOs in Tribal Development in India.

Economic Survey, 2007-08, 2008-09, Government of India, Ministry of Finance, Economic Division.

Kulamani Padhi—Orissa Review, February-March – 2005 Tribal Development in India—A Study in Human Development.

Pradip Kumar Singh (2004), Journal of Social Research, Vol. 26 I and II, Department of Anthropology, Ranchi. On Tribal Development in India: What Went Wrong? http://www.kvic.org.in

S. (Roy) Mukherjee#, N. Ali* and B. Ghosh# Consumerism in Tribal India: A Case Study from Arunachal Pradesh.

Department of Economics, University of North Bengal, NBU, Darjeeling, India.

* Department of Economics, J.N. College, Pasighat, Arunachal Pradesh.

Socio-Economic and Educational Development Society (SEEDS), Planning Commission, Government of India (2006) Status Study of Tribal Handicraft—an option for livelihood of tribal community in the states of Arunachal Pradesh, Rajasthan, Uttaranchal and Chhattisgarh.

Tribhuvandas Foundation, Annual Report, 2005-06, 2006-07, 2007-08, 2008-09, Rajodpura, Anand, Gujarat. http://tfoundation.blogspot.com (Development and Regulation Act, 1951) (SIDBI Report, 2000).

Taori, Kamal (1990), "Need for separate identity of rural industries", Khadi Gramodyog, XXXVII: 1, Oct., pp.10-13.

Taori, Kamal and S. N. Singh (1991), "Marketing Rural Industry Products—Experiments and Experiences in Uttar Pradesh", Khadi Gramodyog, XXXVII: 8, May, pp. 295-311.

3

Pragmatic Model for the Development of KVI Sector in Arunachal Pradesh

DEBABRATA MAJI

Khadi History

During the Freedom Struggle, Mahatma Gandhi, the Father of the Nation, was witness to the grinding poverty of our people, and realized that the poor could not be organized for the struggle, without the problem of hunger, poverty and unemployment being addressed first. He conceived of the development of Khadi and Village Industries (KVI) which involved processing and conversion of agricultural produce into final goods by the villagers/locals themselves. During the Freedom Movement, the development of KVI was used as an instrument to meet the twin objective of self-reliance through local production and seeking active participation of the poor in the struggle for Independence through removal of hunger and unemployment.

During 1920 of the Nagpur Session the Indian National Congress decided to encourage 'Khadi' and the first Khadi Production Centre was established at Katiawad, Gujarat. The Father of the Nation, Mahatma Gandhi describes the 'Khadi' as "The livery of freedom" which was later part of Swadeshi Spirit to boycott foreign goods. Khadi rendered an opportunity to every man, woman and child to cultivate self-discipline and self-sacrifice as a part of the non-cooperation movement. Year-wise developments of khadi movement are shown as under:

1923	-	Development of All India Board under the Indian National Congress by Gandhiji
1925	-	Setting up of All India Spinners Association (AISA)/ Akhil Bharat Charkha Sangh
1935	-	All India Village Industries Association (AIVIA) was formed
1946	-	Govt. of Madras sought the advice of Gandhiji and set up a Department for Khadi
1948	-	Govt. of India recognized the role of Rural Cottage Industries in the Industrial Policy Resolution, 1948. Constituent Assembly included Cottage Industries in Rural Areas among the directive Principles of the Constitution in Article 43. These ideas were elaborated in the First Five-Year Plan, which laid down the Policy framework for setting up of a body for Khadi and Village Industries. Central Govt. also recommended for setting up of a Board.
1953	-	Govt. of India set up All India Khadi and Village Industries Board in January
1955	-	A statutory body replaces the Board
1956	-	Khadi and Village Industries Commission Act, 1956 was passed
1957	-	Khadi and Village Industries Commission came into effect

Source: http://www.kvic.org.in/v4/KHADI2.ASP

Introduction

Govt. of India and the Planning Commission has introduced the Khadi and Village Industries within the framework of Five-Year Plans in post-Independence era for poverty alleviation. A Statutory body called the Khadi and Village Industries Commission (KVIC) was created by an Act of Parliament in 1956 to plan, promote, organize and assist in the implementation of the programme by financing of eligible units; training of persons for employment; ensuring supply of raw materials to units/ entrepreneurs; promotion of sales of Khadi and Village Industries (KVI) products; and undertaking research and development activities for the growth.

The implementation of KVI Programme in our country is a joint effort of the Khadi and Village Industries Commission, which are an Apex Organization at the Central level and the State Khadi and the Village Industries Boards functioning in various States and Union Territories. The primary responsibility to carry out the KVI programme lies with State Khadi and Village Industries Boards as per direction from Central as well as State Governments for the proper development of this sector. Subsequently, the State Khadi and Village Industries Boards were constituted in all States and Union Territories. Presently, there are 30 State KVIBs functioning all-over India. About 77.96 per cent of KVI Programme are implemented by State Khadi and Village industries Boards in the areas of Mineral Based Industry (MBI), Forest Based Industry (FBI), Food Processing and Agro Based Industries (FP/ABI), Polymer and Chemical Based Industry (PCBI), Rural Engineering and Bio Technology (REBT), Hand Made Paper and Fibre Industry HMP/FI) and Sericulture and Textiles (S/T).

Status of KVI During 8th Plan

Table 3.1 shows an overview of employment scenario of KVIC during 8th Plan. The village industries sector has shown steady increase during 1992-93 and 1995-96 but, the Khadi Sector has shown negative growth during 1993-96. The employment figures constitute both full-time and part-time employment which does not reflect the real employment scenario especially in Khadi Sector where the employment depends on seasonality, supply of raw material, infrastructure, etc.

Table 3.1: Employment in KVIC during 8th Plan

Year	*Khadi (in lakh)*		*Village Industries (in lakh)*		*Total Employment*
	Full-time	*Part-time*	*Full-time*	*Part-time*	*(in lakh)*
1991-92	4.19	10.01	15.80	20.16	50.16
1992-93	4.31	10.14	17.22	20.83	52.50
1993-94	4.10	9.77	18.76	20.65	53.28
1994-95	4.06	9.13	18.80	21.47	53.46
1995-96	4.28	9.69	19.46	23.29	56.72
1996-97	4.47	10.32	19.73	23.65	58.17

Source: KVIC, Annual Report, 1996-97.

During the 8th Plan period, employment in Khadi Sector remained stagnant. A constituted Working Group and High Power Committee of 8th Plan period analyzed the problem and recommended to increase in production and financial support as there is scope for employment generation. Accordingly, financial support was raised in the 8th Plan period through special allocation for Rural Employment Generation Programme (REGP). The financial assistance by KVIBs in some selected states is shown in Table 3.2.

Table 3.2: Financial Assistance by KVIB in some states (Rs. in lakh)

State	*Sector*	*Average*	
		Grant	*Loan*
Andhra Pradesh	Khadi	0	22.61
	Village Industries	11.24	690.9
Assam	Khadi	8.28	53.9
	Village Industries	0	0
Bihar	Khadi	0	0
	Village Industries	1.9	2.4
Gujarat	Khadi	0	0
	Village Industries	1379.2	45.60
Himachal Pradesh	Khadi	0	0
	Village Industries	13.55	172.8
Jammu and Kashmir	Khadi	-	-
	Village Industries	11.60	106.17
Meghalaya	Khadi	-	-
	Village Industries	12.9	140.4
Tripura	Khadi	10.41	10.41
	Village Industries	4.5	36.87
West Bengal	Khadi	16.9	488.4
	Village Industries	-	-

Source: KVIC, Annual Report, 1996-97.

Table 3.3 shows the wages per worker per annum has increased 1.5 times in Khadi and 1.3 times in Village Industries for both part-time and full-time category of workers which indicates a steady growth in both the sectors especially in Khadi.

Table 3.3: Income per Worker in KVIC during 8th Plan

Year	*Khadi (Rs. per annum)*		*Village Industries (Rs. per annum)*	
	Part-time	*Full-time*	*Part-time*	*Full-time*
1992-93	287	3223	1340	3289
1993-94	299	3662	1495	3478
1994-95	323	3954	1598	3916
1995-96	380	4468	1588	3935
1996-97	433	4835	1770	4323

Source: KVIC, Annual Report, 1996-97.

From the above figures and data indicates that Arunachal Pradesh was out of KVIC map up to 8th Plan period after 50 years of Independence of the country.

Present Status of KVI in N-E States

Since the commencement of REGP, 2,09,705 projects have been financed and 28.05 lakh job opportunities have been created up to 31.3.2005. Keeping in view REGP potential, the Government revised the target of creating 20 lakh to 25 lakh additional jobs during the 10th Plan period. During 2004-05, under REGP 5.30 lakh job opportunities has been generated against the target of 5.25 lakh which is 12.5 per cent growth in employment generation as compared to 2003-04 (4.71 lakh against the target of generating 5 lakh job opportunities). The target for generating additional employment opportunities for 2005-06 and 2006-07 are 5.50 lakh and 5.90 lakh respectively. Table 3.4 shows the achievements during the 10th Plan period.

Table 3.4: Achievements during the 10th Plan Period

Year	*Target for employment generation (in lakh)*	*Employment generated during the year (in lakh)*	*Number of projects set up*	*Margin Money Released (in crore)*
2002-03	4.00	3.61	21024	193.71
2003-04	5.00	4.71	24747	264.38
2004-05	5.25	5.50	23454	292.36
2005-06 (up to Jan'06)	5.50	3.33	14808	322.47

Source: Ministry of Agro and Rural Industries, Annual Report, 2005-06.

Table 3.5: Project set up during 2005-06 (up to January 2006)

State	*FP/ABI*	*FBI*	*HMP/FI*	*MBI*	*PCBI*	*REBT*	*S/T*	*Total*
Arunachal Pradesh	15	12	0	7	0	3	14	51
Assam	494	76	40	159	101	228	180	1278
Manipur	2	3	0	3	0	5	2	15
Meghalaya	18	19	3	19	5	4	29	97
Mizoram	22	8	5	6	2	36	42	121
Nagaland	17	5	2	4	2	16	54	100
Tripura	23	5	9	8	7	15	44	111
Sikkim	10	5	1	1	0	8	30	55
Total	601	133	60	207	117	315	395	1828
All India	4037	955	404	2214	1010	2608	3580	14808

Source: Ministry of Agro and Rural Industries, Annual Report, 2005-06.

During 2005-06 (up to January 2006), 14,808 projects have been set up which generated 3.33 lakh employment opportunities against the target of creation of 5.50 lakh jobs. State-wise performance in respect of project sanctioned, margin money utilized and employment generated during 2005-06 are shown in Table 3.5, Table 3.6 and Table 3.7 respectively.

Table 3.6: Margin Money (in lakh) under REGP during 2005-06 (up to January 2006)

State	*FP/ABI*	*FBI*	*HMP/FI*	*MBI*	*PCBI*	*REBT*	*S/T*	*Total*
Arunachal Pradesh	27.50	19.88	0.00	13.51	0.00	7.88	23.19	91.96
Assam	497.32	81.22	42.47	157.85	102.70	231.95	167.67	1281.18
Manipur	0.75	2.10	0.00	1.64	0.00	2.70	0.75	7.94
Meghalaya	26.04	22.40	3.85	32.94	3.29	0.95	26.19	115.66
Mizoram	41.72	16.10	11.13	9.77	3.47	44.49	62.53	189.21
Nagaland	19.88	4.93	2.80	4.02	2.06	17.20	49.38	100.27
Tripura	24.15	5.95	3.90	9.17	9.82	16.20	44.61	113.80
Sikkim	12.68	8.80	1.29	2.15	0.00	10.35	23.21	58.48
Total	650.04	161.38	65.44	231.05	121.34	331.72	397.53	1958.50
All India	5456.33	1042.22	590.37	3287.04	1489.06	3595.31	3406.04	19008.19

Source: Ministry of Agro and Rural Industries, Annual Report, 2005-06.

Table 3.7: Employment (no. of Persons) REGP during 2005-06 (up to January 2006)

State	*FP/ABI*	*FBI*	*HMP/FI*	*MBI*	*PCBI*	*REBT*	*S/T*	*Total*
Arunachal Pradesh	340	287	0	239	0	103	424	1393
Assam	8886	1439	762	3380	1529	4096	3776	23868
Manipur	11	34	0	39	0	18	16	1187
Meghalaya	338	308	33	654	23	13	409	1778
Mizoram	397	168	150	204	24	731	1240	2914
Nagaland	198	65	17	57	14	207	917	1475
Tripura	361	97	63	220	68	240	904	1953
Sikkim	80	53	8	10	0	59	397	607
Total	10611	2451	1033	4803	1658	5467	8083	34106
All India	88114	18432	9595	69662	19212	56956	70643	332614

Source: Ministry of Agro and Rural Industries, Annual Report, 2005-06.

Since inception of REGP there has been set up 2,09,705 units up to 31.3.2005 out of which 12.4 per cent of the project benefited from Schedule Castes community, 5.7 per cent Scheduled Tribes and 23.8 per cent from OBC. 26.8 per cent women entrepreneurs has benefited for gainful employment. Table 3.8 shows the project sanctioned to different communities.

Table 3.8: Project Sanctioned under various Communities during 2005-06

Category	*No. of projects*	*Percentage*
Scheduled Castes	893	6.0
Scheduled Tribes	984	6.7
OBC	3143	21.3
Minority Community	1900	12.8
Ex-Servicemen/Physically handicapped	226	1.5
General	7662	51.7
Total	14808	100
Women	3972	26.8

Source: Ministry of Agro and Rural Industries, Annual Report, 2005-06.

KVIC have established a Zonal Office at Guwahati and other field offices in all the North-Eastern States. KVI programmes are being implemented through State KVI Boards, registered institutions, cooperative societies and entrepreneurs. The rural industries like pottery, beekeeping, processing of cereals and pulses, fibre, fruit and vegetable processing industries, soap along with other activities like carpentry, blacksmith, and polyvastra has been set up in hilly and backward areas of North-Eastern States to augment the earnings of artisans, weavers, spinners and individual entrepreneurs with high quality KVI products from this region. There has been considerable increase in production and employment in the KVI sector in the North-Eastern States. The achievements made in terms of production and employment in the KVI sector during 2006-07 and 2007-08 are shown in Table 3.9.

Table 3.9: KVI Production, Sales and Employments in North-Eastern States (up to Dec.'07)

States	*Production (Rs. lakh)*		*Sales (Rs. lakh)*		*Employment (in lakh)*	
	2006-07	*2007-08*	*2006-07*	*2007-08*	*2006-07*	*2007-08*
Arunachal Pradesh	1925.21	1447.44	2914.34	2151.92	0.07	0.08
Assam	30328.99	22802.34	47337.39	34953.46	2.48	2.65
Manipur	7336.19	5515.59	7557.24	5580.19	0.66	0.71
Meghalaya	6423.52	4829.42	9003.30	6647.95	0.35	0.37
Mizoram	14239.61	10705.81	20220.03	14930.27	0.64	0.68
Nagaland	7747.68	5824.96	10077.24	7440.94	0.44	0.47
Tripura	5470.01	4112.53	6815.19	5032.27	0.45	0.48
Sikkim	2336.86	1756.93	4819.05	3558.34	0.19	0.20
Total	75808.07	56995.02	108743.78	80295.34	5.28	5.64

Source: MSME, Chapter 11, pp. 117-121.

Table 3.10 shows the number of projects set up along with Margin Money (MM) utilization and gainful employment in the North-Eastern States during the year 2007-08 (up to December 2007).

Table 3.10: Performance under REGP during 2007-08 in North-Eastern States

Sates	Target for 2007-08			Achievements (up to 31.12.07)		
	No. of projects	MM (in lakh)	Employ-ment (in no.)	No. of Projects	MM (in lakh)	Employ-ment (in no.)
Arunachal Pradesh	116	132.96	2214	55	99.09	621
Assam	2344	2678.38	44602	1703	1875.68	31421
Manipur	209	238.55	3973	21	21.45	157
Meghalaya	342	391.07	6513	76	121.03	821
Mizoram	682	797.38	12806	328	402.99	5597
Nagaland	283	322.90	5377	194	81.12	1343
Tripura	246	281.57	4689	77	87.81	1968
Sikkim	122	138.85	2312	24	48.70	168
Total	4344	4981.66	82486	2478	2737.87	42096

Source: MSME, Chapter 11, pp. 117-121.

Backward and Forward Linkages

The KVIC provided financial assistance to its State Offices as well as the State Khadi and Village Industries Boards for establishing backward and forward linkages of the entrepreneurs/institutions. These linkages include EDP trainings, exhibitions of products manufactured by REGP entrepreneurs, district/state level workshops and awareness camps, identification of success stories and its dissemination, etc. An amount of Rs. 667.84 lakhs have been released towards backward-forward linkages which has utilized to train 8712 persons under EDP and organizing 55 workshops, 215 awareness camps and 40 exhibitions during the year 2005-06 (up to January 2006).

New Initiatives in North-Eastern States

- To increase the number of khadi institutions in North-Eastern States.
- KVIC has removed the ban on registration of new khadi institutions located in the NER.
- To improve the technology used in the KVI sector and the quality of products, the KVIC has entered into an arrangement with IIT, Guwahati for S and T interfaces.

- The Indian Institute of Entrepreneurship (IIE), Guwahati has been recognized as the Nodal Agency for North-Eastern States with the objective to implement and monitor REGP projects being set up in the Region and to impart training to the beneficiaries.
- 10 per cent space is reserved in all Departmental Khadi Gramodyog Bhawans for the products from North-Eastern States for marketing of KVI products.

Demographic of Arunachal Pradesh

65 per cent of the Arunachalis belong to 20 major-collective tribes and 82 tribes, who had a heritage of a diverse and rich culture, language and beliefs. Most of them are either of Tibetan or of Tai-Burmese origin. Another 35 per cent of the population are immigrants, including 30,000 Bangladeshi, Bodo Hajong and Chakma expatriates, and immigrants from other parts of India, notably Assam and Nagaland. The most notable tribes include the Adi, Nishi, Monpa and Apatani. The literacy of the State rose to 54.74 per cent from 41.59 per cent in 1991. Today, the number of literates is 487,796. Recent statistics shows that 36 per cent of Arunachal's populations are Animist, who follows Animistic religions such as Donyi-Polo and Rangfrah. 37 per cent are Hindus. Tribes who follow Hinduism include the Nocte and Miri. Another 13 per cent are practicing Buddhists. Tibetan Buddhism predominates in the districts of Tawang, West Kameng and isolated regions adjacent to Tibet, and Theravada Buddhism is practiced by tribal groups living near the Burmese border. Christians mostly Baptist are present since 1961, claim to be 13 per cent of the population. There are some non-Baptist groups active since 1990. Christianity is widely practiced by several Naga tribes in Changlang and Tirap adjacent to Nagaland, although many Nagas in these areas remain followers of traditional beliefs. Though not common, a few tribal groups combine the Christian and traditional belief systems together. Table 3.11 shows the demographic of Arunachal Pradesh.

Women Population and literacy in Arunachal Pradesh

According to Census 2001, the literacy rate of women in Arunachal Pradesh was 43.5 per cent, which was 10 per cent lower than the national average of 53.70 per cent. However, the State has made

Table 3.11: Demographic of Arunachal Pradesh
(As per 2001 Census)

Districts	*Areas (in sq. km)*	*No. of Villages*	*Forest Cover (%)*	*Populations as per 2001 Census*			*Decadal growth rate (1991-2001)*	*Sex Ratio (females per 1000 males)*	*Density (person per sq. km)*	*Literacy rate (%)*
				Persons	*Male*	*Female*				
Anjaw	NA	NA	NA	18428	10164	8277	NA	816	NA	31.32
Changlang	4662	336	93.35	125435	65821	59601	31.30	906	27	51.30
D/Valley	13029	213	72.23	7272	4286	2986	34.00	697	4	53.00
E/Kameng	4134	310	88.56	57179	28802	28377	13.50	985	14	40.60
East Siang	4422	212	78.33	87397	45265	42132	21.60	931	22	60.70
K/Kumey	8818	NA	NA	42518	21117	21401	18.10	1013	5	25.70
Lohit	11402	493	68.06	125086	67150	57936	30.80	863	13	58.70
L/Dibang V.	NA	NA	NA	50448	27156	23292	34.00	858	NA	59.80
L/Subansiri	1317	652	92.04	55726	28425	27301	18.10	960	42	59.40
Papum Pare	2875	267	94.74	122003	64184	57819	67.60	901	35	69.30
Tawang	2172	181	55.94	38924	21846	17078	37.60	782	18	47.30
Tirap	2362	167	80.74	100326	52537	47789	17.30	910	43	41.07
Upper Siang	6188	92	79.42	33363	18057	15306	20.10	848	5	49.80
U/Subansiri	7032	398	81.63	55346	28240	27106	10.50	960	8	50.30
W/Kameng	7422	212	88.56	74599	42542	32057	32.20	754	10	60.80
West Siang	7643	398	88.26	103918	54349	49569	15.50	912	13	59.50
Arunachal Pradesh	**83743**	**3863**	**81.22**	**1097968**	**579941**	**518027**	**26.85**	**894**	**13**	**54.74**

Source: http://databank.nedfi.com; State of Forest Report, 2001, Forest Survey of India.

rapid progress in raising women's literacy from 14.02 per cent in 1981 to 43.5 per cent in 2001. In rural areas, women literacy rate is as low as 36.90 per cent and the rural-urban gap in female literacy continues high. In 2001, the literacy rate among urban women was as much as 69.5 per cent almost double the literacy rate of rural women. Among the Scheduled Tribes population, literacy for women went up from 7.31 per cent in 1981 to 24.94 per cent in 1991. The adult literacy rate for women went up from 11.01 per cent in 1981 to 23.59 per cent in 1991, whereas in rural the adult female literacy rate is only 19.13 per cent, which is much lower than that in the other states of North-east India. Women literacy rates are also vary in district-to-district e.g. 60.4 per cent in Papum Pare, 28.6 per cent in East Kameng and 28.8 per cent in Tirap.

Status of Women in Arunachal Pradesh

The earnings and other opportunities, which are normally associated with employment, are generally influenced by the quality of employment. Although, enough data are not available to objectively assess the quality of employment of female workers in the state, indirect evidence clearly suggests that female workers in the state generally work in low-paid jobs with little job security. An overwhelming majority of female workers in the state work in the unorganized sector. When they are employed in non-agricultural occupations, such as government services, a higher proportion of women workers are found in the lowest ranks of the job hierarchy. The share of female workers in the service sector is expanded more than the male workers during 1971-91. The skill level of the female workforce, along with gender-based discrimination, may be the reasons for this. In 1991, while 55.9 per cent of the male workers were illiterate, 87.9 per cent of the female workers were illiterate. In rural areas, the percentage of illiterates among the female workers was as high as 90 per cent. Only 1 per cent of the female workers had studied up to graduation and above. Even among the women workers who were engaged in the non-agricultural sectors, the percentage of illiterates was as high as 54.06 per cent in 1991. Thus, there is a limited degree of diversification of occupation among the female workers, and typically secure jobs in the low-skill, low-earning end of the spectrum.

Traditional Skill Potential in Arunachal Pradesh

Weaving

The spider was the first weaver in the world. By watching the spider spins its web that the women became proficient in the art of weaving, and the men learned to span rivers with cane suspension bridges (Singphoo folklore). In the beginning, only Donyi Polo—the Sun Moon God—knew the art of weaving. He taught it to a female spirit, who taught the wife of the first man to weave (Boori Adi folklore). Arunachal Pradesh has a rich tradition of crafts such as weaving, pottery, smithy work, and basketry. Most women are skilled weavers. Each community has a distinct pattern or design and, it is often possible to tell a person's tribe by looking at the Galle (a sarong like wrap-around skirt) worn by the women or by the jackets and shawls worn by the men. The designs reflect the social and religious systems from which they emanate. Motifs are drawn from everyday life, and from the world around them, from myths and legends. Many of the designs reveal the spiritual and religious beliefs of the people and reflect their belief in the cosmic order. In recent years, the importance of weaving as a livelihood option is being recognized, given the demand for hand woven fabric in the domestic and the international market. According to the Census of Handlooms (1987-88), nearly 47,000 workers in the state were engaged in weaving on a part-time or full-time basis. However, there were only 500 full-time workers in weaving, and another 200 workers engaged in preparatory work. This is because this activity is largely in the non-formal sector. On the 46,000 looms in the state, the average production was only 1.26 metres of cloth per loom, as against the national average of 5.12 metres. This shows that there is significant scope for expanding weaving as a livelihood option for women.

Art and Crafts Industry

Arunachal Pradesh is a land of beautiful handicrafts comprising wide range in variety. All the people have a tradition of artistic craftsmanship. A wide variety of crafts such as weaving, painting, pottery, smithy, basketry, woodcarving etc. are found among the people of Arunachal Pradesh. On the basis of the art and cultural pattern, the indigenous inhabitants of the state may be divided into three distinct groups: (i) the group comprising Bodice tribe like Monpa, Sherdukpen, Memba, Khamba, Khamti and Singphoo, (ii) group including the Aka, Miri, Miji, Sulung, Nishing, Adi, Apatani, Hill Miri, Tagin, Mishmi, Tangsa, Nah, (iii) and the Nocte and the Wancho. All of these groups have some speciality in their art items. The members of first group are good in art of woodcarving and painting works. The second group is widely known for their weaving and cane and bamboo works. The third group viz. Nocte and Wancho are also good wood carvers but their style and motifs are quite different from the other groups. They also specialize in beads works. Apart from these, carpet making, scratch painting, tattooing, pottery, smithy and ivory works are also practiced by some of the tribesmen, which assume significance of their respective society. Weaving forms part of the major occupation for the women folk. Most woven products use natural dyes and have geometric designs. Some noteworthy products such as: Shawl, Jacket, Bag, Scarves etc.

Tie
Wool (Cashmilon)
Length: 52″
A Tie as a fashion statement
Hand-woven woollen tie with traditional Apatani motif.

Ladies Woollen jacket
This is a hand woven traditional ladies waistcoat made of wool, worn by ladies of the Apatani tribe particularly during Dree festival

Bag
Length: 30″
Breadth: 12″
Handwoven woollen bag with traditional Apatani motif.

Cane and Bamboo Industry

Cane and bamboo industry of Arunachal Pradesh is of very high standard. Most of the domestic requirements are made of cane and bamboo. Hats of different sizes and shapes, various kinds of baskets, cane vessels, a wide variety of cane belts, woven and plains, elaborately woven brassier of cane and fibre, bamboo mugs with carvings, a variety of ornaments and necklace are some of the products that deserve special mention. The technique of basketry is also worth mentioning. The two basic techniques are twill and hexagon both open and closed. Arunachal basketry is beautiful not only because of the fine texture but also because of the unusual shapes. Many a baskets have pleasing forms. There is definite correlation between the shape and the topography and climatic condition of the region. The angular and curveting nature of some of the baskets has definite functional value. Some noteworthy products such as: Hat, Basket, Cane vessels, Cane belts, Bamboo mugs and Carvings, Ornaments and Necklaces etc.

Carpet Industry

Carpet making is the speciality of the Monpas. They weave lovely colourful carpets with dragon, geometric and floral designs. The choice of colour and the colour combination is unique. Though originally they weave carpet for domestic use, it has now become an item of trade. Along with increase in demand, production has also been made in large scale. Carpet Making is one among the speciality occupations. Carpets are woven with varied colours, designs (geometric, dragon, floral) and shapes. With increase in demand, carpets have become an item of trade and a major occupation for some women folk.

Wood Carving Industry

Wood carving is a tradition with some of the tribes of Arunachal Pradesh. The Monpas, Khamtis, and Wanchos occupy significant place in this art. The Monpa wood carvers make beautiful cups, dishes, fruit bowls and carve magnificent masks for ceremonial dances and pantomimes. The Khambas and Membas of West Siang also carve wooden masks. The Khamptis make beautiful religious images figures of dancers, toys and other objects. Very beautiful woodcarvings are made by the Wanchos of Tirap. Some noteworthy products such as wooden cups, dishes, fruit bowls, masks (for ceremonial dances and pantomimes).

Status of Women Entrepreneurs

Women Entrepreneurs are the women or a group of women who initiate, organize and operate a business enterprise. The Government of India notes women entrepreneurs as 'an enterprise owned and controlled by women saving a minimum financial interest of 51 per cent of the capital and giving at least 51 per cent of the employment generated in the enterprise to women'. In Arunachal Pradesh, there are 1411 Nos. of SSI (presently MSME) units in both registered and unregistered, out of which 281 units are managed by women with a 19.91 per cent which is greater than the national average.

State	*No. of Units*	*Unregistered Units*		*Registered Units*		*Percentage*
Arunachal Pradesh	1411	Enterprises Managed by women	Women Enterprises	Enterprises Managed by women	Women Enterprises	19.91
		80	87	51	63	

Source: Ministry of SSI, GoI, Annual Report 2005-06.

Role of NGOs/SHGs

With the emphasis on empowering the poor and marginalized, many NGOs concentrate on 'the poorest of the poor'. In Arunachal Pradesh, there are 400 registered NGOs working in different parts of the state. Approximately 162 SHGs (SGSY), 35 SHGs (APSS) and other similar organizations are working in Arunachal Pradesh for micro-credit, income generation activities, education and health and women's development. Some are known for advocacy to mobilize the poor to pressure their governments to act promptly on important issues. Many NGOs work through Self-Help Groups. In fact, these have become alternative power centre to the feudal and entrenched powers in their villages. NGO lobbying and advocacy has prompted agencies and governments to reassess their policies and to introduce necessary amendments. Economic empowerment is a central focus of NGO and SHG concern. Poverty alleviation, provision of micro credit, employment in the informal sector, supply of improved seeds and other agricultural implements to increase income and employment is the key for the rural areas.

Role of Arunachal Pradesh Seva Sangh

Arunachal Pradesh Seva Sangh is the first NGO in Arunachal Pradesh, registered under section 3 of the Societies Registration Act, 1860 on June 17, 1979 with the aim to promote self-sustenance among rural people, particularly women through promotion of Khadi and Village Industries; to educate and train rural people for socio-economic upliftment; to develop Khadi and Village Industry network in remote parts of the state and promote village cottage industries; to promote land based developmental activities and agro-based industries; to preserve ecology and healthy living among rural masses; to strengthen National Emotional Integration through seminars, meetings, workshops and educational tours and to design and promote programmes for rural development and make alliances with other agencies in similar areas through its various activities like Skill Development Training programme; Production of Khadi Materials, Cane furniture, Mustard Oil and Spices; Demonstration of low cost Agriculture development using contour-hedgerow-farming-system technology; promoting of animal husbandry and dairy farming; Biogas, bio-composer and vermin-compost making; raising of quality seedling using green house and poly-houses and demonstration of water harvesting for mult-purpose uses; demonstration of sanitary latrines and solar lighting in different villages of Arunachal Pradesh. It is collaborative partners with KVIC, CSWB, Ministry of Tourism and Culture, GBPIHED and TAGS. It has strong 35 registered SHGs through the Arunachal Pradesh. So far, it has trained more than 2424 rural youth through Skill Development Training Programme under Multidisciplinary Training Centre (MDTC), Doimukh Centre and other extended programme in different parts of Arunachal Pradesh till 2006-07. Total 10 Nos. of project prepared by the APSS through its RICS Centre and the entire project are sanctioned by the KVIC and are functioning well. It has trained 45 string NGOs from NE region.

KVIC in Arunachal Pradesh

The Arunachal Pradesh has a great diversity in respect of culture, tradition and ethnicity. They have a tradition of artistic craftsmanship and are engaged in various activities such as weaving, painting, pottery, smithy work, basketry, woodcarving, etc. Therefore, development of KVI activities in Arunachal Pradesh is to be considered priority area under KVI programme. KVIC has introduced a Margin Money Scheme through which nationalized banks can make credit available to the enterprises directly up to Rs. 10 lakhs for individual units and up to Rs. 25 lakhs for institutions, for which 25 per cent of project outlay would be the margin money granted by the KVIC/state KVIB. KVI provides immediate employment, ensuring more equal distribution of wealth. This sector is labour intensive with less capital and less skill, and has short gestation period and advantage of decentralization. KVI programme is good for accelerating the tempo of rural industrialization in the state. Market is not necessarily confined to any particular geographical location in which buyer and seller are brought into contact with each other. What is essential for a market is that the buyers and the sellers are able to get in touch with each other and that the exchange of goods and services for money is affected between them. In the process of industrial development, the importance of cottage industries should not be ignored. Setting up a heavy industry is not possible in different places of this state, as its major portions are not easily accessible. But setting up small-scale industries in the state is not difficult.

Need to Strengthen the SHG through Multi Skill

The nature of skill mix in building trades is of significance. The skills required to perform building trades vary considerably. A 'mazdoor' could easily be used to assist a mason, concreter, painter or a carpenter. But the skill requirements begin to increase as one move up the technological ladder. Skills required to become a formwork and centering carpenter, are different from those required in a furniture making carpenter. Similar is the case in masonry, plumbing, etc. Each of these trades is semi-dependent, though a part of the construction process. Entry in the building job market is easy and quick at the bottom-end of the skill; the exit at this end is also easy though not as rapid. Unskilled workers keep moving in and out of the industry. But as the level of acquired skill grows, the opportunity for movement out of the industry declines. This is inevitable, as there is no demand for building skills in any other industry. They may change jobs from a contractor to an independent entrepreneur.

Social Partners for Skills Development System

A range of social partners has an important role to play in skills development sector. Social partners refers primarily to Employers in the public and private sectors, however, it can include in a broad sense Training Providers, Professional Societies, and NGOs/Civil Society Institutions. They can provide support by way of physical, financial and human resources, sharing of expertise and experience, and, above all, building a conducive environment and continued commitment to skill development. They can contribute through participation in identification of competencies, setting competency standards, skill-gap studies, curriculum development, assessment, delivery of training, monitoring and evaluation, and providing work place experience, equipment and trainers, and various incentives to promote skills development. Most of all, they provide a touchstone to base skills development initiatives in contextual reality and relevance. Involvement of social partners is thus an important strategy.

Public Private Partnership

The task of building a skills development system adequate to the size of potential requirement is just too large for the public sector to achieve on its own. Stimulation of private sector participation is thus an imperative. There are many opportunities for public private collaboration which are mutually beneficial:

- Provide greater space for private sector participation, and encourage and enable the private sector by dismantling undue procedural and policy barriers;
- Focus much more on establishing 'institutional mechanisms' and 'framework' aimed at the development of the system, than on direct delivery, but it would not abdicate its responsibility to set up lead institutions of excellence which serve as beacons and role models.
- Play a more 'strategic' than 'comprehensive' role.
- Adopt a more promotional role rather than regulatory and control.
- Extend to the private sector institutions, on par with public sector institutions, access to schemes and programmes that are aimed at quality improvement - such as curriculum

development, trainers' development, learning resource material development.

REGP and PMEGP

The Rural Employment Generation Programme (REGP) has been implemented by KVIC to generate additional employment opportunities in rural areas through setting up micro enterprises and helping in reduction of migration of people from rural to urban areas. The Prime Minister's Employment Generation Programme (PMEGP) is the merger of two schemes e.g. Prime Minister's Rojgar Yojana (PMRY) and The Rural Employment Generation Programme (REGP). Under the scheme, the beneficiary is required to invest his/her own contribution of 10 per cent of the project cost and in case of Scheduled Castes/Scheduled Tribes/Minority/OBC etc., it will be 5 per cent of the project cost. The remaining 90 per cent and 95 per cent of the project cost, as the case may be, is granted by banks specified under the scheme. The beneficiaries under the scheme are refunded a certain amount of the loan 25 per cent for general and 35 per cent for weaker sections in rural areas which is credited after two years from the date that the loan was extended.

Convergence of Collaborative Agencies

The KVIC has built up a large network of rural cottage industrial units producing a wide range of goods and articles catering the rural and partly urban markets. Some of them have achieved high standards for export but majority of them lack support in maintaining standard quality for want of technical back-up to upgrade the quality of their products. Keeping in view, KVIC should set up technical back-up units which will provide science and technology inputs to the entrepreneurs engaged in KVI activities. The KVIC have also undertaken certain activities in various outsourcing interfaces at engineering and technological institutes of Arunachal Pradesh to meet perceived needs to make the products more marketable either through design interventions or quality assurance system.

A MoU has signed between KVIC and ITC Ltd. (Agarbatti Division) envisages marketing of "MANGALDEEP" Agarbatti manufactured by Khadi and Village Industry units. The MoU envisages with:

Title	REGP	PMEGP
Objectives	To develop entrepreneurial skill among the rural unemployed youth. To achieve the goal of rural industrialization. To facilitate participation of Financial Institutions for higher Credit to rural industries.	• To generate employment opportunities in rural as well as urban areas of the country through setting up of new self-employment, ventures/ projects/ micro enterprises. • To bring together widely dispersed traditional artisans/ rural and urban unemployed youth and give them self-employment opportunities to the extent possible, at their place. • To provide continuous and sustainable employment to a large segment of traditional and prospective artisans and rural and urban unemployed youth in the country, so as to help arrest migration of rural youth to urban areas. • To increase the wage earning capacity of artisans and contribute to increase in the growth rate of rural and urban employment.

Financial Assistance	Beneficiary's contribution	Margin Money	Beneficiary's contribution	Rate of Subsidy Urban	Rate of Subsidy Rural
General Category	10%	25%	10%	15%	25%
Special Category [SC/ST/OBC/ Minorities, etc.]	05%	30%	05%	25%	35%
Beneficiaries	Any individual above 18 years of age; Individual Entrepreneurs; Self-Help Groups; Institutions; Co-op. Societies; Trusts and Public Limited Companies owned by State/Central Government.		Any individual, above 18 years of age; Self-Help Groups (including BPL); Institutions registered under Societies Registration Act,1860; Production Co-operative Societies, and Charitable Trusts. **Note:** Project costing above Rs.10 lakhs in the manufacturing sector and above Rs. 5 lakhs in the business/service sector, the beneficiaries should possess at least VIII standard pass educational qualification.		
Financial Institutions	27 Public Sector Banks and their sponsored Regional Rural Banks; Private Sector Banks approved by the State/UT KVI Boards and Co-op. Banks approved by the State/UT KVI Boards.		27 Public Sector Banks; Regional Rural Banks; Co-operative Banks approved by State Level Task Force; Private Sector Scheduled Commercial Banks approved by State Level Task Force and Small Industries Development Bank of India.		

Contd...

Village Industry	Any Village Industry including Coir based projects located in the rural area which produces any goods or renders any service with or without the use of power and in which the fixed capital investment per head of a full time artisan or worker does not exceed Rs. 50,000.	Any Village Industry including Coir based projects located in the rural area which produces any goods or renders any service with or without the use of power and in which the fixed capital investment per head of a full time artisan or worker i.e. Capital Expenditure on workshop/ workshed, machinery and furniture divided by full time employment created by the project does not exceed Rs. 1 lakh in plain areas and Rs.1.50 lakh in hilly areas.
Rural Area	Any area classified as Village as per the revenue record of the State, irrespective of population. It also includes an area even if classified as town, provided its population does not exceed 20,000.	Any area classified as Village as per the revenue record of the Union Territory, irrespective of population. It will also include any area even if classified population does not exceed 20,000 persons.
Entrepreneurship Development Programme (EDP)	The objective of EDP is to provide orientation and awareness to various managerial and operational functions like finance, production, marketing,	The objective of EDP is to provide orientation and awareness to various managerial and operational functions like finance, production, marketing, enterprise

	enterprise management, banking formalities, book-keeping, etc. The duration for EDP under REGP was only 3 days. EDP will be mandatory for all the REGP beneficiaries.	management, banking formalities, book-keeping, etc. The duration for EDP under PMRY will be 10 days. EDP will be mandatory for all the PMEGP beneficiaries.
Marketing Support	Marketing support for the products, produced by the units REGP may be provided through KVIC's Marketing Sales outlets. KVIC will reserve the right to provide such a support based on quality, pricing and other parameters to be separately circulated by KVIC to KVIBs/DICs.	Marketing support for the products, produced by the units PMEGP may be provided through KVIC's Marketing Sales outlets. KVIC will reserve the right to provide such a support based on quality, pricing and other parameters to be separately circulated by KVIC to KVIBs/DICs.
Product Promotion	REGP Exhibition will be organized by KVIC in coordination with KVIB in State/ District levels to promote product produced by REGP Units.	PMEGP Exhibitions will be organized by KVIC at National, Zonal, State and District Levels and special exhibitions for North-Eastern Zone in coordination with KVIBs and DICs, to promote products produced by PMEGP units.

Contd...

Registration	Registration with the KVIC/ KVIBs under the Scheme is mandatory. Beneficiary will have to register either with KVIC or KVIB. The application should be accompanied by registration fee @ 1 per cent of the project cost. Registration is valid for 3 financial years. For further renewal of the registration, registration fee @ 0.5 per cent of the project cost is to be paid to the KVIC.	Registration with the KVIC/KVIBs/State DICs under the Scheme is voluntary. No registration fee will be charged from the beneficiaries and the funds available under Forward and Backward linkage will be utilized to meet expenses on documentation cost, etc.
Evaluation of the Scheme	A Comprehensive evaluation of the scheme was there without rigidity.	A comprehensive, independent and rigorous evaluation of the scheme will be done after two years of its implementation. Based on the findings of the evaluation study the scheme would be reviewed.

- One of the manufacturing units functioning as the nodal agency for quality assurance, perfuming and packaging of the product in accordance with ITC's specifications and
- ITC buying the entire produce of agarbatties from these KVI units and undertaking their marketing through its own outlets and the outlets in KVI sector. It is expected that this MoU would be beneficial to the KVI units concerned by assured off take of the product, additional marketing channels becoming available to the KVI units, promotion of the product as a distinct brand, expansion of production base resulting in employment generation a sustainable basis in the rural areas, etc.

The State Office of KVIC in Arunachal Pradesh should take initiative from the above MoU for the sustenance of local artisans in the globalization era.

Raw Materials Store at KVIC State Office

In order to facilitate continuous off take of slivers/roving by khadi institutions faced with resource crunch, the KVIC operated local godowns during the year 2004-05 in the states of Rajasthan, Maharashtra, Gujarat, Uttar Pradesh, Andhra Pradesh, Tamil Nadu and West Bengal. Therefore, similar pattern of raw materials store in the state KVIC Office is urgently needed for continuous supply of raw materials to the SHGs through DIC/District Centre of APKVIB and simultaneously to collect the products from SHGs to easy bulk transfer of product materials to KVIC Store for further transfer to the different outlet in the state as well as other states also. This may give a new era to the local artisan of Arunachal Pradesh for long time sustainability of their venture.

Restructuring Marketing Facilities

The world is moving towards natural and eco-friendly products. More and more people are becoming conscious of responsibility towards the environment and ecology. The products like plastic, etc. are highly looked down upon and demand is being generated for bio-degradable and eco-friendly products. The KVI Sector produces a wide range of exclusive products which have distinct characteristics. There is urgent need of a number of marketing organizations in the State like the State Trading

Corporation, Industrial Marketing Federation. In addition, Marketing and Export Promotion Council (MEPC) as apex agency is highly essential to support the sale of goods within and outside the State. The existing organizations have to encourage continuing their operations and taking up marketing of the hitherto neglected products. The MEPC may be entrusted for marketing and export of the local produce and provide guidelines for establishment of marketing infrastructure, roadways, warehouses etc. and provide directions for efficient functioning of the marketing agencies. A Market Information Cell is essential component to provide the most up-to-date market trends on various goods. The Government should make an attempt to reduce the cost of the production and transportation and enhance the overall competitiveness of the products manufactured in the State. The KVIC has launched a massive marketing development plan throughout the country to generate interest, awareness and attraction amongst the masses about khadi and village industries products. To create a market-niche for eco-friendly, pure and bio-degradable natural products, the KVIC have introduced two new brands 'Sarvodaya and Khadi'. The KVIC has worked out a plan to supply KVI products in a big way to Central and State Government Organizations and to set up show windows in Indian Missions abroad, as well as, to open Khadi Gramodyog Bhawans in Australia, Germany, UK, USA, Canada, Dubai and Singapore. To review these schemes and to give a major thrust to marketing efforts, the scheme should be revised with the following:

- To assist in marketing and boost the sale of Khadi and V.I. products including handicrafts,
- To facilitate the consumer to purchase genuine Khadi and V.I. products brought from different parts of the country under one umbrella,
- To serve as a window for promoting awareness among the consumers about the latest designs and varieties of fabrics, products etc.,
- To disseminate knowledge about the latest designs developed amongst artisans,
- To create mass awareness about the KVI Programme/KVI products,

- To bring the rural traditional skill of artisans and help in promoting the image of the organization,
- To liquidate the accumulated stocks of Khadi and V.I. products available with the implementing agencies of KVI sector,

To help the Institutions / Artisans in the areas affected by natural calamities viz., Earthquake, Cyclone, Floods etc.

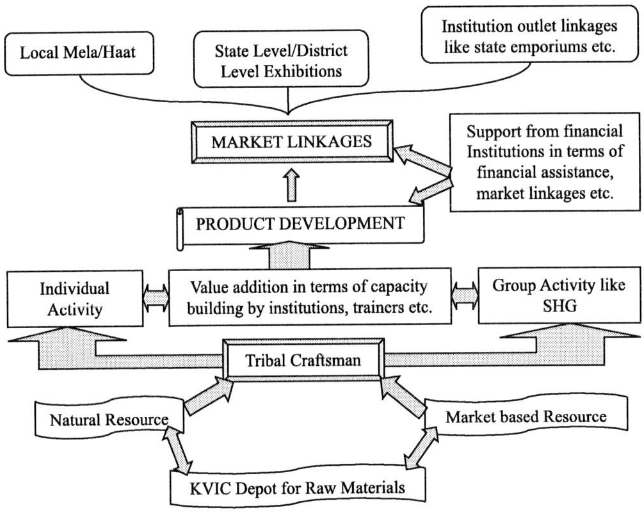

Fig. 3.1: Marketing Model

Pragmatic Model Approach

The Pragmatic Model has been developed based on a recent survey undertaken during a SHG product at State level REGP Exhibition held at Itanagar during February 20-29, 2008. The survey was conducted through business proponents used questionnaires as the main form of gathering the data needed for the study. The proponents used the questionnaire with personal suggestions of the respondents and marketing aspect like product, price and promotion. The proponents applied the descriptive method in presenting data that was gathered from 399 respondents composed of several households. This method was used to assess, analyze and interpret the respondents' perceptions on a candle and candle stands (both metallic and wooden). The study was made in order to know whether the consumers would accept the candles with candle stand and to identify their preferences when purchasing Candle. The representative sample size of respondents was determined by Sloven's formula:

$$n = N/1 + Ne^2$$

where, n = representative
N = size of total population
e = margin of error (assumed to be 5% or 0.05)

$$n = 122003/1 + 122003\ (0.05)^2 = 399$$

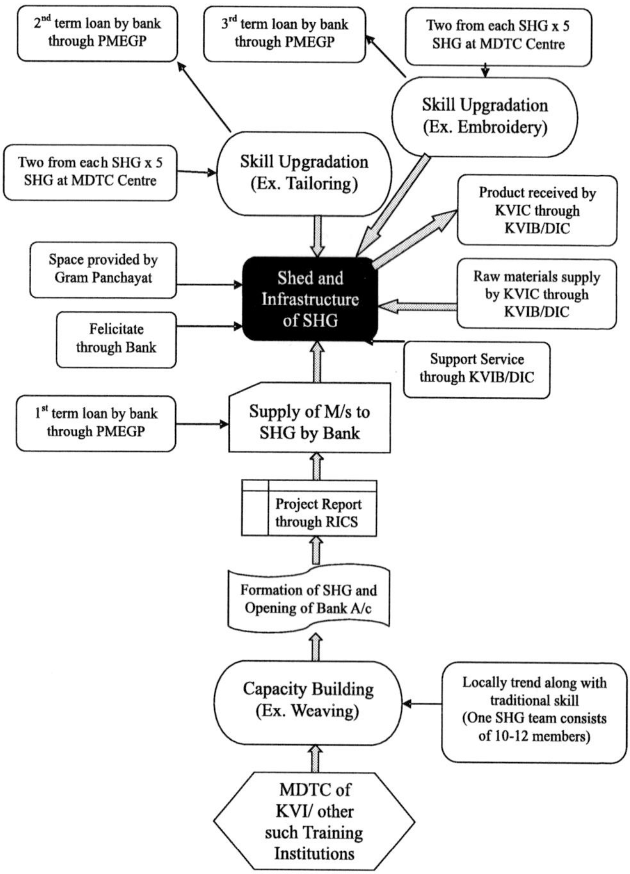

Fig. 3.2: Pragmatic Model

Flow Chart for Delivery of Product

The flow chart represents the delivery of product by the SHG in a convenient manner and also receiving the required raw materials for their unit. The system has developed in such a way that no body need to handle cash, as the whole system will be done through banking system. The KVIC state office would be sole responsibility to deposit the earning money (Product Cost – Raw materials) to the bank directly where the Bank accounts of SHG are maintained. The Bank also has no problem to deduct their loan amount from the SHG A/c. Fig. 3.3 shows the delivery of product to the outlets of KVIC to sustain SHG.

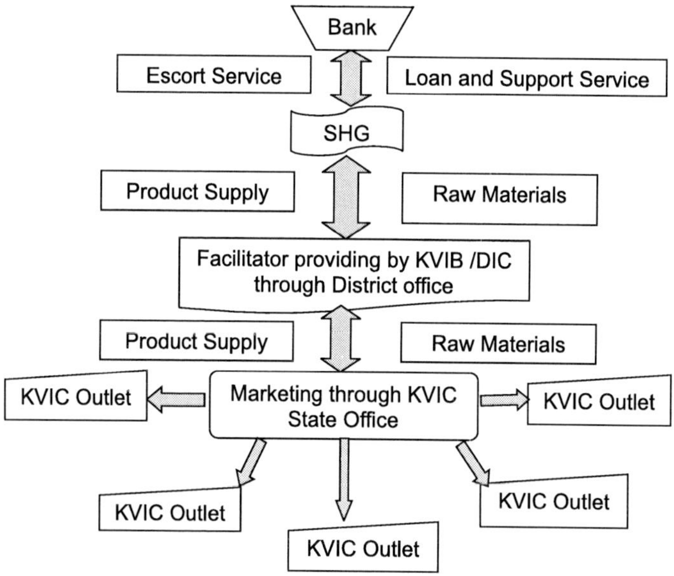

Fig. 3.3: Delivery of Product to outlets of KVIC.

Recommendations

- The khadi programme should be ensuring that production of goods actually takes place on a sustainable basis, so that its main objective of generating employment opportunities for the unskilled/ rural poor is met.

- The overhaul of the marketing strategy for khadi products, product development and marketing need a professional approach.
- It should concentrate on technological upgradation and diffusion to continually raise labour productivity and improve product mix of units.
- To ensure supply of raw material and other inputs to all units at fixed terms.
- To ensure delivery of output by the units to KVIC as per cost charts and inputs supplied, by linking release of concessional funds to delivery of output;
- To impart train to artisans and technicians more effectively than being done at present. The entire cost of such training should be borne by KVIC and should also provide the necessary financial help to the units /institutions to bring about an improvement in the hygienic conditions of the work places (such as providing pollution mask for khadi workers).
- To monitor input delivery, output quality, assessment of needs of the units in response to changes in market demand.
- To develop an appropriate MIS to get market information feedback from the private sector on the desired product mix, output quality, demand pattern and respond to the changes by reorienting production pattern of the units.
- To constitute a Committee to examine the feasibility of the proposed model and to suggest suitable measures.

Conclusion

The Khadi and Village Industries programme holds great potential for generating gainful employment opportunities for the rural poor, arresting migration of rural unskilled workers to urban areas and for promoting the strategy of sustainable development. It can also be a viable and effective social safety net to enable the poor to ward off the adverse impacts of structural adjustment and economic reforms on their well-being. However, this potential cannot be realized without addressing some basic weaknesses with regard to the design and implementation of the programme and without making it fiscally sustainable.

REFERENCES

Acharya, S. and Mitra, A. (2000), "The Potential of Rural Industries and Trade to Provide Decent Work Conditions: A Data Reconnaissance in India", *SAAT Working Papers*, International Labour Organization, New Delhi.

Arunachal Pradesh Seva Sangh, 'Brief profile', 2007.

Bandyopadhyay, D., Yugandhar, B. N., Mukherjee, A. (2002), "Convergence of Programme by Empowering SHGs and PRIs", *Economic and Political Weekly*, Vol. 37(26), pp. 2556-2561.

Basant, R., Kumar, B. L. and Parthasarathy, R. (1998), *Non-Agricultural Employment in Rural India: The Case of Gujarat*, Rawat Publications, Jaipur, India.

Bhattacharya, B. B., Bhanumurthy N. R. and Sakthivel, S. (2004), "Economic Reforms and Structural Changes in Employment: A Comparative Analysis of Gender Specific Employment Behaviour in Organized and Informal Sector in India", an unpublished report submitted to *Institute of Economic Growth*, Delhi University Enclave, Delhi-110007.

Biswas, N. B. (1996), *Development of Education in Arunachal Pradesh: A Critical Study*, Arunachal University Research Journal, Vol. I.

Chadha, G. K. (2001), "Impact of Economic Reforms on Rural Employment: No Smooth Sailing Anticipated", *Indian Journal of Agricultural Economics*, Vol. 56, No. 3, pp. 491.

Cohen, J. M. and Uphoff, N.T. (1997), *Rural Development Participation: Concepts and Measures for Project Design, Implementation and Evaluation*, New York.

Das, Gurudas (1995), *Tribes of Arunachal Pradesh in Transition*, Vikas Publishing House, New Delhi.

Elwin, V. (1988), *The Art of North-East Frontier of India*, Directorate of Research, Government of Arunachal Pradesh, Itanagar.

Fisher, T. and Mahajan, V. (1998), *The Forgotten Sector: Non-farm Employment and Enterprises in Rural India*, Intermediate Technology Publications, London.

Haq, Mahbub Ul. (1996), *Reflections on Human Development*, Oxford University Press, New York.

http://dkvib.delhigovt.nic.in/aboutus.html

http://en.wikipedia.org/wikiKhadi_and_Village_Industries_Commission

http://www.ari.nic.in/RevisedKVICACT2006.pdf

http://www.indianchamber.net/new/northeast ARUNACHAL PRADESH.pdf

http://www.indianexpress.com/news/msme-ministry-asked-to-redraw-rebate-scheme/471467/

http://www.kirjasto.sci.fi/gandhi.htm

http://www.kvic.org.in/v4/KHADI4.ASP

http://www.kvic.org.in/V4/OVERVIEW.ASP

http://www.msme.gov.in/Chapter%205.pdf

Kulkarni, A. P. (1993), "Employment in Informal Sector: Some Issue", *The Indian Journal of Labour Economics*, Vol. 36, No. 4.

Kundu, A. and Sharma, A. N. (2001), "Informal Sector in India: Perspectives and Policies", *Institute of Human Development and Institute of Applied Manpower Research*, New Delhi.

KVIC (1995), *Guidelines on Rural Employment Generation Programme (REGP)*, Mumbai.

KVIC (2008), *Guidelines on Prime Minister's Employment Generation Programme (PMEGP)*, Mumbai.

KVIC, *Annual Report*, 1996-97.

Mahendra, D. (2000), "Economic Reforms, Poverty, Income Distribution and Employment", *Economic and Political Weekly*, March.

Maji, D. (2008), Decentralization: Role of NGOs/SHGs in Rural Development, in the NABARD and NEITCO sponsored One day State Level Seminar on 'Rural Development in Arunachal Pradesh' organized by State Institute of Rural Development, Itanagar, Arunachal Pradesh on July 9, 2008, pp. 5-6.

Maji, D. (2008), Experimental Analysis of EQ as Tools for Quality Workplace, Proc. of the International Conference on 'Management' Bhadu, S. S. (ed.), Mohanlal Sukhadia University, Udaipur, Rajasthan, September 22-24, 2008.

Maji, D. (2008), Role of CATRD in Social Development, in the NABARD and NEITCO sponsored One day State Level Seminar on 'Rural Development in Arunachal Pradesh' organized by State Institute of

Rural Development, Itanagar, Arunachal Pradesh on July 9, 2008, p. 11.

Maji, D. (2008), Work Motivation: A Culture Based Approach, in the 'Humanizing Work and Work Environment', Eds. Abhyankar, H. K. *et al.*, ISBN 978-81-906198-2-0 published by Vishwakarma Institute of Technology, Pune, 2008, pp. 571-576.

Maji, D. (2009), Knowledge Management: A Typical Application for Planning, in the Book of Abstracts of National Conference on 'Emerging Trends in Mechanical Engineering', Eds. Mehta, A. and Desai, D. published by GCET, Vallabh Vidyanagar, Gujarat during March 20-21, 2009, p. 49.

Maji, D. (2009), Micro Finance through SHG for Poverty Alleviation in Arunachal Pradesh, in the Souvenir of National Seminar on 'Micro Finance and Women Empowerment' held at Yogi Vemana University, Kadapa, Andhra Pradesh during March 12-13, 2009, p. 17.

Ministry of Agro and Rural Industries, *Annual Report*, 2005-06.

Ministry of Development of North-Eastern Region and North-East Council, *North-East Region Vision 2020*, Volume-1.

Ministry of Rural Development (1994), *Report of the Technical Committee on DPAP and DDP*, Government of India, New Delhi.

Ministry of Small Scale Industries, *Annual Report*, 2005-06.

Mishra, P. K. (1995), *50 years of Independence: Programmes for Change*, New Delhi, Ministry of Rural Areas and Employment, Government of India.

Mishra, P.K. (1995), *Linkages with Self-Help Groups, NGOs and Cooperatives for provision of Micro Credit*, New Delhi.

NABARD (1992), *Refinance Assistance for Non-Farm Sector Activities*, Mumbai.

NIRD-NERC, Summary Paper on "Poverty Eradication/Alleviation in North-East India: An Approach", Guwahati.

Pandey, D. and Tripathy, B. (1997), *A Comprehensive History of Arunachal Pradesh*, Bani Mandir Publications, Pasighat, Arunachal Pradesh.

Planning Commission (2001), *Evaluation Study on Khadi and Village Industries Programme*, Government of India, New Delhi.

Planning Commission (2001), *Report of the Task Force on Employment Opportunities*, Government of India, July, New Delhi.

Planning Commission (2002), *Report of the Special Group on Targeting Ten Million Employment Opportunities per Year*, Govt. of India, New Delhi.

Ramakrishna, P. S. (1992), *Shifting Agriculture and Sustainable Development: an inter-disciplinary study from North-Eastern India*, Wiley Eastern.

Saleth, R. M. (1999), *Strategic Linkages in Rural Diversification: Empirical Analysis and Policy Issues*, Commonwealth Publishers, New Delhi.

Sarkar, Goutam K. (2001), *Agriculture and rural transformation in India*, Oxford University Press, Calcutta.

Srivastava, R. (1997), "Poverty Reduction in India: Economic Growth, Human Development and Anti-poverty Programme", *A background paper for the World Bank.*

Uma, R. and Jeemol, U. (2004), "Unorganized and Organized Manufacturing in India-Potential for Employment Generating Growth", *Economic and Political Weekly*, October, pp. 4568-4580.

Upadhyay, V. and Mishra, D. (2004), "Micro Enterprises in Hill Economies: A Study on Arunachal Pradesh", *The Indian Journal of Labour Economics*, Vol. 47. No. 4, pp. 1027-38.

World Bank (2000), *India: Reducing Poverty, Accelerating Development*, Oxford University Press, New Delhi.

4

Small-scale and Village Industries in Economic Development of Nepal

UDAYA RAJ REGMI AND ARJUN KUMAR BARAL

Introduction

The growth and development of small and village industries in Nepal may be traced back to the *Kiratee* Empire which ruled the country several centuries before the Christian era. By the fourth century B.C. and afterwards, various types of artistic goods requiring high degree of craft used to be produced and exported to India and Tibet which were highly admired for their high craft and artistic beauty. The department of cottage industry established in 1939 with the aim of propagating crafts and small industries in general and the cottage handloom industries in particular is conceived to be the landmark in the development of small and village industries in Nepal. Owing to the slow rate of capital formation, persistence of disguised and seasonal unemployment, local utilization of raw materials, small and disintegrated domestic market, high potentiality of earning foreign exchange, lack of appropriate technology and inefficient human resources, small and village industries still play a crucial role in the national economy.

Methodology

"Industrial policy should increase both the importance and productivity of the manufacturing sector. Industrial policy may affect manufacturing-wide productivity by increasing the importance of industries whose *TFP* growth is above average, by altering the structure of manufacturing sector, or by stimulating TFP_i itself" (Pack, 2000). As used in the literature, following model has been employed:

$$IP = \Sigma_i (VA_i / VA)\, TFP_i$$

where subscripts i indicates individual industries such as food processing, textiles, wearing apparel within the manufacturing sector, VA_i is value added originating in sector i, VA is manufacturing-wide value added, TFP_i is the rate of total factor productivity in sector i, and IP is the Industrial Policy index. The ratio of value added in each sector to value added in all manufacturing (VA_i / VA) represents the industrial structure where sectors with high ratios are more prominent than sectors with low ratios. Industrial policy index is the sum of *TFP* growth in each sector weighted by a measure of the importance of that sector. If the calculated effect is large and positive, there may be a basis for least developed countries embarking on more intensive industrialization.

The present study seeks to estimate *TFP* growth with the help of Divisia Tornquist approximation from a transcendental logarithmic (translog) production function. In such a formulation, Total Factor Productivity Growth (TFPG) can be expressed as:

$$Ln(Y_t / Y_{t-1}) = Q_K ln\, (K_t / K_{t-1}) + Q_M ln\, (M_t / M_{t-1}) + Q_L ln\, (L_t / L_{t-1}) + TFPG$$

$$TFPG_{t-1,t} = ln\, (Y_t / Y_{t-1}) - Q_K ln\, (K_t / K_{t-1}) - Q_M ln\, (M_t / M_{t-1}) - Q_L ln\, (L_t / L_{t-1})$$

where $Q_t = (Q_{it} + Q_{it-1})/2$, Y denotes output, K denotes capital input proxied by gross fixed asset, M is the intermediate input, L is the labour input proxied by total number of employed persons and Q_K, Q_M, Q_L denote factor share of capital, factor share of intermediate inputs, and factor share of labour respectively.

In order to estimate the technical efficiency of each industrial sub-group, the stochastic production frontier model developed by Aigner, Lovell, and Schmidt (1977) and applied by Cornell, Schmidt and Sickles, 1990; Krishna and Sahota, 1991; Fecher and Pestiean, 1993; Wu, 1995) has been employed which is defined as:

$$ln\, Y_i = \alpha + \Sigma_j \beta\, ln\, X_{ji} + \varepsilon_i$$

where ln Y_i is logarithm of output of industry i, $ln\, X_j$ is a vector of logarithm j inputs is vector of unknown parameters to be estimated. The error term ε_i is composed of two components, a symmetric random component ($v_i \neq 0$) and a one-sided component ($u_i \geq 0$) representing technical inefficiency. Technical efficiency is obtained from the following relation:

$$TE_i = Y_i / Y_i^* = \exp(u_i)$$

where Y_i is the observed level of output and Y_i^* is the frontier level of output, and $du_i/dt = TE_i$. Technical efficiency lies in the interval 0 and 1, $0 \leq TE \leq 1$, where 1 indicates full efficiency. Output growth is equal to the rate of technological change, input growth, and the rate of change in technical efficiency (TE) it is expressed as:

$$Y_i = \alpha + \Sigma_j \beta_j X_i + TE$$
$$TFPG = \alpha + TE$$

Productivity will depend on both technology and the efficiency with which factors of production are used (Landau, 1986). Hence, *TFPG* is the summation of the rate of technological progress or regress and the rate of change in technical efficiency (*TE*).

In order to compare the level of industrialization among five regions, composite indices, deviation indices, and A/E ratio have been computed. The Composite index has been computed by converting the entire data of five development regions into scoring system for which six variables of industrialization namely number of factories, manufacturing employment, value added, percentage of manufacturing employment to total workers, percentage of manufacturing employment to total population, and value added per employee are added. The maximum 100 point score has been allotted to the region having the highest value of the indicator. Then, Composite index for each region is calculated by dividing total scores by the number of indicators. Likewise, deviation index has also been calculated. The mean value of each indicator has been assumed as unity. The value of each indicator for each region has been converted into index by dividing the value of each indicator for each region by corresponding mean values. Then, the sum of the index value of all indicators for each region is divided by the number of indicators to get the Deviation index. The regional imbalances in regional industrial development have also been computed by Area-Employment (*A/E*) ratio as follows:

A/E ratio = (Percentage value of area of a particular region/ percentage value of number of persons engaged in manufacturing industries in that region).

The sum of Total Factor Productivity (*TFP*) growth in each sector weighted by a measure of the importance of that sector has been used as an indicator of industrial policy. The weighted total factor productivity (*TFP**) growth has been regarded as an index of industrial policy (Pack, 2000) on which this analysis is based. In mathematical terms, this can be expressed as: $TFP^* = \Sigma_i (VA_i/VA)\, TFP_i$, where subscripts *i* indicates individual industries such as food processing, textiles, wearing apparel within the manufacturing sector, VA_i is value added originating in sector *i*, *VA* is manufacturing-wide value added, TFP_i is the rate of total factor productivity in sector *i*, and *IP* is the Industrial Policy index. The ratio of value added in each sector to value added in all manufacturing (VA_i/VA) represents the industrial structure where sectors with high ratios are more prominent than sectors with low ratios. If the calculated effect is large and positive, there may be a basis for least developed countries embarking on more intensive industrialization.

This study is based on secondary information. The main data sources are the Census of Manufacturing Establishments, 1981/82, 1991/92, and 2001/02 prepared by Central Bureau of Statistics. These Censuses report data on number of establishments, output, input, value added, number of persons employed, wages and salaries, and fixed assets for organized manufacturing establishments engaging ten or more persons. The other data source includes the regular issues of "Economic Survey" published by Ministry of Finance. Besides, some international sources like "Global Development Finance" published by the World Bank, and "Handbook of Statistics" published by United Nations have been used. These publications report data on Gross Domestic Product and Foreign Direct Investment.

Present Situation

Small Scale and Village Industries in the National Economy

Although Nepalese economy is dominated by agricultural sector, small-scale and village industries are also playing an important role in income-generation programme of the country. The overall scenario of these industries has been presented in Table 4.1.

Table 4.1: Contribution of Small-scale and Village Industries

Year	*National GDP (Rs in Millions)*	*Manufacturing Sector*		*Small Scale and Village Industries*	
		GDP (Rs. in Millions)	*%*	*GDP (Rs. in Millions)*	*%*
1964-65-1968-69	6815.80	126.80	1.82	459.4	6.73
1969-70-1973-74	10170.40	280.80	2.72	690.0	6.78
1974-75-1978-79	19426.00	497.60	2.60	248.8	1.30
1979-80-1983-84	30596.00	908.80	2.92	392.0	1.29
1984-85-1992-93	84819.88	4188.00	4.60	1518.0	1.83
1999-2000-2007-08	494374.00	40603.44	8.35	7460.56	1.55

Source: Authors' calculation based on *Economic Survey* (various issues), Ministry of Finance, Government of Nepal.

Table 4.1 presents the information that the contribution of small-scale and village industries during the period 1964-65 to 1973-74 to the GDP was more than 6 per cent. But its contribution has been significantly declined from 1974-75 till now. It has been contributing only by less than 2 per cent to the GDP.

Performance of Small-scale and Village Industries in the Process of Industrialization

The performance of these industries has been analyzed on the basis of number of industries, employment, production and investment. The overall scenario of these industries has been presented in Table 4.2.

Table 4.2: Performance of Small-Scale and Village Industries

	Year	*All Industries*	*Middle and Large*	*Small Scale and Village Industries*	*% of Small Scale and Village Industries*
No. of Industries	1977-78	75445	3570.00	75057	99.49
	1991-92	50689	4271	46418	91.57
Employment	1977-78	1271340	56340	1215000	95.57
	1991-92	310166	223463	86703	27.95
Production	1977-78	3288141	2575140	713901	21.71
(Rs.'000)	1991-92	16213450	13649922	2563528	15.81
Investment	1977-78	826050	485000	341050	41.29
(Rs.'000)	1991-92	25038150	20087126	4951024	19.77

Source: Authors' calculation based on *Census of Manufacturing Establishments* (Various Years), Central Bureau of Statistics, Government of Nepal.

Table 4.3: Annual Average Rate of Growth of the Small-Scale and Village Industries

	1977-78	*1991-92*	*1999-2000*	*Average Annual Growth Rate (1977-78-1991-92)*	*Average Annual Growth Rate (1991-92-1999-2000)*
No. of industries	750575	46418	43671	–16.93	–6.75
No. of persons engaged	1215000	86703	121270	–16.14	3.80
Gross fixed assets	341050	4951024	8165338	19.52	5.72
Output	713901	7530981	25945645	17.00	14.73

Source: Authors' calculation based on *Census of Manufacturing Establishments* (Various Years), Central Bureau of Statistics, Government of Nepal.

Table 4.2 shows that the number of industries, employment, production and investment seems to have been significantly declined during 1977-78-1991-92. Though the number of industries has been declined from 99.49 per cent in 1977-78 to 91.57 per cent in 1991-92, it has occupied a major position in the industrial sector of the country. The average annual growth rate is negative and even declining further during the latter period. The average annual growth rate of the number of small-scale and village industries declined from –16.93 per cent in 1977-78-1991-92 to –6.75 per cent in 1991-92-1999-2000. These industries have created employment opportunities to 95.57 per cent of total employment opportunities from the industrial sector in 1977-78 which has declined sharply to 27.95 per cent in 1991-92. The number of persons engaged sharply declined during the former period and increased a little bit during the latter period. The average annual growth rate was –16.14 per cent during 1977-78 -1991-92 which increased to 3.8 per cent during 1991-92-1997-98. The production has also declined from 21.71 per cent of the total industrial sector in 1977-78 to 15.81 per cent in 1991-92. The average annual growth rate of output also declined from 17.0 per cent during 1977-78-1991-92 to 14.73 per cent during 1991-92-1999-2000. As a result, the investment has also declined from 41.29 per cent of the total industrial sector in 1977-78 to 19.77 per cent in 1991-92. The average annual growth rate of gross fixed assets also declined sharply from 19.52 per cent in 1977-78-1991-92 to 5.72 per cent in 1991-92-1999-2000. Thus, the overall performance of these industries looks gloomy and dismal in Nepal in recent times.

Output Growth and Total Factor Productivity of Small-scale and Village Industries

The sources of output growth and Total Factor Productivity have been decomposed as material input growth, capital input growth, labour input growth and total factor productivity growth of small-scale and village industries in Nepal. The analysis of such decomposition has been presented on the basis of various natures of industries which have been shown in Table 4.4.

The results show that the contribution of total factor productivity to output growth is appreciably high whereas the contribution of capital and intermediate goods seems extremely low. In contrast, labour has negative contribution to output growth in small-scale and village industries during 1991-92-1999-2000.

Table 4.4: Sources of Output Growth and Total Factor Productivity in Small-scale and Village Industries in Nepal (1991-92-1999-2000)

Name of Industries	*Output growth*	*Material input growth*	*Capital input growth*	*Labour input growth*	*TFPG*	*% Share of VA (1991)*	*% Share of VA (1999)*	*Industrial Policy*	*Rate of change in TE*	*Technological progress/ regress*
Food	1.6542	0.3492	0.1811	0.0010	1.1229	0.3676	0.5801	0.7820	0.028	1.096
Tobacco	0.5981	0.0687	0.2484	–0.0388	0.3198	0.0046	0.0023	0.0010	–5.653	5.948
Textiles	–0.1767	0.0034	–0.382	–0.1369	0.3393	0.1066	0.0209	0.0185	–1.141	1.389
Wearing Apparel	–0.6426	–0.0520	–0.277	–0.1387	–0.174	0.0277	0.0070	–0.0033	–9.845	9.573
Leather Footwear	1.5047	0.1831	0.1190	0.1294	1.0732	0.0057	0.0248	0.0438	0.431	0.766
Wood	1.1659	0.2059	0.0379	0.0144	0.9078	0.0333	0.0424	0.0491	0.180	0.739
Paper	1.3752	0.1978	–0.435	–0.0263	1.6392	0.0458	0.0111	0.0210	2.183	–0.565
Printing and Publishing	–0.2501	–0.0401	–0.243	–0.1622	0.1959	0.0076	0.0201	0.0083	0.074	–0.019
Chemical Products	0.0795	–0.0910	0.1424	0.0227	0.0054	0.0076	0.0057	0.0000	2.974	–2.949
Rubber and Plastics	1.8177	0.3109	0.6629	0.0967	0.7472	0.0039	0.0109	0.0093	–1.793	2.632
Non-metallic Mineral	0.7954	0.0729	0.2547	0.0760	0.3919	0.0031	0.0216	0.0113	–1.829	2.272

Fabricated Metal Products	0.2266	0.0020	0.1131	–0.0997	0.2112	0.0308	0.0186	0.0097	2.151	–2.027
Electrical Goods	–0.7770	–0.1134	–0.4584	–0.0864	–0.1188	0.1040	0.0022	–0.0008	–5.338	5.138
Radio and TV	–1.2880	–0.4080	0.1220	0.0133	–1.0153	0.0110	0.0001	–0.0157	–125.582	124.579
Furniture	0.6473	0.1063	0.6162	0.0478	–0.1230	0.0246	0.0834	–0.0151	–0.289	0.211
Total	1.2370	0.2515	0.1960	–0.0078	0.7972	1.0000	1.0000	0.9191	–0.008	0.798

Source: Authors' calculation based on *Census of Manufacturing Establishments* (Various Years), Central Bureau of Statistics, Government of Nepal.

During this period the total growth rate of output is 1.23 per cent out of which the contribution of *TFPG* is 0.7972 whereas material input and capital input have contributed by 0.2515 and 0.1960 respectively. This also holds in almost all the industries. Though the small-scale and village industries are technically inefficient, the technological progress is single most important factor that contributes considerably to the total factor productivity growth which ultimately leads to output growth. Although the share of value added declined in almost all the industries, the food industries are playing a dominant role. Hence the basic structure of these industries remains the same in almost all the industries.

Contribution of Small-scale and Village Industries in Foreign Trade

Small-scale and village industries were playing a vital role in export trade of Nepal from manufacturing industrial sector. Though the current situation is not satisfactory, its contribution in export trade cannot be underestimated. The contribution of these industries has been presented in Tables 5 and 6.

Table 4.5: Share of Small-scale and Village Industries in foreign trade of Nepal (1993-94 and 2006-07)

Year	*Total Export*	*Manufactured Exports*	*Export from small and village industries*
1993-94	19293.4	17546.2 (90.94%)	7811.507 (44.52%)
2006-07	59383.1	46481.2 (78.27%)	6512.989 (14.01%)

Source: Authors' calculation based on *Census of Manufacturing Establishments* (Various Years), Central Bureau of Statistics, and *Economic Survey* (various issues), Ministry of Finance, Government of Nepal.

From the Table 4.5, it has been found that the share of manufacturing industries in total exports was very high (90.94 per cent) in 1993-94 out of which 44.52 per cent contributed by small and village industries. But in 2006-07, the share of manufacturing industries in total exports declined to 78.27 per cent

Table 4.6: Commodity-wise Share of Small and Village Industries in Foreign Trade of Nepal (1993-94 and 2006-07)

Commodities	*Total Export*		*Large and Medium Manufactured Export from*		*Small_X*		*%LM_X*		*%Small_X*	
Year	1993-94	2006-07	1993-94	2006-07	1993-94	2006-07	1993-94	2006-07	1993-94	2006-07
Woollen Carpets	9534.1	5600.2	2328.751	2302.435	7205.349	3297.765	24.43	41.11	75.57	58.89
Readymade garments	5943.2	5212.9	5217.741	1442.93	725.459	3769.97	87.79	27.68	12.21	72.32
Handicrafts	91.5	250.2	0	0	91.5	250.2	0	0	100	100
Jewellery		325.4	0	0		325.4		0		100
Pasmina		931	0	0		931		0		100

Source: Authors' calculation based on *Census of Manufacturing Establishments* (Various Years), Central Bureau of Statistics and Economic Survey (various issues), Ministry of Finance, Government of Nepal.

out of which the contribution of small and village industries declined sharply to 14.01 per cent. Table 4.6 gives the information that small and village industries are providing 100% contribution in the total exports of Handicrafts, Jewellery and Pasmina. Similarly, the contribution of woollen carpets and readymade garments produced by small and village industries occupied a lion's share in total exports of these commodities. The contribution of woollen carpets declined slightly (from 75.57 per cent in 1993-94 to 58.89 per cent in 2006-07) but the contribution of readymade garments improved significantly (from 12.21per cent in 1993-94 to 72.32 per cent in 2006-07). Though these commodities have significant role in export trade but the overall contribution of small and village industries has been declined sharply.

Regional Analysis

In order to generate employment opportunities, reduce income inequality, mobilize local resources and reduce poverty incidence, the Government has aimed at achieving balanced regional development for which small and village industries should be developed to support the goal. However, there has been a continuing tendency for spatial concentration of small and village industries in Nepal which seriously handicap the industrial development effort of the country. Regional indices of small and village industries have been shown through Table 4.7.

Table 4.7: Regional Indices of Small and Village Industries in Nepal

Development Regions	*Composite Index*	*Deviation Index*
Eastern Development Region	66.14	1.23
Central Development Region	100.00	1.97
Western Development Region	58.21	0.87
Mid-western Development Region	32.27	0.51
Far-western Development Region	29.41	0.43

Source: Authors' calculation based on *Census of Manufacturing Establishments* (Various Years), Central Bureau of Statistics and Economic Survey (various issues), Ministry of Finance, Government of Nepal.

Among the regions, CDR is the highly industrial region as indicated by the highest composite index followed by EDR, WDR, MWDR, and FWDR respectively. Likewise, as indicated by the highest mean value of deviation indices, it is clear that CDR is highly industrialized region followed by EDR, WDR, MWDR and FWDR. The remarkably wider gaps between CDR and other development regions regarding index values indicate that the region-wise small and village manufacturing activities in the country remained unbalanced in 1999-2000. Despite the Government efforts for reducing industrial disparity, the persisting distribution patterns of industrial growth obviously indicate a uneven development in the country.

Problems

- **Raw Materials:** Most of the Small-scale and Village industries in the rural areas are scattered. A regular and unhindered supply of raw materials for the small-scale and village industries is very essential. Non-availability of raw material is a serious handicap for small and village industries. Though the availability and potentiality of raw materials is very high but the indigenous raw materials have not been utilized adequately for the promotion and development of small and village industries. Moreover, raw materials available at one part of the country cannot be transported to another part due to transportation difficulties. Storage facilities for raw materials are also scanty. Hence, these industries are bound to use imported raw materials which are not available in sufficient quantity and cannot be acquired through simple procedures. Many industries are forced to run below capacity or closed due to non-availability of imported raw materials.
- **Finance:** Credit is required to start a new project or improve an existing project. Financial constraints have been the principal handicaps in the development of small and village industries. The loans provided to these industries are more collateral oriented than project oriented. Banks are in no position to grant credit without collateral. Since the banking procedures are based on collateral basis, small and village entrepreneurs do not have sufficient land and buildings,

banks do not accept their property for collateral due to their location in rural areas and they get small amount of loan because these properties are valued not more than 50 per cent of the market price. High interest rate, red tapism and bureaucratic hurdles rampant in financial institutions are discouraging the entrepreneurs to get loans hence more than 70 per cent of the industries are sick.

- **Market:** The products of these industries have to compete with the products of large and medium domestic and foreign industries. Low quality, negative attitude of Nepalese consumers towards these products, lack of appropriate technology and trained manpower, non-availability of suitable distribution channels and low promotion efforts have created obstacles to sell the products of these industries. Similarly, the absence of national market due to the lack of transportation network has created the problems of transporting and selling goods produced by these industries.
- **Labour Unrest:** Labour unrest and conflicts with management are frequent phenomena in these industries in general and carpet and readymade garments in particular. Workers have been organized and trade unions have been formed. Strikes and lockouts have been staged frequently for demanding higher wages and fringe benefits which hamper the production and profitability of these industries.
- **Unfavourable Government Policy:** Government's policy is not favorable for the promotion and development of these industries. The entrepreneurs have to spend most of their time in fulfilling government formalities and getting loans rather than managing the enterprises and involving in productive activities. The government is still not positive towards a one window system which is essential to providing required machinery, raw materials, foreign exchange, tax and credit facilities, market protection from imports, export facilities, information and training in an integral manner.

REFERENCES

Aigner, D. C., A. K. Lovell, and P. Schmidt (1977). "Formulation and Estimation of Stochastic Frontier Production Function Models", *Journal of Econometrics* 6: 21-37.

Bajracharya, P. (1990). "Efficient Market Management for the Development of Cottage and Small Industries", *Cottage and Small Industries Souvenir*, FNCSI, Kathmandu, Nepal: 6-16

Bista, N.K and Shrestha, B.K. (2000.). "Entrpreneurship and Enterprise Development on SMEs in Nepal: Challenges and Opportunities", *Economic Journal of Development Issues*, 1(2): 59-71.

Corneiwell, C., P. Schmidt, and R.C. Sickles (1990). "Production Frontiers with Cross Sectional and Time Series Variation in Efficiency Levels", *Journal of Econometrics* 46: 185-200.

Fecher, F. and P. Pestiean (1993). "Efficiency and Competition in OECD Financial Services"; in Harold O. Fried, C.A. Knox Lovell and Shelton S. Schmidit (eds), *The Measurement of Productivity, Efficiency, Techniques and Applications*, New York: Oxford University Press: 374-85.

Kansakar, V. (1996). "Role of Rural Development Projects in the Growth of Cottage and Small Industries in Nepal". M.K. Dahal and H. Mund (Eds.) *Social Economy and National Development*. NEFAS: 138-59.

Khatiwada, Y.R. (1997). "Financial Problem of Cottage and Small Industries: Structure and Remedies", *Cottage and Small Industries Souvenir*, FNCSI, Kathmandu, Nepal: 12-28.

Krishna, K. L. and G. Sahota (1991), "Technical Efficiency in Bangladesh Manufacturing Industries", The Bangladesh Development Studies 19: 89-101.

Nepal Law Society (1992). *Cottage and Small Industries in Nepal: An Overview*, Kathmandu, Nepal.

Shrestha, S.H. (1998). *Economic Geography of Nepal*, Kathmandu: Educational Enterprise Pvt. Ltd.

Wu, Y. (1995), "Productivity Growth, Technological Progress and Technical Efficiency Change in China: A Three Sector Analysis", *Journal of Comparative Economics*, 21: 207-29.

5

KVI and the Socio-economic Development of Assam

MOUSUMI BORAH AND SANGEETA KAKOTY

The various development programmes which were prepared after independence of the country, with a view to raise progressively the standard of living of the people included the promotion of cottage industries on individual or co-operative basis. In this context, the role of the Khadi and Village Industries (KVI) in the development of the economy was assessed by the Planning Commission.

Khadi is a cloth woven by hand using handspun yarn only. Natural fibres namely cotton, wool and silk are used in spinning and the production activity is carried out in rural areas. A Village Industry means any industry located in a rural area which produces any goods or renders any service with or without the use of power and in which the fixed capital investment per artisan or a worker does not exceed [one lakh rupees] or such other sum as may, by notification in the Official Gazette, be specified from time to time by the Central Government.

In the Gandhian vision of "Gram Swaraj", the basic building blocks of sustainable economy and a humane civilization is constituted by self-reliant villages . In this model, "Gramodyog" or village industries are expected to be the main engine of economic development.

India has been urbanizing rapidly and this process is unlikely to be reversed. However, the growth of mega cities creates problems which need to be tackled at various levels. One of the factors responsible for rural-urban migration is the lack of economic opportunities in the rural areas. After India's independence, the Indian leaders concentrated on the development of modern industries at the expense of village industries. On the contrary, villages were encouraged to supply cheap raw materials and semi-finished products like dairy products such as milk and agriculture products such as vegetables, oils, seeds, cotton and foodgrains to the urban organized sector. At the beginning of the twentieth century village industries accounted for about 40 per cent of the labour force. By the middle of the twentieth century this had decreased to 10 per cent and by the end of twentieth century it was 2 per cent. But even in the 21st century more than half of the total population of India still lives in the villages. This is the reason Gandhiji's ideas are worth revisiting especially since most of the people living in the villages live in poverty.

KVI with their stunning simplicity and wholesome adaptability has occupied a unique position in the rural economy of the country by not only contributing substantially towards strengthening the economic base of the villages but also by effecting utilization of the vast natural resources untapped hitherto.

Significance of KVI

- Production by the masses rather than in mass.
- Providing employment at the doorstep.
- Eco-friendly hence preserves environment.
- Imparting dignity of labour.
- Low cost technology instead of capital intensive technology.
- Ensuring participation of women and backward classes in economic activity.
- Promoting decentralized economic activities.
- Acting as bulwark against migration of population to city slums.
- Rejuvenating rural economy.

Objectives of the Study

- To try and analyze the important role that KVI has been playing in the Socio-Economic Development of Assam.
- To study the contribution of KVI in the growth of production and employment generation in the state of Assam.
- To try and locate the loopholes and suggest remedial measures.

Methodology

This study is primarily based on secondary data. However, oral interviews of both KVI officials as well as beneficiaries had been undertaken to collect relevant information regarding the functioning of KVI.

Assam is situated in the Himalayan foothills and is richly endowed with natural resources. Well known for its extensive forests with varieties of flora and fauna the landscape consisting of hills and valleys is a treasure house of natural beauty. The women of this region weave fairy tales on the loom, one of the world's finest artistic traditions finds expression in their exquisitely woven endi, muga and pat fabrics. The handicrafts for which this region is equally famous are also made mostly in the villages from jute, wood, cane and bamboo. Both Khadi and Village Industries have got a large potential in almost all the districts of Assam.

In fact KVI has been working through various schemes and programmes in Assam, along with the rest of the North-Eastern states like Rural Employment Guarantee Programme (REGP), Khadi Grant, Khadi Loan, Village Industry Grant, Science and Technology Grant, A Scheme of Fund for Regeneration of Traditional Industries (SFURTI) etc.

Table 5.1 shows the production, sales and employment achieved in Assam by KVI during the period 2005-06 to 2007-08.

Table 5.1: Production, Sales and Employment Generation of KVI in Assam

(Rs. in lakhs)

Sl. No.	*Year*	*Production*	*Sales*	*Employment (Nos.)*
1.	2005-06	473.64	382.36	11,466
2.	2006-07	490.86	424.12	11,573
3.	2007-08	618.00	455.68	14,000

Source: Annual Report of KVI.

Table 5.1 clearly shows that there has been a substantial increase in all the three departments. Thus it may be concluded that there has been an increase in the production and sales of KVI and there has also been an increase in employment generation which has played an important role in the socio-economic development of the region.

Production, Sales and Employment of KVI in Assam

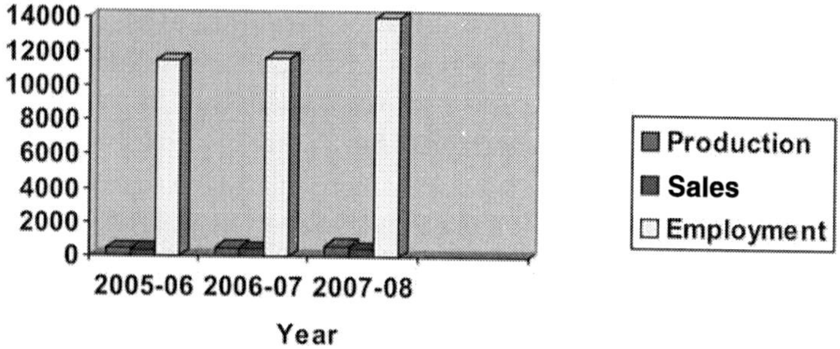

Fig. 5.1

Table 5.2 presents the targets and achievements of KVI in the state of Assam during the period 2006-07 and 2007-08.

Table 5.2: Targets and Achievements of KVI

Sl. No.	Year	Targets			Achievements		
		No. of Projects	Margin Money	Employment (in Nos.)	No. of Projects	Margin Money	Employment (in Nos.)
1.	2006-07	1468	1694.25	27,263	1599	1717.35	30,912
2.	2007-08	2120	2678.38	44,602	2560	2887.94	48,303

Source: Annual Report of KVI.

Table 5.2 clearly shows that KVI has been successfully achieving more than the targets sought.

KVI has designed various programmes and schemes for the development of the North-Eastern region as a whole. Under its Transport Subsidy Scheme, to and fro fare along with freight charges are provided from KVIC for participation in the exhibition and fairs in other parts of the country. Further during the year 2007-08, 10 per cent of space in the Khadi Gram Udyog Bhavan, New Delhi was reserved for the products produced by the units of the North-Eastern region.

For ensuring better appeal of Khadi the role of design input has been widely recognized. This scheme Product Development, Design Intervention and Packaging (PRODIP) envisages hiring of professional designers to improve the salability of Khadi and Village Industries products. In 2006-07, of the 4 PRODIP projects sanctioned for the North-East, 3 were allocated to Assam and 1 to Meghalaya. Again, in 2007-08 of the 6 projects sanctioned for the North East, 5 were allocated to Assam and 1 to Arunachal Pradesh.

Furthermore, creation of the Artisan Welfare Fund is one of the inbuilt components of the cost chart that regulates the cost of Khadi products. In fact an Artisan Welfare Fund has been registered in Assam.

Yet another welfare measure that has been adopted for Khadi artisans is the Khadi Karigar Janashree Bima Yojana (KKJBY). In Assam this Yojana has been successfully implemented. Table 5.3 shows the performance of KKJBY from 2005-06 to 2007-08.

Table 5.3: Performance of KKJBY in Assam

Sl. No.	*Year*	*No. of Institutions*	*No. of Artisans*
1.	2005-06	15	1446
2.	2006-07	14	1427
3.	2007-08	15	1511

Source: Annual Report of KVI.

Table 5.3 shows that this scheme has benefited a substantial number of artisans in rural Assam and has contributed towards their economic development.

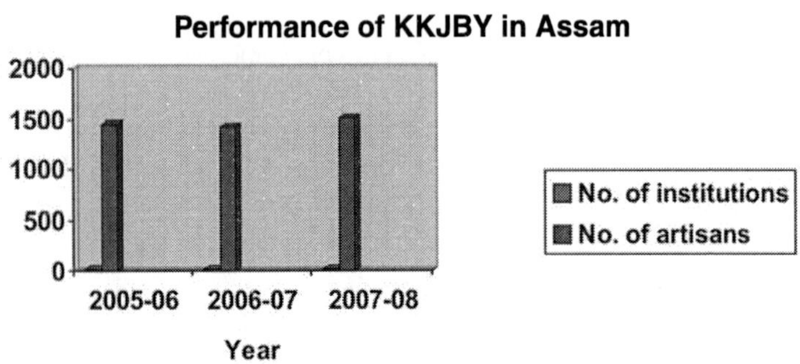

Fig. 5.2

The Rural Industry Service Centres (RISC) cater to the need for various common facilities such as infrastructure support necessary for individual units to upgrade their production, quality, skills, marketing etc. Financial support up to 90 per cent of the project cost is provided to the beneficiaries from NER as against the 75 per cent to other parts of the country.

Table 5.4 shows the state-wise position of RISC projects sanctioned and KVICs share released during 2007-08.

Table 5.4: State-wise position of RISC projects sanctioned and KVICs share released during 2007-08

(Rs. in lakhs)

Sl. No.	*State*	*Sanctioned by SLAC No. of Projects Target*	*Sanctioned by SLAC*	*KVIC share*
1.	Arunachal Pradesh	2	2	9.00
2.	**Assam**	**5**	**5**	**20.25**
3.	Manipur	2	0	4.50
4.	Meghalaya	4	4	22.50
5.	Mizoram	3	3	13.50
6.	Nagaland	3	2	9.00
7.	Sikkim	2	0	2.25
8.	Tripura	1	0	4.50
	Total	22	16	85.50

Source: Annual Report of KVI.

During the year 2007-08, KVIC put concrete effort for implementing the Rural Employment Guarantee Programme (REGP) in the region. As a result REGP exceeded the target set for the year. Table 5.5 shows the Targets and Achievements of REGP for all the NER states during 2007-08.

Table 5.5: Targets and Achievements of REGP for all the NER states during 2007-08

(Rs. in lakhs)

Sl. No.	*Year*	*Targets*			*Achievements*		
		No. of Projects	*Margin Money*	*Employment (in Nos.)*	*No. of Projects*	*Margin Money*	*Employment (in Nos.)*
1.	Arunachal Pradesh	200	132.96	2214	186	325.67	1783
2.	**Assam**	**2120**	**2678.38**	**44602**	**2560**	**2887.94**	**48303**
3.	Manipur	31	238.55	3973	77	82.39	1105
4.	Meghalaya	186	391.07	6513	409	512.55	3509
5.	Mizoram	610	500.00	8326	1290	1125.97	17299
6.	Nagaland	306	322.90	5377	462	471.18	6910
7.	Sikkim	200	138.85	2312	143	273.58	2260
8.	Tripura	475	281.57	4689	608	681.83	14178
	Total	4128	4684.28	78006	5735	6361.11	95347

Source: Annual Report of KVI.

Backward and forward linkages to projects are an integral part of REGP. As such financial assistance is provided to conduct various activities like awareness camps, exhibitions, market promotions and workshops. In the year 2007-08, 24 awareness camps, 5 banker's meetings and12 exhibitions were organized in Assam. Under EDP 2546 persons were trained in the state and this entire venture incurred a total expenditure of Rs. 45.97 lakh.

During the year 2007-08, a total number of 7125 candidates were trained under Khadi and other Village Industries in the North-Eastern region. In Assam, 34 SC candidates, 147 ST candidates, 88 OBC candidates, 2582 General candidates and 120 women candidates were trained under this programme.

Major Impediments to KVI which needs urgent Attention

- **Easy access to bank credit:** Lack of credit has been a serious hurdle in the path of growth of KVI. Initiatives have to be taken for providing micro finance and it must also be ensured that it is being passed to the beneficiary without any legal and statutory delays.
- **Rationalization of Corporate as well as Commodity Taxes:** Rationalization of the indirect tax structure is the need of the hour. Given the multiplicity of taxes as they exist today, the incidence on the final price of commodities is way too high and in turn reduces demand. Rationalization of commodity taxes would accelerate manufacturing activity by boosting demand and would also enhance the competitiveness of India's Export.
- **Provision of adequate infrastructure and SEZ:** While initiatives to provide infrastructure in general are important, they should be supplemented by efforts to promote infrastructure development in local areas such as Special Economic Zones (SEZ) and Special Economic Regions.
- **Improved Technology:** Technological modernization will be of vital importance to high industrial growth.
- **De-Reservation:** Another constraint affecting the growth of labour-intensive manufacturing is the reservation in many of these industries for the small-scale sector. With reduced barriers to trade and the negotiation of free trade agreements with neighbouring countries and with the ASEAN countries,

domestic producers have to compete with imports even if they do not aim for export markets. They cannot do so if reservation limits their ability to modernize. The policy of progressive de-reservation of industries for small scale production has reduced the list of reserved industries to a substantial number. This policy should continue at an accelerated pace.

- **Easy entry and Exit:** Many units are suffering from regulatory hassles. All entry barriers should be removed and business risks for start-ups mitigated.

Conclusion

It is evident that KVI has given a huge contribution to the industrial economy of Assam. At the outset it becomes imperative to look after this sector with great honour and precision while framing policy for its development. In the recent past various measures have been taken by the government to safeguard the KVI. Among the six basic principles of governance underlying the National Common Minimum Programme (NCMP) of the Government, "sustained economic growth in a manner that generates employment" has a very important place. The NCMP also describes the micro and small enterprises and the KVI as "the most employment-intensive segment". Thus the special thrust to this sector has been with the multiple objectives of employment generation, regional dispersal of industries and as a seedbed for Entrepreneurship.

Both Khadi and Village Industries have got a large employment potential in almost all the districts of Assam. Assam is the only state where Muga Cocoon is available which has much impact on the rural economy and socio-cultural activities in the rural areas of Assam. Eri Cocoon is also available in plenty in Assam. But due to lack of appropriate technology the earnings of the spinners both in the field of Eri and Muga are very low. It is therefore very essential to improve the technology by undertaking special R&D programmes.

REFERENCES

Annual Report, KVI (2005-08).

Annual Report, Reserve Bank of India (1998-2004), Mumbai.

Economic Survey (1991-2007); Ministry of Finance, Government of India.

6

Socio-economic Development of North-Eastern States: Role of Khadi and Village Industries

R.P. BHATTACHARJE

Introduction

The North-Eastern Region consists of eight states. These are Arunachal Pradesh, Assam, Manipur, Meghalaya, Mizoram, Tripura, Nagaland, and Sikkim. The region is isolated geographically as the region is land locked having 98 per cent of its border being international. Only 2 per cent of NER borders tagged with mainland through North Bengal Corridor. The region is sensitive geographically due to natural isolation amidst rugged terrain. The North-Eastern States, recently, became more sensitive internationally after the claim of China over Arunachal Pradesh on the eve of recent visit of His Holiness Dalai Lama.

This region is having a geographical area of 262,179 sq. km. (NEC-2006) which is 7.98 per cent of total geographical area of all India (32,87,263 sq. km). The NE states are covered with dense forest and its 66.1 per cent of geographical area is having forest covered. The least forest covere is in Assam (35.48 per cent) and highest forest cover is in Mizoram (87.42 per cent) compared to 20.64 per cent in all India.

The population of NE states is 388.58 lakhs which is 3.78% of total population of India (2001). Thus the area is sparsely inhabited with a density of 148 person per sq km compared to 313 in all India. Arunachal Pradesh is having lowest density of 13 while Assam is having highest density of 340 in this region.

Despite being rich in natural resources with fertile land, rich forest and mineral deposits, development of the region has lagged behind from the rest of the country due to historical reasons. The per capita income of Arunachal Pradesh at current prices during 2005-06 was Rs.23,788 compared to Rs. 25,716 in all-India. The per capita income in Assam was Rs.18,598 while in Manipur, it was Rs. 20,326, Meghalaya with Rs.23,420, Mizoram with Rs. 22,417 (during 2004-05), Nagaland with Rs.20, 998 (during 2004-05) and , Tripura with Rs. 24,706 are lagging behind the national average while Sikkim with Rs. 26,412 per capita income, is the only state in North Eastern States having higher income compared to all-India (*Economic Survey*, 2007-08).

The traditional Economy in North-East is simple and shifting cultivation is still practiced. Economic growth has picked up recently due to various plans and programmes of the Govt. Both for proper socio-economic development, it is essential to remove infrastructure bottlenecks, human resource development, health care, provision of basic minimum services, creating conducive environment for private investment, control illegal immigration etc. We know that peace and development go hand in hand. There is urgent need to bring back insurgent groups to the national mainstream and involve them in developmental activities through rehabilitation plans. The problems should be studied in coordination with social scientists, NGOs etc. better counselling, education, health care and employment opportunities can surely enhance their participation in developmental activities(*Yojana*, 2005).

Socio-Economic Development

In North-Eastern States, 84% of population live in rural areas with a large chunk of workable population are unemployed. As a consequence there is unrest and terrorism. It is a general feeling of this area that NER is neglected by the mainstream and there is lack of socio-economic development. Here Khadi and Village Industries can play a major role provided KVI compete with the globalized economy. The emphasis on inclusive growth and emancipation of the common man was perhaps the dream of Mahatma Gandhi when he sketched Swaraj of the common man especially at rural area through village administration or Panchayati Raj Institutions (PRI). Presently devolution of power to PRIs is the panacea of inclusive growth at grass roots level. The increased focus is on mainstreaming rural India. Thus there is a need of bridging gap between urban-rural divide. These can be done if our rural areas given sufficient attention in respect of socio-economic development. The 11th Five-Year Plan (2007-12) is expected to have a growth of 7.5 per cent compared to 5.5 per cent during 9th plan and 7.2 per cent during 10th plan in our country.

This reflects strengths of our economy and the dynamism of the private sector in relation to public sector in many areas. Yet it is true that economic growth has failed to be sufficiently inclusive. Agriculture has lost its growth momentum. Jobs in the organized sector have not increased despite faster growth. The percentage of BPL is declining slowly. There is still lack of access to the basic services such as health, education, clean drinking water and sanitation facilities. There is a need of all-round participation and collective action to improve the socio-economic conditions especially of NE States. Empowerment of rural mass especially of PRIs is ongoing but yet to give full empowerment.

The NE States have some unique economic problems arising out of remoteness, poor connectivity, hilly and often inhospitable terrain, a week resource base, poor infrastructure, sparse population low population density, shallow markets, inadequate administrative capacity, low skill development and finally, low and order problem and low economic activity. Connectivity is the key issue for the NE States.

A sense of isolation prevails due to this and adds to transportation, cost making trades and investment uncompetitive and a low volume of success.

Let us find a few socio-economic indicators of this region in Table 6.1.

Here we find that Sikkim has better Socio-Economic infrastructure in the NE- states – while infant mortality is not good compared to other NE States. Growth rate of SDP is again better during 9th plan although Tripura, Manipur and Meghalaya having poor growth rate. In HDI, it is Mizoram, Manipur and Nagaland who had relatively better position in the North-Eastern States. Except Mizoram, all the states have higher poverty ratio while Arunachal Pradesh have lowest road density in the region. Mizoram, Sikkim and Meghalaya have lower road density compared to all-India.

Table 6.1: Socio-Economic Indicators of NE- States

States	*Index of socio-economic infrastructure (1999)*	*IMR (2001) (%)*	*Growth rate of SDP (9th plan)*	*PCI at current prices (2004-05)*	*Percentage of under-weight children (1998)*	*HDI rank of (32 States/ (UTs)*	*BPL*	*Road density*
Arunachal Pradesh	69.71	44	4.4	22,542	24.3	29	33.47	168
Assam	77.72	78	2.1	16,825	36.0	26	36.09	872
Manipur	75.39	25	6.4	18,386	27.5	9	28.54	490
Meghalaya	75.49	52	6.2	21,915	37.9	24	33.87	379
Mizoram	82.13	23	-	22,417	22.7	7	19.47	229
Nagaland	76.14	-	2.6	20,998	24.1	11	32.67	1107
Sikkim	108.09	52	8.3	23,791	20.6	18	36.55	258
Tripura	74.87	49	7.4	22,836	-	22	34.44	1405
All India		71	5.3	22,946	47.0		26.1	749

Sources:

1. Annual Report, 2004-05, Ministry of DONER, quoted from *Yojana*, Vol. 49, December, 2005, p. 12.
2. *Economic Survey*, 2007-08, p. A-13.

Role of Khadi and Village Industries in Socio- Economic Development of NER

During the freedom struggle, the development of Khadi and Village Industries was an instrument to meet the twin objective of self-reliance through local production and seeking active participation of the poor in the struggle for Independence through removal of hunger and unemployment. This potential as an instrument of poverty alleviation was also recognized by our early planners. Accordingly, the Khadi and Village Industries Commission (KVIC) was created by an act of Parliament to plan, promote and organize their systematic development and expansion (PC:2001).While the output and employment of KVI have grown manifold during the last four and a half decades, their role in the context of the new paradigm of development has been questioned. In particular, the effectiveness of the programmers in terms of its employment generation capacity, resource use, efficiency and sustainability has come under attack from various quarters. Before independence, development of Khadi and Village Industries was entirely a non-governmental effort under the guidance of Mahatma Gandhi.

Government had an evaluation of the performance, adequacy, and effectiveness of the implementation mechanism and impact of the KVI programmes (1992-1997). As per KVIC's statistics, during 8th plan, only 8 lakh jobs were created against a target of 20 lakh. Recently, a task force committee was constituted for revision of working capital norms for Khadi and Village Industries sector by the Ministry of MSME under the chairmanship membership of chairperson KVIC at Mumbai in which RBI, SBI, NABARD, IBA and khadi exports held a meeting during January, 2009. Thus, there is scanner on the development of KVI in the country. Let us now find the status of production, employment, sales and earnings of KVI which is shown in Table 6.2.

Table 6.2: Production, sales, employment and earning of KVI in NER

States	*Production*	*Sales*	*Employment (nos. in lakhs)*	*Earnings*
Arunachal Pradesh				
1988-89	0.13	0.13	-	0.08
1997-98	86.24	87.83	0.01	35.74
1998-99	35.91	37.40	-	9.27
2002-03	317.88	446.40	0.01	150.86
2003-04	468.54	583.21	0.01489	185.42
2006-07	1925.21	2914.34	0.07	-
2007-08	1447.44	2151.92	0.08	-
Assam				
1988-89	1411.90	1350.00	1.10	454.17
1997-98	4066.55	3468.73	1.10	1177.05
1998-99	4379.30	3499.73	1.25	1149.97
2002-03	6084.08	5731.09	1.12	2418.68
2003-04	8017.93	9981.51	1.26950	3446.50
2006-07	30328.99	47337.39	2.48	-
2007-08	22802.34	34953.46	2.65	-
Manipur				
1988-89	1290.59	1357.00	0.32	400.08
1997-98	2978.57	3151.84	0.42	962.13
1998-99	4457.27	4602.41	0.42	1385.01
2002-03	6000.85	5661.92	0.61	2632.68
2003-04	6029.24	6069.49	0.62095	2690.18
2006-07	7336.19	7557.24	0.66	-
2007-08	5515.59	5580.19	0.71	-
Meghalaya				
1988-89	380.03	450.00	0.06	182.41
1997-98	1411.87	1774.47	0.13	874.87
1998-99	1202.98	1547.92	0.11	709.61
2002-03	3101.61	3842.64	0.25	1950.24
2003-04	3202.03	3297.21	0.26455	1998.65
2006-07	6423.52	9003.30	0.35	-
2007-08	4829.42	6647.95	0.37	-

Mizoram				
1988-89	80.53	77.00	-	32.21
1997-98	2085.46	1962.73	0.12	541.52
1998-99	2412.76	2273.09	0.15	578.96
2002-03	3769.44	5063.82	0.23	1492.67
2003-04	4057.80	4218.02	0.24645	1661.08
2006-07	14239.61	20220.03	0.64	-
2007-08	10705.81	14930.27	0.68	-
Nagaland				
1988-89	163.90	180.00	0.04	67.20
1997-98	1946.13	2162.00	0.19	1064.21
1998-99	1816.92	2008.03	0.19	956.00
2002-03	4583.94	5509.06	0.03	3011.71
2003-04	4773.70	5200.28	0.30353	3155.35
2006-07	7747.68	10077.24	0.44	-
2007-08	5824.96	7440.94	0.47	-
Sikkim				
2002-03	373.51	222.90	0.06	104.96
2003-04	441.18	532.45	0.06804	134.84
2006-07	2336.86	4819.05	0.19	-
2007-08	5824.96	7440.94	0.47	-
Tripura				
1988-89	1324.20	1390.00	0.44	503.19
1997-98	1245.46	1284.92	0.27	468.56
1998-99	1186.89	1282.46	0.23	381.89
2002-03	2235.29	2379.85	0.28	647.36
2003-04	3603.89	4255.19	0.30246	1252.43
2006-07	5470.01	6815.19	0.45	-
2007-08	4112.53	5032.27	0.48	-
NER@				
1988-89	4651.28	4804.13	1.96	1639.34
1997-98	18471.56	13892.52	2.25	5124.08
1998-99	15492.03	15251.04	2.35	5170.71
2002-03	26466.60	28833.01	2.85	12409.16
2003-04	30594.72	34137.75	3.09037	14524.46
2006-07	75808.07	108743.78	5.28	-
2007-08*	56995.02	80295.34	5.64	

* up to December, 2007; @ excluding Sikkim

Source(s):

1. NEC, *Basic Statistics of NER*, 2002 (p. 215) 2006 (pp. 314-15).
2. *Annual Report*, 2007-08, KVIC. p. 118.

In Table 6.2, we find that there is improvement in the activities of KVI in NER in recent years. If production, sales, employment and savings are assumed to be a few socio-economic indicators, we find that except Assam, other States does not play any major role and that is pertinent due to population size.

However, there is a need of improvement in the States of AP, Mizoram and Sikkim. In the States of Assam, Manipur, Nagaland and Meghalaya, there is some consistency in the activity of KVIC.

Suggestions

1. There is a need to increase the number of KVI Institutions in NER.
2. The technology in the production of KVI products needs immediate improvements to compete with globalised world. In this region, there is a few technical institutions like IIT (Guwahati), NERIST (Nirjuli), NIT (Silchar, Agartala) and few Central Universities pursuing technical courses who may play a major role in developing technology for KVI.
3. There is a need of training to the KVI workers and there is only one IIE at Guwahati. There is a need of more such Institutions in NER to impart training to the beneficiaries.
4. The REGP entrepreneurs may be provided more incentives to play a major role in socio-economic development in this region.
5. There is a need to enhance sales of KVI products within the country and abroad.
6. The KVI units needs to be self-sufficient and shrugged off any subsidy.

REFERENCES

NEC: "Basic Statistics of NER, 2006", pp. 3-171.

GOI : "Economic Surevey, 2007-08", p. A-13.

Yojana, Vol. 49, December, 2005, p. 1.

Planning Commission :"Evaluation Study on Khadi and Village Industries Programme", March, 2001.

SECTION - II

Challenges and Opportunities

7

Problems of Khadi and Village Industries in Arunachal Pradesh

SUKAMAL DEB

The Arunachal Pradesh Human Development Report, 2005 says the people of the state have enormous traditional skill and knowledge. Arunachal is poised at a critical juncture and is in position to make a crucial choice, regarding development path it wants to pursue. Here at this juncture, the Village Industries can intervene positively for the inclusive development of the state. There was no developmental activity and as such no means of communication till the last quarter of the 20th century. During the reorganization of the states in the North East, a pertinent criterion was rashly ignored that the territory in question must have revenue resources to meet its administrative and other non-developmental expenditure. The regional imbalance of North East is expressed in terms of frustration and insurgence. Youths who were supposed to be productive entrepreneurs mould them to violence entrepreneur.

Outline of Arunachal Pradesh

Arunachal Pradesh situated in the north-eastern part of India is 83,743 km in area and has a long international border with Bhutan to the west (160 km), China to the north and north-east (1,080 km) and Myanmar to the east (440 km). It stretches from snow capped mountains in the north to the plains of Brahamaputra valley in the south. Arunachal Pradesh is the largest state of the North East with a sparse population. The state has the highest forest cover in the country and boasts over five hundred species of orchids. Its 'hydropower', largely untapped has the potential to become powerhouse of the country by providing sizeable hydro-electricity.

The territory was known as no man's land (*terra incognita*) till the beginning of the 20th century. There was no developmental activity and as such no means of communication till the last quarter of the 20th century. This was because of the fact that the Ahoms, who ruled Assam for about 600 years, followed a policy of non-interference in internal affairs of the tribes. The British Indian Government which succeeded the Ahoms after the Yandaboo treaty in 1826 continued the same policy (Begi Joram, 2008, *Education Scenario in A.P.*, IPR, Government of A.P.). Arunachal Pradesh acquired an identity for its own for the first time in 1874 when some tribal areas from Assam's Darang and North Lakhimpur districts were separated to form the North East Frontier Tract (NEFT). The NEFT was further sub-divided into Balipara, Sadia and Tirap tracts between 1914 and 1943. The Abor Hills district, the Mishmi Hills district and the Naga Tribal areas were furthermore amalgamated and renamed as North East Frontier Agency (NEFA) in 1951. In 1954, NEFA was reconstituted into Kameng, Subansiri, Tirap, Siang, Coleit and Tuensang Frontier Divisions but the Tuensang Frontier division was separated in 1957 and merged with the newly constituted Naga Hills Tuensang area which is today's Nagaland. Administrative responsibility for Arunachal passed from the External Affairs Ministry to the Home Affairs Ministry in 1965 leading to the five frontier divisions of the territory becoming the five original districts which have been further sub-divided with the passage of time into today's sixteen districts. The NEFA was subsequently upgraded to Union Territory and renamed as Arunachal Pradesh. The first election of a 30 member Assembly was held in 1978 leading to the Union Territory replaced by full-fledged statehood on 20th February, 1987 with the state assembly of 60 elected members. The basic data of the state as on today are as follows (Table 7.1):

Table 7.1: Basic Data of Arunachal Pradesh

1.	Area	:	83,743 sq. km.
2.	Districts	:	16
3.	Additional Deputy Commissioner (Independent)	:	11
4.	Sub-division	:	20
5.	Extra Assistant Commissioner	:	17
6.	Circles	:	106
7.	Number of towns	:	24
8.	No. of villages	:	3863
9.	Population (2001 Census)	:	10,97,968
10.	Males	:	5,79,941
11.	Females	:	5,18,027
12.	Density of population	:	13.096
13.	Sex Ratio	:	901 (Female per 1000 males)
14.	Literacy rate	:	54.74%
15.	Mineral resources	:	Limestone, Dolomite, Graphite, Coal, Oil, Quartzite, Natural Gas, Yellow Ochre, Marble.
16.	Existing Industries	:	Medium Industries -17, SSI - 2526.

Source: Industrial Policy of Arunachal Pradesh, 2001.

KVI implementing Agencies

The nodal agency for implementation of KVI programmes in the State is Arunachal Pradesh Khadi and Village Industries Board. The KVIC is the national nodal agency to promote KVI and to support efforts of state KVIBs. Organizationally, the Board is in a poor condition to play its role effectively. The State Government's funding to the KVI sector is abysmally meagre. There appears to have no long-term plan on anvil and KVIC role also appears to be insufficient. Organizational weakness, lack of trained manpower and technical expertise, inadequate support from the State Government or the KVIC are some of the reasons for inability of the sector in making any significant impact.

Other factors in adverse includes lack of entrepreneurial knowledge, lack of technical know-how, taking undue benefits of subsidy linked scheme, license issuing system, lack of dignity of labour, banking scenario, absence of good vocational training institutes in the State, limitation of the State Industrial Policy, culture of working in isolation to line organizations, having no reach out with the PRIs etc.

Specific threats for Khadi programme are, lack of interest of weavers and spinners as minimum wages prevailing in these states are much higher than wages payable to Khadi spinners and weavers as per Khadi cost chart provision, lack of raw materials, lack of working capital or timely finance, lack of marketing facilities which include competitions from the handloom and power loom sector.

It has been observed that the present mindsets are not to establish their own enterprise but to venture either in politics, contract business, or government services to earn *"easy money"*. This mindset can be termed as psychological barrier which has emerged very strongly in the present socio-economic context of the State. This has been in quiet adversely affecting the rest of the society.

A prescription towards solution of problems in effective implementation of Khadi and Village Industries Programmes could be: Strengthening APKVIB; KVIC may come up with simple schemes and modalities friendly for the rural entrepreneurs; KVI needs advertisement and priority to develop border trades, To undertake a Comprehensive Techno-Economic Survey to find out potential area; To modernize the Craft Centres; Declaration of uncovered banking service areas and to arrange financial support not linked with bank finance for them; Arranging flow of relevant information relating to Village and Small Industries, to keep entrepreneurial world abreast with the recent trends.

The Department of Industries may launch a periodical bulletin and ensure its circulation to all far and wide prospective entrepreneurs. Any good development, success stories, whatsoever minute it may be, around the entrepreneurial world in the State need to be highlighted through this periodical. This doses a moral boost and confidence building. The banks and Financial Institutions should play more constructive role in lending credit support to viable proposals, APIDFC needs revival. Tourism/Eco-tourism may be encouraged which will have ripple effect on the Village and Small Industries sector and the ancillary activities. Single item can be identified which could be synonymous with the name of the

State. The existence of Inner Line System appears to be irrelevant in present global scenario and therefore authority may contemplate twice on its continuation. It needs a careful analysis that if such restrictions are in counterfeit to socio-economic development. The design of grabbing benefits by a middle layer (neo-aspirant class) has to be under strict vigil and such attempts and approach has to be eliminated out in totality.

For the North-Eastern Region in general or the state in particular, the unemployment problem has become a paradox because the unemployment in the region is growing, not because there is lack of opportunities, but because the unemployed youths have failed to take advantage of the opportunities available. It is an accepted fact that the availability of entrepreneurship is the most important determinant in the process of industrialization. The Government in its efforts to create entrepreneurship provides for various monetary and non-monetary incentives like the development of an infrastructure, assistance in marketing and procuring raw-materials, providing finance or granting subsidies on investment. Various state and central organizations have accordingly been created to cater to the needs of entrepreneurs. But reality in field draws blurry picture of entrepreneurs. The State Government has to play the real role of facilitator to promote this social sector as 'development of Village Industries' has been included in the Directive Principles of the State policy listed in the Indian Constitution.

Problems faced by KVI in the State

In analyzing the investigation the problems that the sector face may be presented in the following way : The Khadi and Village Industries in the State are not commercially viable due to (i) lack of interest of weavers and spinners as minimum wages prevailing in these states are much higher than wages payable to Khadi Spinners and Weavers as per Khadi cost chart provision, (ii) lack of raw materials, (iii) lack of working capital or timely finance, (iv) lack of marketing facilities, (v) lack of capacity utilization, (vi) lack of technical know-how, (vii) devoid of organizational strength, (viii) competition on Khadi (hand spun and hand woven) from power loom (machine spun and machine woven) and hand loom (machine spun and hand woven),

(ix) lack of entrepreneurial knowledge, (x) lack of power, (xi) lack of transport etc. We can elaborate the problematic areas as follows:

1. Market: The KVI sector is not accessible to the modern means of marketing. In modern days marketing the buyer and seller are able to get in touch with one another so that the exchange of goods and services for money takes place between them. This can also be done through E-mail, internet, telephone, courier, speed post and ordinary mails. It is undisputedly accepted that success of an industry depends on market of its products. It has no well organized market outside this state and even inside the state. It has no world-wide Website and no advertisements through electronic or print media. The field study says entrepreneurs are given opportunities to participate to various exhibitions etc. Owing to intrinsic reasons the opportunities are not availed to full extent. There has to be a proper market assessment. Designing a product well, having a right brand name, having appealing packaging for different quantities, buying specific raw materials, employing right people, establishing required distribution system, having effective advertising and promotion, deciding right price, deciding terms and conditions for the middlemen and deciding about product life and precautions and notifying relevant information on the pack will be key factors for sustainable markets. Obtaining the Fruit Processing Order (FPO) number, Bureau of Indian Standard (BIS) specifications, ISO certificates are prerequisite for quality conscious standard markets. But, exceptionally, the state has so far failed to produce enough industrial products for which additional efforts of marketing needed.

The hypothesis that says the KVI units in the State produce products to meet-up selective demands and not in adequate quantity to create market demand appears to be in conformity with the investigation. Moreover, the hypothesis that said the impact of liberalization, privatization and globalization is yet to influence the people of Arunachal Pradesh also appear to be justified. It makes an indication that initially, efforts needed to produce enough marketable industrial produce. This should essentially follow the well knitted marketing strategy.

2. Inner-line System: Inner-line System that was introduced in 1873 still exists even in the present changed scenario. This restricts the free movement of non-Arunachalees to the State as we witnessed from field data. A non-Arunachalee who wants to cross beyond the Inner-line has to get the Inner Line Pass (ILP) issued for a limited period with certain conditionality as it is viewed that the territory is located at strategic location from the defense point of view. Besides, the Government of India feels it necessary to protect the tribal, their land and forest, who has a vivid socio-economic and cultural dimensions, from the Non-Arunachalees' hunger of grabbing. The hypothesis that speaks about the ethnical similarities, distinctive characteristics even the artistic craftsmanship of the Arunachalee Tribes are in concurrence to the ILP policy of the Government as the Government seems to be scared of for its need of preservation.

We should also look into the other aspects of the ILP policy. Globalization refers to a process of increasing economic integration and growing economic interdependence between the contemporary world economies. It is associated not only with increasing cross-border movement of goods, services, capital, information technology, and people but also with an organization of economic activities which crosses national boundary. To get the good effect of globalization in the State it needs to first cross the State flow among the other states of India. In fact the Inner-line system posing as a major hindrances for free flow industrial environment. This seems, *inter alia*, that attempts to blend the ethnic designs with contemporary world taste has not been taken place and no effective steps are being initiated in this direction, which again in unison to the hypothesis made in the thesis.

The North-Eastern Region is isolated, landlocked which shares only 2 per cent of its border with the country and rest with Bhutan, Bangladesh, Myanmar and the Tibetan region and China. For most of this international border has been artificially created. The result has been the elimination of the region's trade, commerce and other linkages, which existed in the pre-independence days. These North-Eastern States are very close to the dynamic South-East and East Asian economics. It is imperative to develop a coherent policy linking this area. (Sachdeva, JNU, 2005). The observation is in factual fitness to the State or the region as revealed from the investigation.

3. Entrepreneurial lack: In the North-Eastern Region, the unemployment problem has become a paradox because the unemployment in the region is growing, not because there is lack of opportunities, but because the unemployed youths have failed to take advantage of the opportunities available. It is an accepted fact that the availability of entrepreneurship is the most important determinant in the process of industrialization. The Government in its efforts to create entrepreneurship provides for various monetary and non-monetary incentives like the development of an infrastructure, assistance in marketing and procuring raw-materials, providing finance or granting subsidies on investment. Various state and central organizations have accordingly been created to cater to the needs of entrepreneurs. But reality in field draws blurry picture of entrepreneurs.

It can be argued that lack of entrepreneurial skill of the local people and their deficient interest to invest and innovate has contributed in preventing the evolution of modern economic system in the State. One example of their lacking interest in setting up enterprises is that those tribal boys/girls who go for craft training do not want to have their own business but like to join as craft teachers in government organizations. The mindset of the most of the contemporary tribal of the State are not to establish their own enterprise but to venture either in politics, contract business, or government services to earn "*easy money*". This mindset can be termed as psychological barrier which has emerged very strongly in the present socio-economic context of the State. Some tribal people within a very short period of time have experienced income and wealth inequalities to a high degree. Very few of them have been found to become very rich overnight and enjoy luxurious life and prefer conspicuous consumption which has been adversely affecting the rest of the society. The income inequalities in the tribal society are very strong. Some are very rich and some are stark poor. The presence of high degree of corruption at all levels and existence of underground economy is also a deterrent to State's economy (Mandal, 2007).

4. Taking undue benefits of subsidy linked Scheme: It has been in common practice that the persons seeking financial assistance under Government sponsored schemes normally prepare their scheme proposal by considering only the upper financial limit as it has direct bearing with the quantum of subsidy entitled. This fact has clearly emerged through field investigations as bigger projects have higher failure rates. It is commonly observed that the beneficiaries, sometimes even the implementing agencies do not consider the economic viability of the proposed projects. The concerned financial institution gets limited scope to appraise the projects to suit their prescribed norms. As a result in the present practice, majority of Government sponsored schemes fail miserably. Considering the intensity of the problem and also to have a clear picture of the viability of a project, assigned Professional Management Network (PMN) to prepare 20 project profiles 10 for each district of Kamrup and Nagaon, Assam as revealed from their official letter No. TEDF/F-14/No. 464 dated July 13, 2001. This report contains only the project profiles of Kamrup district. The projects profiles were prepared with an objective to give only a guideline to NEDFi at the time of appraising a project for finance. One should not consider these projects as Detailed Project Report (DPR). Respective beneficiary have to collect latest information regarding market, technology, raw materials, manpower infrastructure etc. at time of preparing their individual project report (Documents IIE, Ministry of MSME, Government of India, Guwahati, 2005). This is an innovative step from NEDFi in injecting professionalism which the State has been lacking.

5. Licence issuing system: The outsiders who want to venture business in the State are to obtain licence in the name of some Arunachalees who get rent from the concerned businessman for the licence. These trading people earn money and mostly siphon off in their respective home because they don't get the right to buy property for independent business. This status largely refrain the private investors in coming and opening up ventures in Arunachal Pradesh. Institutional credit for trade and industries are available to the local people but they lack entrepreneurial skills and show hardly any interest in industrial activities. Therefore, like Inner Line permit, the Licence issuing system of the Government has also discouraged the opening up of KVI units in the State.

6. Lack of dignity of labour: The contemporary Arunachalee, mostly, oblivious of their age-old pride of dignity of labour and even for petty household works they depend on assisting hands. This has quietly uprooting the habit of doing productive works on self-help basis and making them dependent on others. This is contrary to the entrepreneurial trait. The concept of depending too much on servants for the whole lot of household chore has become almost a glamour or vanity of neo-status concern tribal families. Even those who are marginally in the middle income group or doing an ordinary grade government job can't think of maintaining the family chore without depending on maids. During the field visits it had been a common scene that the workers were outsiders.

7. Power: Power is one of the major infrastructures for the growth of industrial activities of any size. Arunachal Pradesh has a huge potential for the development of hydroelectric power because of its many torrential rivers. The State has the potential to supply one-third of total hydroelectric requirement of the country. The per capita consumption of electricity in A. P. was 86.9 kWh in 2001-02 against the all-India average of 335 KWh. In addition to water resource, the state has oil, natural gas and coal resources that can be used in the production of electricity. The Government of India has taken initiative for large scale production of hydropower. Such initiative will also have the spin-off benefits like employment avenues, increase in consumption of industrial products, roads, schools, banks, health care, postal facilities, and training centres etc. In 1971-72 only 37 villages were electrified. By March, 2001 this has rose to 2,506 out of 3,649 villages. The state having untapped estimated hydropower potential of 49,000 MW, may emerge as powerhouse of India when this potential is fully harnessed. In the study 72.5 per cent respondents opined that their activities are hampered by power supply irregularities.

8. Transportation: The service of transportation is a prerequisite for economic development. The road density in the state is very low. In 2001, the road density was 17.36 km per 100 sq. km of area as against the national average of 82 km per 100 sq. km. The main reasons for this low density are: the difficult topography and undulating terrain, the late start of development process, and the high cost of construction in the inaccessible and remote areas. The states does not have lateral roads connecting districts, since roads run vertically connecting places in Assam with districts or sub-divisions in A.P. This has not only resulted in high transportation costs but also affected by disturbed law and order situation and insurgency problem of Assam. The State at all has no railways except 1.26 km metre gauge railway line laid in 1989 connecting Bhalukpong with Indian railway map. This is a major handicap and supplemented by the field feedback.

9. Banking Scenario: The KVI activities come under the priority sector vide Reserve Bank of India's circular No.RPCD.PLNFS.BC.84/06.0612/93-94 (RBI, 1994). The REGP, now revised as PMEGP, is the only flagship scheme of KVIC in common to be offered for setting up Village Industries units. Under this scheme major assistance has to come from bank as loan. This scheme has its inherent lacuna to get handy to State's unemployed for couple of reasons. There are vast areas in the State where either there is no any bank or is a single-man branch which is obviously not equipped to go beyond the normal banking transactions of drawal and deposits. Even, as a whole, the banking scenario of the region has not been promising. For example, in 1969 Assam had 74 branches of scheduled commercial banks giving 1 branch for 1, 88,000 people. The Branch licensing policy of the RBI increased the number to 1242 in 1999 providing a bank for every 17,000 people. Still it lags all-India average. Thus, a vast interior of the North-Eastern region is practically a not covered area. In developing countries like ours, the failure to promote Financial Institutions in rural area has lead to failure of bank policies in these areas. Banks and Financial Institutions always point to the low recovery rate never thinking the mode of operation of the system imposed and associated maladies might led to the situation. The state financial Institutions like State Industrial Development Corporation, Industrial Financial Corporation are mostly in doldrums. Entrepreneurs have no other alternative than to approach the National Institutions for help whose contribution is also low ranking. The North Eastern Development and Finance Corporation Limited (NEDFi), Guwahati, under the Ministry of Finance, Government of India was positioned to care and foster the aspirations of the Region. However, the regional institute also could not fully rise to the much expected occasion. It is necessary for the authorities to establish a rapport with the beneficiaries but in the North-Eastern Region this gap always existed. The bank officers who are mostly outsiders appear to have no natural concern in advancing loans to the local entrepreneurs for taking up industrial ventures. One reason which adds to the cause adversely is the past records of recovery of bank loans which are pitifully low. It will be perhaps an expectation beyond the reality that a Bank Manager who is transferred to the branch for a limited tenure will normally put his service records at stake by granting unsecured loans rather he would opt for a safe passage in spending the tenure. The RBI has issued directives to all public sector banks to ensure 20 per cent year to year growth in credit to Micro Small and Medium Enterprises, which has never been achieved in the state. Around 85 per cent field responses say getting loan is a tough experience.

10. Need to strengthen the Single Window Scheme: Single Window Coordination Mechanism is a boon to the First Generation Entrepreneurs. Like Gujarat model (Industrial Extension Bureau) it is necessary for the region to have Single Window Coordination Mechanism in every state. It should guide in obtaining the Statutory License/clearance. The role of Department of Industries is not perceptible or not visible in advancement the cause of rural industrialization in the State and here the role of Department of Industries has always been scored average. The hard fact then remains that it has failed to come up as a true facilitator and path finder guide to the youths to venture in entrepreneurial career. Getting an appropriate project formulated, obtaining detailed information came in the way of expectations of the aspirants as substantiated by field data. Around 78 per cent respondents said they face problem for project formulation and 57 per cent explained inconvenience in getting explanation on scheme guidelines etc.

11. Vocational Training/Education: The State Government has a network of 88 craft centres, earlier called Cottage Industries Training and Production Centres (CITPC). Lack of modern tools and equipments, poor physical infrastructure, shortage of competent training instructors, outmoded curriculum and training methods, neglect of skill upgradation, low stipend offered to trainees etc. are some of the reasons for the suboptimal performance of the craft centres (Majumdar, 2000).Field study revealed the trained persons are not getting timely financial and other supports.

The dropout rates in Arunachal Pradesh at the primary and upper primary level in 2003 were 20 per cent and 36 per cent respectively (Arunachal Pradesh Human Development Report, Summary, 2005). The Arunachal Pradesh Human Development Report, 2005 advocates that after primary school, vocational streams should be available to train the boys and girls in the local context so that they find education is relevant and employment oriented. The State of Arunachal Pradesh is below the National level in female literacy (National Human Development Report, 2001). This is a case of gender disparity contrasting women empowerment.

12. Limitation of the Industrial Policy of the State: The policy document fails to give a clear road map for development of the KVI sector. In fact the policy documents remain handicap as it do not have any mention of the KVI sector. Generally in such documents of other States a chapter is devoted for the sector. On persuasion to the Department it appears that they have an indifferent and lukewarm attitude towards the KVI sector. Thus the non-inclusive Industrial Policy of the State has resulted directly or indirectly many hindrances towards promotion of this sector. As already dealt upon, the set up of APKVIB, the nodal agency for development of the KVI sector has been tragically weak. The government doesn't provide any Non-plan fund for its establishment charges. The lion's share of funds under Village and Small Industries Head of Account (VSI) are earmarked to Small Industries Sub-head under the cover of VSI. Even in the APKVIB the statutory posts are not being filled up. The plan document has hardly any mention of KVI sector. It appears that the Government and Administrative department is not very buoyant about its role. The study revealed that the Annual Reports of the APKVIB were never being tabled in the Assembly, which is must as per the provision of the Board Act. Even the Audits are not conducted regularly. The State Government has no developmental scheme for the sector and thus it solely depends on KVIC's developmental schemes which remain mostly unavailed. The APKVIB is not included in the standard mailing list of the Government. There has been a poor psyche about the status of the APKVIB and its employees. All these issues prompt one to conclude that perhaps the existence of the Board is not fully recognized.

13. No District level or Sub-divisional set up of APKVIB: In the absence any district level or block level set up, the KVI sector faces a severe setback in reaching out to the grass roots level person which is a precondition for success of this social sector. The claim of the State Government that the district level officer of the Textile and Handicrafts Department as nodal officer is totally ineffective and serves hardly any purpose for various limitations, the vital being non-orientation or non-induction of such officers to the KVI activities, its policies and guidelines and the Board can't have any administrative control on such officials. For absence of extension workers in the implementing agency, no rapports are built-up with NGOs, social activists. Thus outreach of the organization is confined. There is also scarcity of sincere NGOs in the State to be messengers of KVI sector. The abysmally poor condition of the APKVIB in terms of staff strength, infrastructures, lack of funds for establishment or field visits, unavailability of simple scheme to support the needy or deserving candidates makes the presence of APKVIB cool. Perhaps ignorance or intentional indifference of the Government towards the small economy that revolve round the KVI sector makes the sector unappealing. Field study reports that KVI information is scarce and wanting.

14. Khadi weaving vis-à-vis Handloom weaving: Handloom weaving is much popular in the State whereas Khadi spinning or weaving is nearly absent. An inquisition to the cause has been made. It appears that the Khadi activities are not open up to undertake as in case of handloom. It suffers from a plethora of rules. The stringent norm of Khadi Certification with its (Khadi Certification Code, 2003) and set norm of taking up Khadi at institutional level i.e. not at individual level, rules governing categorization of Khadi Institutions, unavailability of Khadi yarn in the open market, imposition of provision of cost charts, unavailability of financial assistance easily, unfriendly mode of extending rebate on Khadi products, as followed by KVIC has fettered the growth of Khadi Programme in the State. Few weavers also complained weaving in Khadi yarn is more cumbersome than Handloom yarn. The spinning process which has to be done manually with the help of Charkha as a distinguishing feature of Khadi is a tedious job with meagre wages. The welfare schemes for unorganized sector and those for Khadi workers like Khadi Karigar Group Insurance Scheme (launched from 15-8-2003), Khadi Artisan Welfare Fund Trust, and Incentives available under Quality Implementation Programme that has been introduced by the Government of India are not at all known to the target group (A Short Anthology of Initiatives in Service of Khadi – a Heritage Product, 2004, KVIC).

It is not that Khadi do not have its intrinsic merits over the Handloom or the Power loom. Khadi is the only fabric that is used for production of India's national flag (BIS specification No.IS:1-1968). The peoples having proximity to the Khadi world believe it as a supreme handicrafts; hand spun, hand woven cloth is a fabulous texture cool in summer and warm in winter. It is environment friendly cloth, the production of which does not deplete the basic scarce resources of the world. The Gandhian philosophy advocates that 'Hand Spinning' is a great mental therapy and creative outlet. Gandhi used to say 'Wearer of Khadi is wearer of freedom'. It has a universal appeal about it believing its creative force will bring people together against violence and division. The essence of Khadi is self-reliance and it gives us pollution free environment and violence free human mind. Moreover, we know times change and taste change. Today we live in a hurried world where convenience seems to call the shots. The primary users of handloom and Khadi no longer find it viable to wear them. Globalization brings with it a homogenizing of tastes. But it also brings with it the problems of eco-destruction, overuse of earth polluting chemicals, and energy guzzling factories. And it is here where handlooms and Khadi must make a renewed entry. The Khadi textiles offer environmentally friendly beauty which also gives livelihoods to millions, offers limitless design innovations and short exclusive runs. For designers who are looking for new, different and earth nourishing fabrics there can be no better option. And for consumers who care for the world and their environment, for the livelihood of millions and for preserving culture, Khadi is the cloth with a conscience. It also unites us again against our common enemies like poverty, pollution and unemployment.

Not hurting this supreme philosophy which is highly ethical and egalitarian, even in minute, however, one is perhaps constraint to say in the State of Arunachal Pradesh handloom has occupied an unmatched triumph over Khadi taking benefits of various weaknesses.

15. No relation with Panchyati Raj Institutions (PRI): The Board has been working in total isolation to the People's Organization. The KVI sector comes under the purview PRI institutions. In the Schedule-I of the Arunachal Pradesh Panchyati Raj Manual, 2002 (Arunachal Pradesh Panchyat Raj Act, 1997) published by the Department of Panchyat, the sector is placed under the Panchyati Raj Institutions. As per this provision, the activities which are to be undertaken by the PRI includes (1) Promotion of rural and cottage industries, (2) Organization of conferences, seminars and training programmes, agricultural and industrial exhibitions for the benefit of the rural areas. By failing to unite the PRI and KVI movement together Gandhi's view of Gram-Swaraj gets defeated. There is hardly any KVI scheme in the State where PRI can be involved effectively.

8

Khadi and Village Industries in Arunachal Pradesh

SARITA SRIVASTAV AND MANAS KUMAR JANA

The village and small-scale industries and traditional un-organized industries constitute an important segment of Arunachal's planned economy. This sector has not only continued to play a vital role in fulfillment of socio-economic objectives but also offers an excellent opportunity for industrial self-employment. The aim and objective of the planned economy in the state is to promote the industrial activities in the state, thereby to provide employment opportunities to the rural and urban, and to improve the economic conditions of the people. About 94 per cent population of Arunachal Pradesh lives in the rural belt making agriculture the main occupation. The principal crop of this area is rice, and other important crops include maize, millets, wheat, pulses, potato, sugarcane and oilseeds. The ecological conditions are suitable for horticulture and fruits like pineapple, orange, lemon, papaya, plum, pear, guava, cherries, walnut and peach thrive here. The Government of Arunachal Pradesh formulated the Agricultural Policy, 2001 with the need for achieving higher economic growth and creating job opportunities for the rural unemployed through Agriculture and allied sectors via a massive and gigantic entrepreneurship development programme.

A number of policy measures have been taken to promote entrepreneurship in the State. The Government is focusing on entrepreneurship development through institutional support from organisations like Khadi and Village Industries Commission (KVIC), District Industries Centres (DIC), Development Commissioner

(Handlooms), Development Commissioner (Handicrafts), Small Industries Development Organisation (SIDO), etc. In this paper, a sober attempt has been made to analyze the role of Khadi and Village industries in the entrepreneurship development process of Arunachal Pradesh *vis a vis* fulfilling the condition of sustainable development. There are many poverty alleviation programmes under implementation by the Government of India, which have a bearing and effect on promotion of entrepreneurship development.

Jawahar Gram Samridhi Yojana permits creation of infrastructure for education, health, roads etc. Swarnajayanti Gram Swarozgar Yojana (SGSY), aims at development of a large number of micro enterprises in rural areas with an emphasis on the cluster approach, focusing on organisation of the rural poor in Self-Help Groups and on their capacity building, planning of activity clusters, infrastructure build up, technology, credit and marketing, etc.

The Swarna Jayanti Shahari Rozgar Yojana seeks to provide gainful employment to the urban unemployed or underemployed poor through encouraging the setting up of self-employment ventures or provision of wage employment. Under the recently launched National Programme for Rural Industrialisation (NPRI) 100 rural clusters are to be set up or strengthened every year to give a boost to entrepreneurship development and to provide benefits to rural artisans and unemployed youth. The Khadi and Village Industries Commission (KVIC) assists in the promotion and development of khadi and village industries with the main objectives of rural industrialisation, skill development, transfer of appropriate technologies to rural industries income generation and promotion of self-reliance among the rural people. Under the Rural Employment Generation Programme (REGP), the KVIC has aimed at creating 10 lakh new jobs, most of them through village or rural industries by the end of the Tenth Plan. The expansion of cottage and small scale industries depends upon a number of factors like provision of raw materials, availability of power, technical advice, organised marketing of their produce and where necessary, safeguards against unequal competition from large scale manufacturers and above all an authoritative policy statement for strengthening the Small Scale sector is expected to be made by the State Government.

Village Industries

A "**Village Industry**" means – (i) "any industry located in a rural area which produces any goods or renders any service with or without the use of power and in which the fixed capital investment per head of an artisan or a worker does not exceed [one lakh rupees] or such other sum as may, by notification in the Official Gazette, be specified from time to time by the Central Government":

Provided that any industry specified in the Schedule and located in an area other than a rural area and recognised as a village industry at any time before the commencement of the Khadi and Village Industries Commission (Amendment) Act, 1987 shall, notwithstanding anything contained in the sub-clause, continue to be a village industry under this Act:

Provided further that in the case of any industry located in a hilly area, the provisions of this sub-clause shall have effect as if for the words "one lakh rupees", the words "one lakh and fifty thousand rupees" had been substituted.

(ii) ...any other non-manufacturing unit established for the sole purpose of promoting, maintaining, assisting, servicing (including mother units) or managing any village industry.

There is a wide scope of employment opportunities — rather self-employment opportunities, through KVIC in the State. Entrepreneurship development is possible through KVIC's Margin Money Scheme (MMS). This is a bankable scheme. Only enterprising entrepreneurs should take the opportunity of MMS. The Government of Arunachal Pradesh and the Khadi and Village Industries Board have taken steps to introduce MMS among the rural artisans of the State.

But much work remains to be done in the formation of clusters of handicrafts and pottery. The sense of loan repayment is gradually coming to the actual entrepreneurs. KVIC's schemes are best suited for industrialisation of rural Tripura. The approach to the KVIC is changing to ensure full utilisation of the schemes.

Village Industries under KVIC Purview

The KVIC has broadly re-grouped various village Industries under seven heads for the purpose of implementation of its programmes. The list of industries including the newly added ones is depicted in Table 8.1.

Table 8.1: Khadi and village Industries

Mineral Based Industry
1. Pottery
2. Lime

Agro Based and Food Processing Industry (ABFPI)
1. Pulses and Cereals Processing Industry
2. Gur and Khandsari Industry
3. Palmgur Industry
4. Fruit and Vegetable Processing Industry
5. Village Oil Industry

Polymer and Chemical Based Industry (PCBI)
1. Leather Industry
2. Non-Edible Oils and Soap Industry
3. Cottage Match Industry
4. Plastic Industry

Forest Based Industry (FBI)
1. Medicinal Plants Industry
2. Bee Keeping Industry
3. Minor Forest Based Industries

Hand Made Paper and Fibre Industry (HMPFI)
1. Hand Made Paper Industry
2. Fibre Industry

Rural Engineering and Bio Technology Industry (REBTI)
1. Non-Conventional Energy
2. Carpentry and Blacksmithy
3. Electronics

SEP/Service Industry
1. V. I. Co-ordination

Credit to SSI Sector from Public Sector Banks

Table 8.2 below gives the status of credit flow to Village and Small Industries (VSI) Sector since 1991.

Success Story of KVIC (Shri L. Ngamboi)

In the hilly and tribal inhibited areas in Churachandpur town which is a district place as well, one comes across a small Offset Printing Press owned and operated by Shri L. Ngamboi who himself belongs to a scheduled tribe. His M/s. Marantha Offset-cum-Stationery Shop became a reality when he was conferred with a

Table 8.2: Credit Flow to Village and Small Industries

Year	*Net Bank Credit (in Rs. crores)*	*To SSI (in Rs. crores)*	*Share of SSI*
March 1991	1,05,632	16,783	15.89%
March 1992	1,12,160	17,398	15.51%
March 1993	1,32,782	19,388	14.60%
March 1994	1,40,914	21,561	15.30%
March 1995	1,69,038	25,843	15.29%
March 1996	1,84,381	29,485	15.99%
March 1997	1,89,684	31,542	16.60%
March 1998	2,18,219	38,109	17.50%
March 1999	2,46,203	42,674	17.33%
March 2000	2,92,943	45,788	15.6%
March 2001	3,40,888	48,445	14.2%
March 2002	3,96,954	49,743	12.5%
March 2003	4,77,899	52,988	11.1%
March 2004(P)	5,58,849	58,278	10.4%
March 2005(P)	7,18,722	67,634	9.4%

Source: RBI.

loan of Rs. 9.81 lakhs by Punjab National Bank under REGP. He set for meeting orders for the printed material and stationery from nearby offices and institutions. With a turn over of Rs. 3 lakhs in the first year, Shri Ngamboi's unit has now become a talk-of-the-hill-town. His firm now is a supplier of documents, books of account, note and exercise books, letter heads, VCs, etc. to the educational institutions. The unit is now a breadwinner for ten including Shri Ngamboi and his wife. He has two girls trained in DTP on his pay roll. The success of the Press lies in the fact that it has cleared the loans drawn from the bank under the scheme. The owner says, "I've paved way for younger generation to get self-employed". He must be having those two girls in front of the Computer trying their fingers on the keyboard on his mind in the backward and tribal hilly area in the North-eastern corner.

Name of Entrepreneur	: **Shri L. Ngamboi**
Address	: Sieltmat, Churachandpur, Manipur
Name of the activity	: Printing and Stationery
Project Cost	: Rs. 9.81 lakhs

Table 8.3: Credit Flow to Tiny Sector

Credit to Tiny Sector	*March* '95	*March* '96	*March* '97	*March* '98	*March* '99	*March* '2000	*March* '2001	*March* '2002	*March* '2003	*March* '2004	*March* '2005
Net Credit To Tiny Sector (Rs. Crore)	7734	8183	9515	10273.13	8837.47*	22,742**	26,019	27,030	26,937	30,826	28,063
Credit of Tiny sector as percentage of net SSI credit	29.93	27.76	30.2	27.0	20.7	54.03	53.7	54.34	50.84	52.9	41.5

* Refers to units with investment in P&M up to Rs. 5 lakhs.

** Refers to units with investment in P&M up to Rs. 25 lakhs.

Table 8.3 gives the status of credit flow to Tiny Sector since 1995.

Commencement of production : 2001-02
Annual Turn Over : Rs. 29 lakhs
Employment Generated : 10 Persons
Monthly Income : Rs.15,000

KVIC Product Range

The world is moving towards natural and Eco-friendly Products. More and more people are becoming conscious of responsibility towards the environment and ecology; and products like plastic, etc. are highly looked down upon and greater demand is being generated for biodegradable and eco-friendly products. The KVI Sector produces a wide range of exclusive products which are having distinct characteristics. Some of the chief KVI products are as under:

Khadi: Hand spun and hand woven Khadi is very comfortable to wear compared to the artificially made synthetic fibres like Nylon, Terene , etc... The products are Cotton, Woollen, Silk and Polyvastra Khadi. Cotton Khadi is 100 per cent cotton, which has a great demand abroad, and it is available in different shades and colours. Attractive readymade garments are being designed in the form of Kurta-pajama, shirts, Ghagra Choli, salwar-khameez and other attractive garments. Khadi can be exported directly by KVIC or through registered merchant exporters registered with the Directorate of Marketing. Trade discount and incentives are available on the Export arranged by the KVIC since Khadi produced in the decentralised sectors requires some time for collection from various producing centres, processing and supplying to the buyers. However, the material as ordered can be supplied as per the specification at predetermined price fixed by the Commission.

Silk Khadi: Silk Khadi comes in various categories like Tussar, Matka, etc. Silk khadi can be converted into shirting, attractive sarees with Zari border or printed saree such as Baluchari sarees, which has rich embroidery or Kanjeevaram with its intricate designs woven in silver or golden thread.

Woollen Khadi: Woollen Khadi items consisting of Sweaters, Mufflers, Blankets, Socks.

Polyester Khadi: Polyvastra Khadi consisting of shirting and suitings in attractive shades and designs including dress materials and sarees.

Fibre: Fibre utility items are made out of Sisal, Banana, Pineapple, Palm and other fibres. Some of the products include bags, table mats, wall hanging, carpets, floor mats, floor pot holders etc. Palm fibre products like fancy bags, baskets, mats etc. are in great demand.

Leather: Leather products range include footwear like Kolhapuri chappals, sandals, shoes and purses, briefcase, jewel bags, vanity bags, attractive readymade garments etc.

Cane and bamboo: Fancy utility articles by using cane and bamboo as raw materials are produced in the North-eastern parts of the country. The items like furniture, sofa set, partition wall mats, handicrafts, items etc. can be supplied in bulk quantity.

Agarbatti: Incense sticks with fragrance are available in different varieties. There is a good demand existing in India and abroad. Incense sticks are made by women workers. Orders can also be executed with buyers brand name and prescribed specifications. In foreign countries, agarbatti is used as incense in place of artificial air purifier.

Processed Fruit Products: This is one of the activity taken up by the institutions and co-operative societies financed by the Commission. Products like Mango pulp, Tomato Pulp, Juices, Chatni etc. can be exported in large quantity. The products are covered under FPO (Food Product Organisation) license. There is good demand in the gulf countries for canned products.

Honey: Honey is natural sweet syrup collected by honey bees. There are 2 types of honey produced. One by the bees produced in forest and another apiary honey produced by installing colonies of bees and maintaining these in a systematic manner. Honey is also used as cough syrup, blood purifier and also as a general tonic. The honey in India is costlier than in the international market. However, this can be overcome by minimizing the wastage and increasing the productivity.

Hand-made Paper: This is a beautiful product uses the cloth rags and waste paper as raw material for production thus contributing in saving the trees, and hence preservation of ecology. The main strengths of Hand-made paper are as follows:

- Long product life. 100 years or more.
- Uniqueness in texture.

- Environment friendly, does not use wood pulp as raw materials and hence save trees.
- Converts waste into wealth, recycling nature.

Hand-made paper products range from stationery items like files, letterpads, envelopes, fancy bags, visiting cards, greeting cards, watermark certificate and decoration materials, photo album etc. There is a good market for these products in particular.

Pottery and Stone Ware items: Clay articles produced in rural areas by potters known as Prajapaties are in great demand in the country as well as abroad. In the market fancy pottery items and terracotta are in great demand.

Papad and Masala: Papad and masala are in great demand in India and abroad. Mahila Griha Udyog Lijjat Papad of KVI , exports papad and masala in a large way to U.K., U.S.A., Gulf countries and New Zealand.

Herbal Products: Number of herbal products like herbal shampoo, tooth powder, health tonic like Chavan Prash and Churnas are being produced by KVI. Herbal products are "in thing" in the foreign market.

Constraints of KVIC Movement

There are several constraints of khadi and village industries movement. Absence of a long-term policy, lack of marketing infrastructure, poor design and quality, shrinkage of markets, inadequacy of working capital and poor initiative are mainly responsible for the downward trend of this sector. A new Rs. 125 crore five-year package with special attention on the North-Eastern States has been unveiled by Union Minister of State for Small Scale Industries, Smt.Vasundara Raje Scindia. Khadi has been designated as a heritage product. Besides, an insurance scheme for workers and a Rs. 390 crore budgetary support apart from an institutional finance of Rs. 825 crore have also been launched. Marketing strategies have been revamped. Quality assurance of khadi is stressed upon. Besides, the Khadi and Village Industries Commission (KVIC) initiated the *Abhyudaya*—Moving Forward—scheme during the Golden Jubilee celebrations of the country's Independence to reach out to certain segments of society normally outside its fold. The programmes under *Abhyudaya* took KVIC out of the typical Government department mode of functioning.

Conclusion

The present global economic scenario which is turning the world into a global village is also bringing in its wake several opportunities for the rural population for developing their entrepreneurial talents, in proper prospective and add to the national gross domestic product.

The Khadi and V.I. Commission, as it has all along been the forerunner in bringing succour to the rural populace with all dignity and self-respect, had launched many a programme on those lines, the latest and the most popular as on today being the Rural Employment Generation Programme.

The Rural Employment Generation Programme (REGP), which is being lauded as the most successful amongst rural development programmes in the country as on today has brought forth many useful innovations and necessities in the purposeful implementation of the programme. Rural Industries Consultancy Services (Rural ICS) is one off-shoot of such an endeavour.

Sustainability of any project depends upon fulfilment of certain basic requirements. Systematic approach, training to entrepreneurs, technology, Quality Control and marketing support etc. if all these will be taken care of adequately, the KVIC can play an exemplary role in the process of entrepreneurship development in Arunachal Pradesh.

REFERENCES

Dr. Kaveri, V.S., "Banking In North East and Suggestion", *SBI Monthly Review*, Vol. XXXVII, Nov. 1999.

Economic Times—Various Issues.

Khanka, S.S. *Industrial Devlopement of Backward Areas*, Himalaya Publishing House, New Delhi , 1994.

Khanka, S.S., *Entrepreneurial Development*, S. Chand and Company Ltd., New Delhi , 2001.

Mail, D.D. and Bandopadhya, R., " Small Industry Development in North East India—Status and Strategy", Omsons Publications, New Delhi , 1993.

NEDFI Data Bank Quarterly, July 2002.

Panda, D.P., and Parida (Dr.) J.K., "Entrepreneurship Development in Tribal Region of India – A Consortium Approach". *The Utakal Business Review*, Vol. XVI, 2002-03, p. 61.

SIDBI, *Development Report*, 2002, p. 57.

Various Issues of *SBI Monthly Review*.

Vernekar, S.S., "Employment Generation and Entrepreneurship Development". *University News*, 41 (42), Oct. 20-26, 2003.

www.sidbi.com

9

Development of Khadi and Village Industries in Manipur : Issues and Challenges

JAYANTI NINGOMBAM AND VICTORIA AYEKPAM

Manipur is a small state in the North-Eastern corner of India bordering with Mynmar on the east, Nagaland on the north, Assam on the west and Mizoram on the south. She has a geographical area of 22,327 sq. km. inhabiting 23,88,634 persons as per 2001 census. About 9/10 of the total area of the state is covered by hills and the remaining 1/10 is covered by valley. On the other hand, 9/10 of the total populations are settled in the valley which indicates the regional disparity, indicating the need of industrialization and entrepreneurship development especially in the rural and hilly areas through Khadi and Village Industries.

Industrialisation through Khadi and Village Industries are inseparable factors in the economic development of rural areas. Because, it can generate large scale employment with relatively low capital investment; promote more balanced development; equitable distribution of income; make use of untapped capital, natural and human resources etc.

Despite massive development efforts taken by both Central and State Governments through various schemes and programmes, the pace of economic and industrial development of the state is very poor. As a result the number of educated unemployed youth of the state has crossed 4,60,143 as in January 2005 of which 1,18,121 were female unemployed youth. The rate of unemployed youth against the total population was 19.26 per cent which is much higher than the national average of 2.81 per cent in 2000.

The growing unemployment problem can be solved only when the educated and uneducated youth of the state are trained and involved in industrial oriented vocations. Because entrepreneurship is a purposeful activity through which it helps in initiating, promoting and maintaining various range of economic activities for the production and distribution of wealth.

Thus, industrial development usually implies development of small scale industries and it has a significant role in the economic development indirectly and directly solving the alarming growth of unemployed educated youth of the backward state like Manipur in particular and the North-Eastern region staying in the "No Industry Category".

Recognising the importance of industrial development for the economic and social development, the Central Government, the State Government, the North-Eastern Council through various agencies such as banks, NGOs, Directorate of Commerce Industries have been organizing various programmes over the past few decades. Such programmes have facilitated direct and indirect training and education about the matter to the potentials especially in the area of techniques of marketing, financial, management, and accounting to the small and medium enterprises. But the development of these enterprises is not encouraging and needs proper attention especially to the Khadi and Village Industries which can be seen from the scenario of KVI in Manipur.

Khadi and Village Industries Scenario in Manipur

The Khadi and Village Industries Commission (KVIC) was established by the Government of India in the year 1957. The Khadi and Village Industries is not only providing employment to people in rural and semi-urban areas at low investment per job, but also utilises local skill resources and provides part-time as well as full-time work to rural artisans, women and minorities. It was only in the year 1966 that the State Board for the development of Khadi and Village Industries was constituted by Government of Manipur. The Traditional sector of industries falls within the purview of organisations such as Khadi and Village Industries Commission. The KVIC include artisans in tiny industrial units and defines it as any industry located in a village or town inhabited by population not exceeding 10,000 which produces goods and renders services with or without the use of power in which the fixed capital per head does not exceed Rs. 15,000. In the State, the KVIC has given special attention for economic upliftment of the Scheduled Castes/ Scheduled Tribes and women.

As the KVI provides the employment to the youths of rural and hilly areas it is necessary to analyse the performance of Khadi and Village Industry in Manipur. Table 9.1 shows the performance of KVI in Manipur.

Table: 9.1: Performance of KVI of Manipur 2002-03 to 2003-04

Items	*Units*	*Year*		*% variation*
		2002-03	*2003-04*	*2002-03 to 2003-04*
Production	Rs. in Lakhs	6000.85	6029.24	0.47
Sales	Rs. in Lakhs	5661.92	6069.88	7.21
Earnings	Rs. in Lakhs	2632.68	2690.18	2.18
Employment	No. in Lakhs	0.61	0.62	1.64

Source: *Economic Survey,* Manipur, 2007-08.

Table 9.1 shows that production of KVI sector was to the tune of Rs. 60.29 crores in the year 2003-04 as against Rs. 60.01 crores in 2002-03 showing an increase of 0.47 per cent over the previous year. The total amount earned in the year 2002-03 was Rs. 26.33 crores whereas the earning was Rs. 26.90 crores in the year 2003-04.

In the year 2006-07, there is increase in production and the sales. The production comes down to Rs. 5515.59 lakhs from Rs. 7336.19 lakhs during the year 2006-07 to 2007-08. Both the production and the sales have decrease in the 2007-08 in comparison with the 2006-07. But one thing which can be noted here is that the amount of sales is more than that of production 2007-08 which shows the maintenance of proper stocking. The amount of production is Rs. 5515.59 lakhs while the sale is Rs. 5580.19 lakh in 2007-08. Coming to the employment, there is increase in employment generation. It increases from .66 to .71 lakhs from 2006-07 to 2007-08. The overall picture can be seen from Table 9.2.

Table 9.2: Performance of KVI of Manipur 2006-07 to 2007-08

Items	*Units*	*Year*	
		2006-07	*2007-08*
Production	Rs. in Lakhs	7336.19	5515.59
Sales	Rs. in Lakhs	7557.24	5580.19
Employment	No. in Lakhs	0.66	0.71

Soure: Planning Commission.

From the comparison of Tables 9.1 and 9.2, it is revealed that in an overall there is increase in production and sales in all the years except 2007-08.

As Finance is the lifeblood of any business enterprise it is a need to note the grants and loans provided by the government here. The amount of loan disbursed during the year 1995-96 was Rs. 322.93 lakhs and it was Rs. 585.84 lakhs in 1996-97 and Rs. 569.55 lakhs in 1997-98. Further during the year 1997-98 a sum of Rs. 70.08 lakhs was also provided as grants. During the year 2003-04 a sum of Rs. 15 lakhs under plan and Rs. 56 lakhs under non-plan were provided as grants-in-aid to meet the establishment charges of the Khadi and Village Industries Board.

As the Khadi and Village Industries provides employment to the people in rural and semi-urban areas at low investment per job, utilises local skill resources and provides part-time as well as full-time work to rural artisans, women and minorities, this sector provides both opportunity and challenges to the Manipuris. It is a challenge as there is need for continuous updating of knowledge, skills and the others. Again, it is an opportunity because of providing employment especially at the rural areas.

Problems of Khadi and Village Industries

Despite of the efforts invested at the state and central level Khadi and Village Industries are suffering from a number of problems such as lack of capital, removal of tariff, use of outdated technology, problem of law and order, inadequate power supply, lack of standardisation etc.

1. One of the most important problems faced by the Khadi and Village Industries in Manipur is inadequate use of working

capital. The poor credit payment ratio of the borrower, lengthy process of getting loans and finances aid, fewer financial instruments and sources of funds are some of the challenges faced by the said sector.

2. Marketing is an important area for proper functioning of any business organization. However, KVI faces different problems in the marketing of products by them. Following are the major problems faced by them:
   - Lack of linkage with the marketing agencies
   - Lack of adequate sales promotion measures
   - Lack of a well defined and knit channel of distribution for marketing
3. Another problem faced by the Khadi and Village Industries in Manipur is the use of obsolescence and outdated technology. Most of the units are unable to replace their units with modernize and sophisticated technology due to the lack of fund and other constraints. Until and unless they change with modernize technology the units will be lagging behind from their competitors qualitatively, quantitatively as well as price and product.
4. Power shortage is also one of the hindrances in development of Khadi and Village Industries. Frequent load shedding, low voltage of power, high power tariff affects the functioning of the said sector.
5. Frequent band, strike, economic blockade, and curfew etc. are also big hindrances while working the industries effectively and efficiently. This is due to the existence of insurgencies problems.
6. Most of the workers working in the Khadi and Village Industries are illiterate causing the unawareness of technological knowledge and marketing knowledge etc.
7. Most of the Khadi and Village Industries in Manipur do not maintain accounts properly which leads to the mismanagement of funds, improper utilization of funds, misuse of the same etc. Thus, lack of maintaining accounts becomes one of the problems for the development of the sector.
8. Lack of information and experience is also another challenge for the selection of technology, market, location tackling the problems relating to labour and finance etc.

Opportunities of Khadi and Village Industries

Several entrepreneurial opportunities are emerging in the Khadi and Village Industries, wholesaling, retailing, handloom and handicraft, and even in agriculture and allied sectors. Old entrepreneurial activities are also undertaken, but new entrepreneurial opportunities are emerging.

In the Khadi and Village Industries Sector, two traditional industries, handloom and handicraft industries offer very good scope for entrepreneurial activities. Handloom is a women's activity which can be carried leisurely. Handicraft is also another entrepreneurial activity which can be done through cane and bamboo. These are locally available materials too.

For the development of the products of khadi and village industries Khadi and Village Industries Commission has introduced a common brand names—***Sarvodaya*** brand for village industry products and *Khadi* brand for Khadi products. Besides, they have introduced ***Deshi ahar*** brand for natural and chemic free organic food products, the demand of which has been constantly increasing. Entrepreneurs in the village industry sector are emerging. This sector has better scope in the North East.

Manipur has large potential for Hydel power resources. The state has hydro power potential of 2241 MW of which only 105 MW Hydro power is generated so far (A Report on Central Electricity Authority, October 2001).Once these resources are tapped fully the power problem of the state can be solved and would facilitate the growth and development of khadi and village industries in Manipur.

Being situated at the border area, there is a chance of developing the khadi and village industries in Manipur. Again, promotion of Indo-Myanmar border trade for solving the unemployment problem is another opportunities area. Strong potential for future trade in both foreign and domestic market is emerging with the new economic policy.

Besides the above-mentioned opportunities, there is the opportunity of developing the KVI in Manipur because of the opening and offering of different subjects relating to foreign trade and others in different levels towards the public at large with which we can have the idea about import and export.

Conclusion

Khadi and village industries not only provide employment to the people in rural and semi-urban areas at low investment per job, but also utilises local skill resources and provides part-time as well as full-time work to rural artisans, women and minorities is considered as an important strategy for developing the economy of Manipur. But, for an effective and efficient functioning of the said sector there is need to provide different infrastructural facilities. Further, there is the need to check whether the facilities, amenities, grants, loans etc. are properly provided to the needy areas.

REFERENCES

Amar Yumnam. *Indo Myanmar Border Trade through Moreh: Status Assessment.* Indo Myanmar Border Trade: Status Problems and Potentials (2005), Akansha Publishing House, New Delhi.

Asha Patil and Anuradha Mathu. *Women an Entrepreneur: Issues and Challenges* (2007), Kalpaz Publication, New Delhi.

Dr. Reddy Ranga A.: *Impact of Globalisation on Indian Economy*, Research Centre for Social Sciences, Journal of Global Economy, Volume 1. No. 2, April-June 2005.

Gaigodin Panmei, *"Indo Myanmar Border Trade"*, Seminar on Indo-Myanmar Border Trade, held at Imphal on 18-10-2004, Organised by Department of Commerce and Industry, Government of Manipur.

G.P. Prasain, *Entrepreneurship and Small Scale Industries* (2006), Akansha Publishing House, New Delhi.

Handloom Export Monthly Newsletter, December, 2004 (HEPC, Chennai), p. 25.

India—At a glance, 2007.

Industrial Policy of Manipur, 1996, Directorate of Commerce and Industries Government of Manipur.

Manoranjan Sharma, *Leading Issues in Indian Economy* (2005) Atlantic Publishers and Distributors, New Delhi.

Planning Commission, Tenth Five Year Plan—2002-07, Vol. 1.

Ruddar Datta and K.P.M. Sundharam. *Indian Economy* (2004), S. Chand and Company Ltd., New Delhi.

Statistical Abstract Manipur 2005, Directorate of Economics and Statistics, Government of Manipur.

Statistical Abstract Manipur 2007, Directorate of Economics and Statistics, Government of Manipur.

10

Khadi and Village Industries in Assam

SWAPNALI BARUAH AND B. D. NAYAK

Introduction

India, with 28 states and 7 UTs, which celebrated its 62nd year of Independence on 15th August, 2009, is still dependent on Agriculture. The country with more than 100 crore of population has considerably improved her economic condition since its independence. Since the country has been practicing Five Year Plans giving utmost importance to the priority sectors from time to time. With "Jai Jawan Jai Kishan" slogan the country boosted the development process of India via the development of the primary sector. In the present era of Globalization, the country is striving hard to develop the secondary and tertiary sector in addition to agriculture. Further, the country has taken several steps for achieving rural development via Rural Industrialisation. The development of rural industries has been the main objective of the Government of India during the Five Year Plan era. Introduction of Khadi and Village Industries Commission (KVIC) and development of Khadi and Village Industries (KVIs) are some of the remarkable initiatives in this direction.

KVIC and KVIs

Development of Khadi and Village Industries (KVIs) is not a recent step. The Khadi and Village Industries Commission (KVIC) have a glorious history behind its origin and development. Under an Act of Parliament (Act. 61) of 1956, the KVIC has been taking over the works of all India KVIs Board. The Khadi industries refer to handspun and hand-woven cloth, in which cotton, silk or wool etc.

(which are spun into threads on Charkha) are used as raw-materials. And Village industries are defined as the rural industry with fixed capital investment up to Rs. 1 lakh, subject to the change from time to time by the Government of India. Objectives behind the development of these two labour intensive industries were many, such as employment generation, providing salable articles, creation of self-reliance among the rural people and building up of a strong rural community spirit. The Government of India has been taking many steps from time to time in its Five Year Plans for the development of these industries. Moreover, "Khadi Bhandars" are made available throughout the country for the sale of the Khadi goods. There are 15,431 sales outlets in India, out of which 7,050 are owned by the KVIC and products of these industries are also sold at international level through various exhibitions.

The KVIs sector makes a significant contribution to the Indian economy. As per available data (Table 10.1), KVIC in the economy has generated a total employment of 82.77 lakh (2005-06) against 76.78 lakh of the preceding year. Against 7.80 per cent employment growth in Khadi industries (2004-05 to 2005-06), the Village industries registered 8.73 per cent growth during the same period. During 2005-06, India produced Khadi cloth worth Rs. 468.30 crore generating employment for 8.68 lakh persons. During 2006-07, the Khadi sector recorded production of Rs. 339.50 crore and provided employment to 8.77 lakh persons up to December 2006.

North-East (N-E) Region of India commonly known as Eight Sisters is an agro-based Region. Governments of this Region has taken steps from time to time for the development of KVIs. Table 10.2 shows that Assam occupied top most position among the entire N-E states of India regarding production, sales and employment in KVIs during the period 2007-08 (estimated up to December 2007). Although achievement of this state is not much remarkable in respect of N-E Region as a whole but Assam showed significant achievement in this respect. However, Mizoram occupied 2nd position, next to Assam regarding the achievements in 2006-07 and 2007-08. Here we shall consider the number of Micro Small Enterprise (MSE) Units and Fixed investment made in KVIs in North-East. As per available data it was found that the number of MSE units is the lowest in Sikkim at 474 and the highest in Assam (2,35,576) with fixed investment at Rs. 14 crores and Rs.1451 crores respectively. Although Arunachal Pradesh occupies higher rank than Sikkim from number of units and fixed investment point of view but achievement of the state during the same is less than Sikkim at Rs. 411.65 lakh (production), Rs.1904.71 lakh in sales and 0.38 lakh persons in employment (during 2006-07). It is found that production of Arunachal Pradesh KVIs has increased from Rs. 86.24 lakh (1997-98) to Rs. 22802.34 lakh (up to December 2007), which is the lowest throughout N-E India during the same period. There are many causes for slow growth of the KVIs in Arunachal Pradesh, say motivation by western culture, which influences people of the state not to use the synthetic clothes and such other products. Moreover, Khadi clothes are used more in the areas characterized by heavy summer, but the N-E Region of India neither so cool nor so hot from climatic point of view for which people are influenced by the products of KVIs.

Keeping in view the performance of the entire North-East, let us now consider the case of Assam, with the help of Tables 10.3(A) and (B). During the years 2000-01 to 2005-06, the sale of these industries has increased from Rs. 3376.05 lakh to Rs. 36135.66 lakh. Similarly, employment generation has increased from 113219 numbers to 215631 numbers, accompanied by the growth of sales from Rs. 1429.91 lakh to Rs. 15557.09 lakh respectively. However, performance of the Village industries was much better than that of the Khadi industries.

Steps taken by Government

The Government of India has been taking initiatives for the growth and expansion of KVIs throughout India. Here we shall mention in brief the steps taken for the N-E Region:

- To increase the number of Khadi institutions in North-Eastern States, KVIC has removed the ban on registration of new KVIs located in NER.
- To improve the technology used in the KVI sectors as also the quality of products, the KVIC has entered into an arrangement with IIT.
- The Indian Institute of Entrepreneurship (IIE), Guwahati has been recognized as the nodal agency for NER with the objective to implement and monitor Rural Employment Generation

Programme (REGP) projects being set up in the Region and to impart training to the beneficiaries.

- 10 per cent space is reserved in all Departmental Khadi Gramodyog Bhawans for the products of the institutions from NER for marketing of KVI products.
- In addition to these initiatives, the Government of India attempted to promote entrepreneurship in N-E Region. For this under REGP, concessional facilities were extended to the weaker sections of NER. Accordingly 30 per cent margin money, as against 25 per cent in the case of beneficiaries from general category, is provided to the entrepreneurs from this region. For setting up of projects in NER, own contribution from entrepreneur is only 5 per cent of the project cost, as against 10 per cent in other area (Table 10.4). Government of India targeted to set up 4344 number of projects with the utilization of Margin Money at Rs. 4981.66 lakhs and generation of employment at 82486 in N-E India. Accordingly up to December, 2007, Government has made achievement at 57.04 per cent in case of number of projects, 54.96 per cent in respect of Marginal Money utilization and 51.03 per cent in case of employment generation in the North-East.

Major findings

Thus, this may be concluded that there is a potentiality for the development of KVIs in North-East. It's the time to find out the ways to utilize these potentialities and promote its contribution to country's National Income. For this, we are to find out the problems working as obstacles in the development of these industries in the North-East India.

- **Costly products:** Free flow of foreign goods to India is likely to kill this labour intensive industry. The foreign products seem to be less costly as compared to that of the KVIs. The cost of one metre Khadi cloth ranges from Rs. 75 to Rs.120 depending on quality, whereas the price of clothes of other industries is comparatively low. Price of every good is likely to increase in the present period of Inflation, but within some limit. The ever increasing price of Khadi products has made it out of the reach of common people. As a result its demand is low in the domestic market. Under such situation, development and expansion of these industries is a matter of doubt.

- **Market potentiality:** Even after 62 years of independence the marketing network is not working strongly enough for the expansion of these industries. Lack of effective distribution system of the products among the masses due to poor market condition is responsible for the slow growth of these industries.
- **Selling cost:** In the present era of Liberalization, Privatization and Globalization (LPG), expansion of KVIs is scanty as compared to the MNCs in India. Lack of selling expenditures is one of the causes responsible for it.
- **Absence of leadership:** In the North-East India, there is absence of leadership for the development of KVIs, as Sailesh Kumar Bandyopadhyay (Eastern zone in-charge of the KVIC and former secretary of Gandhi Smarak Nidhi) said in an interview.

Suggestions

Keeping in view the above-mentioned problems of the KVIs, the following suggestions may be put forward for the revival of this almost dying industry in North-East India:

- The bio-degradable Khadi products can be helpful to counter the burning problem of the current period "Global Warming". Products of these industries are perishable easily and get mixed with soil without leaving any substance, whereas use of synthetic goods are just polluting the environment and adding fuel to the above-mentioned burning problem. So, public consciousness is to be generated among the masses regarding the protection of our environment with the maximum use of Khadi and Village Industry products.
- Before going to expand the Khadi market in abroad, it's necessary to make the khadi industry products popular among the Indian nationals. Government has been sanctioning grants from time to time for this industry, but it needs efficient utilization of sanctioned amount.
- It is not enough just to say that there is absence of leadership in North-East for the development of these industries. Steps for the development of leadership in the region are to be taken, otherwise in near future KVIs in the region will survive only in the "Boards".

- In addition to the grants, Government must provide subsidy for these industries so that people in general can go for the purchase of these goods. Moreover, in the present age of style and fashion, the KVIs must give importance to make their products decorative. Since India is a developing country so majority of total population prefer stylish cheaper goods. This general tendency of the public must be kept in view while new policy measures are implemented for this industry.

Conclusion

So, it's the time to go hand in hand with modern age. Change is necessary no doubt but destruction of our glorious historical industry in the name of change is just like losing our identity. So, it's the right time to think positively for the development of this eco-friendly industry which can counter the burning issue of "Global Warming".

REFERENCES

Anonymous (2002-08): *Statistical Abstract of Arunachal Pradesh Directorate of Economics and Statistics*, Govt. of Arunachal Pradesh.

Anonymous (2002-09): *Basic Statistics of North-East Region.*

Anonymous (2002-07): *Statistical Hand Book of Assam.*

Anonymous (2007): *Assam Economic Journal.*

Jha, J., *Khadi and Village Industries in Economic Development.*

www.kvic.org.in kvic

Table 10.1: Achievements of KVIs in India

Year	*Production (in Rs. Crore)*	*Employment (in lakh persons)*
2002-03	443.07	8.58
2003-04	451.93	8.61
2004-05	461.54	8.64
2005-06	468.30	8.68
2006-07*	485.18	8.80

Source: *Basic Statistics of NER*, 2007.

* Targets

Table 10.2: Achievements of KVIs in North-East India

States	*Production (Rs. Lakh)*		*Sales (Rs. Lakh)*		*Employment (in Lakh persons)*		*No. of MSE units*	*Fixed investment*
	2006-07	*2007-08*	*2006-07*	*2007-08*	*2006-07*	*2007-08*	*2006-07*	*2006-07*
Arunachal Pradesh	1925.21	1447.44	2914.34	2151.92	0.07	0.08	1578	42
Assam	30328.99	22802.34	47337.39	34953.46	2.48	2.65	235576	1451
Manipur	7336.19	5515.59	7557.24	5580.19	0.66	0.71	57171	428
Meghalaya	6423.52	4829.42	9003.30	6647.95	0.35	0.37	28591	202
Mizoram	14239.61	10705.81	20220.03	14930.27	0.64	0.68	14335	167
Nagaland	7747.68	5824.96	10077.24	7440.94	0.44	0.47	19024	601
Sikkim	2336.86	1756.93	4819.05	3558.34	0.19	0.20	474	14
Tripura	5470.01	4112.53	6815.19	5032.27	0.45	0.48	29141	384
Total	75808.07	56995.02	108743.78	80295.34	5.28	5.64	385890	3289

Source : *Basic Statistics of NER*, 2009.

Table 10.3(A): Sales of KVIs in Assam

Year	Sales (in Rs. Lakh) Khadi industries	Village industries	Total
(1)	(2)	(3)	(4)=(2)+(3)
2000-01	87.00	3289.05	3376.05
2001-02	86.99	3405.16	3492.15
2002-03	80.38	3234.22	3314.60
2003-04	67.11	3558.15	3625.26
2004-05	67.99	3013.97	3081.96
2005-06	395.62	35740.04	36135.66

Source: *Statistical Hand Book of Assam*: 2002-07

Table 10.3(B): Employment and wage of KVIs in Assam

Year	Employment		Total	Wage (in Rs. Lakh)		Total
	Khadi	Village		Khadi	Village	
(1)	(2)	(3)	(4)=(2)+(3)	(5)	(6)	(7)=(5)+(6)
2000-01	14710	98509	113219	166.99	1262.92	1429.91
2001-02	17000	103493	120493	164.22	1891.74	2055.96
2002-03	10579	111814	122393	168.02	2248.16	2416.18
2003-04	11134	128000	139134	172.97	4380.14	4553.11
2004-05	11383	154000	165383	251.94	7437.34	7689.28
2005-06	11631	204000	215631	261.57	15295.52	15557.09

Source: *Statistical Hand Book of Assam*: 2002-07.

Table 10.4: Performance of KVIs under REGP during 2007-08 in NER

States	Target for 2007-08			Achievement (up to December'07)		
	No. of Projects	M. M. (Rs. Lakhs)	Employment (in No.)	No. of Projects	M.M. (Rs. Lakhs)	Employment (in No.)
(1)	(2)	(3)	(4)	(5)	(6)	(7)
Arunachal Pradesh	116	132.96	2214	55	99.09	621
Assam	2344	2678.38	44602	1703	1875.68	31421
Manipur	209	238.55	3973	21	21.45	157
Meghalaya	342	391.07	6513	76	121.03	821
Mizoram	682	797.38	12806	328	402.99	5597
Nagaland	283	322.90	5377	194	81.12	1343
Sikkim	122	138.85	2312	24	48.70	168
Tripura	246	281.57	4689	77	87.81	1968
Total	4344	4981.66	82486	2478	2737.87	42096

Source: *Basic Statistics of NER*, 2008.

11

Handicraft and Cottage Industry in Arunachal Pradesh: Challenges and Opportunities

RAM KRISHNA MANDAL

Location and Regional Setting of the State

The state of Arunachal Pradesh is sparsely populated by the indigenous population predominantly. According to 2001 Census, the state has a population of 10,97,968 persons consisting of 5,79,941 males and 5,18,027 females as against 1991 Census of 8,64,558 comprising 4,65,004 males and 3,99,554 females. The tribal population of the State is 64.22 per cent of total population in this state. The state has 0.11 per cent of the All India Population. The decennial growth rate of the population from 1991 to 2001 is about 26.85 per cent against an increase of 21.34 per cent at all-India level. The density of population in the state as per 2001 census is 13 persons/sq.km. as compared to 10 persons/sq.km. in the 1991 census. What is more is that, the population density of the state is the lowest among the states in India. The different census reports have given different classification of total number of tribes and sub-tribes.

According to 2001 census, the state inhabited 25 major tribes and 110 sub-tribes exhibits a distinctive culture, customs and traditions. These tribes are scattered over an area of 83,743 sq. km. in hilly terrain of Eastern Himalayas. The concentration of tribal population throughout the border region though very high is scattered in small villages with uninhabited habitations in higher altitudes. The principal inhabitants of the State of Arunachal Pradesh from east to west are the tribes of Wancho, Nocte, Tangsa, Singpho, Khamti, Mishmi, Adi, Galo, Padam, Minyong, Pailibo,

Bokar, Bori, Memba, Khamba, Apatani, Nyishi, Hill Miri, Nah, Tagin, Aka, Khowa or Bugun, Miji, Sulung, Sherdukpen and Monpa.

The state of Arunachal Pradesh was formed on February 20, 1987, which covers around 2.5 per cent of the total geographical area of our country. The state is predominantly mountainous and like a horseshoe in shape. This state is situated near the tropic of cancer, lying between latitudes 26°28′ N and 29°30′ N and between 91°30′ E and 97°30′ E longitude on the North-East extremity of India. The area falls in the climatic transition between torrid and temperate zones of the Northern Hemisphere. It is surrounded by Bhutan on the West (157 km.), China on the North and the Northeast (1080 km.), Myanmar on the East (441 km.) and Assam and Nagaland on the South. The geo-strategic importance of the state becomes evident from the fact that the state has 1678 kms. International Border. The border is under dispute particularly with Tibet (China) regarding Mac-Mohan Line till date. This border dispute led to the Chinese aggression of India in 1962, which was a turning point not only in the history of India but also in the development of the region under study.

The international border of the state runs from one tri-junction of Tibet (China), Bhutan and India in the north-west to another tri-junction of China, Myanmar and India in the north-east along with high peaks of the Himalayas of more than 1500 kilometres in length. The great Himalayan ranges in the state run from the east of the Himalayas to the Tsangpo up to Mishmi hills. In the extreme east, the state meets another series of mountain ranges where the Himalayan range turns from East-West direction to South-West direction and hastens on, prominently southwards into the hills of Nagaland. Its great range of elevation form the outer Siwalik type hills rises to a height of 300 metres and further in a series of knife like ridges from the plains of Assam to the inner or Greater Himalaya which encompasses heights from 4,900 metres to 7,000 metres along the border of Tibet (China). Though once forbidden and formidable area; it is, at present developing at fast pace and the people are enjoying a better life in social, economic, political and religious spheres.

From the economic point of view, the whole state may be divided into three lateral belts each having a distinct pattern of economic development. The upper belt bordering international frontiers has economic constraints with very little facilities and amenities of modern civilization. The people of this area depend on their own production for their livelihood in many respects. The lower belt consisting mainly of the foothills has intimate economic ties with the adjoining plains of Assam. The people of this belt enjoy almost all facilities of modern life. The middle belt has acted as a bridge between the upper and the lower belts enjoying modern facilities of modern life. The people inhabiting in the three belts are at different stages of economic development. Thus, the socio-economic profiles of the people of these three belts are different from one another.

Arunachal Pradesh is the richest state having the highest per capita availability of natural resources, yet, it is one of the most economically backward regions in India. Out of her total geographical area, 83743 sq. kms., 70 per cent of its topography constitutes broad and narrow valleys, 10 per cent foothills and flat areas and 20 per cent snow clad peak areas.

The main occupation of the local population is agriculture, which is based primarily on swidden cultivation, the slash-and-burn method that is known in North-East India as *jhum*. However, in the foothill and plain areas of the district people are increasingly adopting permanent agricultural practices. Paddy, maize and millets are the main crops. Fruits like apple, pear, plum, peach and almond are grown in the higher reaches of the district whereas pineapple, papaya, litchi, banana etc. are grown in the foothills and plain areas. The climate and soil of the lower parts are suitable for sericulture. People residing in these places grow mulberry and eri silkworms.

The agricultural operations are confined to only 5 per cent of the total geographical area, of which 62 per cent to 65 per cent land are under shifting cultivation (Jhum). It is generally agreed that growing monetization of the economy should lead to the spurt in investment. Nevertheless, due to very low level of farm and non-farm production, output has not registered a noticeable growth that evidently adds to constraints to the economic development. Secondly, social capital of the state has not been utilized to its fullest capacity due to structural and functional inefficiency of the delivery institutions. During the pre-independence era, the North East Frontier Agency (NEFA), now Arunachal Pradesh was only loosely administered and the various tribal communities inhabiting the land were left to manage their own affairs as per their own customary laws and practices.

The tribal communities are extremely self-reliant; they construct their own intervillage path, build their own cane bridge, devise their own indigenous equipments to husk or grind rice and millets, weaving their own cloths, ornaments and jewels, hats, cooking vessels, weapons. Handloom weaving and cane and bamboo works are major traditional village industries in the state. This shows the exceptional similarities of Gandhian concept of self-reliance in the tribal Communities of the state. However, there is hardly any development. The economy and the society at the dawn of independence are primitive. But, now the days are fast moving far from culture of self-sufficiency in this tribal soil.

Handicrafts are hand-made items produced with application of mainly human energy and skills with or without the aid of mechanical devices or handtools for various types of end uses. Handicrafts are categorized as utility items, decorative items and utility-cum-decorative items. By and large, handicrafts are made from almost all commonly available material such as metal, stone, wood, cane, bamboo, straw, grass, textiles, leather, ivory, bones, horns, shells, clay, ceramics, glass, papier machine, paper, zari, etc., using a variety of skills which include casting, engraving, cutting, inlay, marquetry, knotting, embroidery, etching, weaving, polishing, etc. Thus, in the context of changing scenario, the study aims at making a study that the small and village industries are relevant in the tribal soil of Arunachal Pradesh. In view of this, the paper attempts to address the objectives: (i) To investigate the development of Khadi and Village Industries and Employment Scenario. (ii) To find out the major problems faced by Khadi and Village Industries and (iii) To find the probable solutions of the problems in the state.

All-India Scenarios

The first ever initiative to gather comprehensive socio-economic data on the handicrafts sector in India was taken under the sponsorship of Development Commissioner (Handicrafts) when a national census of the handicrafts sector was undertaken by the

National Council of Applied Economic Research (NCAER), New Delhi in 1995-96. In the 24 States in which the survey was conducted, the total number of units producing handicrafts was 12.66 lakh. The artisans working in these units were 41.03 lakh; the estimated value of goods produced was Rs. 26.213 crore. The average size of a unit in these 24 States was 3.24 persons per unit.

Status of Handicrafts Sector

Indian handicrafts have won the admiration of connoisseurs all-over the world. The age-old rich cultural heritage, which is the hallmark of India, manifests in every handicraft produced in any corner of the country. Be it the magnificent brassware of Moradabad, glittering diamond work of Jaipur, exquisite embroidery of Jammu and Kashmir, fine filigree work of Orissa, or the glorious sculpture work of Southern India, handicrafts from India have carved a niche across the world. Every State in India makes a rich contribution to a very wide range of handcrafted articles, which are a class by themselves. While the painstaking labours of India's craftsmen result in unique objects of beauty, the produce is also a creation symbolizing their inner self-expression. Creativity and novelty represents the cultural heritage of our diversified population.

The decade of the nineties has given proof of the global interest in Indian handicrafts through the rising exports that have taken place. Barely Rs. 1800 crore in 1991-92, the turnover of exports in 1999-2000 has crossed Rs. 8000 crore. This impressive trend has helped to provide gainful employment to the nation's expanding workforce and to earn valuable foreign exchange for it, expectedly over US$ 1.9 billion. In the last annual report (1998-99), the Ministry of Textiles has asserted that employment in the handicrafts sector increased from 48.5 lakh in 1991-92 to 81 1akh by 1997-98. But, it is commonly felt that India has not been able to wholly realize her potential through exports of handicrafts in the export market. India's share in world trade of handicrafts is said to be less than two per cent as compared with China's share of 17 per cent.

According to UNCTAD, "the term 'hand-made' should be taken to include those articles produced with or without the use of tools, simple instruments, or implements operated directly by the craftsmen mainly by hand or by foot". At times, handicrafts may have additional attributes such as traditional or artistic features derived from the geographical region of production or production by craftsmen working at a cottage scale. Some goods may be partly machine-made and partly hand-made. For example, hand embroidered table cloth will have a machine-made fabric for ground and exquisite hand embroidery to enhance its appeal, to be ultimately classified as a hand-made product.

In India the Supreme Court has laid down the following tests for an article to be recognized as a handicraft:

- It must be predominantly made by hand; it does not matter if some machinery is used in the process.
- It must be graced with visual appeal in the nature of ornamentation or inlay work or some similar work lending it as an element of artistic improvement; such ornamentation must be of a substantial nature and not a mere pretence.

The Typical Handcrafting Skills involved *inter alia* are:

Casting	Coiling
Engraving	Dyeing
Etching	Tie and Dyeing
Inlaying	Batik
Embossing	Artistic Weaving
Enamelling	Embroidering
Cutting	Knotting
Shaping	Applique
Carving	Felting
Turning	Knitting
Lacquering	Cobbling
Painting	Polishing
Marquetry	Moulding
Weaving	Glazing

A product may be an application of a single skill or a combination of the above skills. In India, the Office of the Development Commissioner for Handicrafts in the Ministry of Textiles groups handicrafts as:

- Carpets,
- Art metalwares,

- Woodwares,
- Hand-printed textiles and scarves,
- Hand-knotted and embroidered goods,
- Shawls as artware,
- Zari and zari goods, and
- Imitation jewellery.

Miscellaneous goods covering musical instruments; lace and lace goods; buttons and studs; hatware; carpeting; articles of stoneware as artware; leather goods; attars; sculpture and statuary; paintings and drawings; pottery articles of fur, skin, human hair; articles of tortoise; articles of horn; articles of grass, straw and fibre; papier machine products; stuffed animals; fancy glassworks; hookahs; trophies; antiques; articles of jute.

Handicrafts Industry in India

Despite the vast prevalence of the handicrafts industry in India, precise statistics on its extent and production were until very recently not available. It was claimed by the Office of the Development Commissioner for Handicrafts that the country accounted for over 80 lakh artisans in various branches of handicrafts and the total value of their production in 1999 was estimated to be Rs. 31,000 crores. However, under the sponsorship of the Development Commissioner for Handicrafts, a national census of the handicrafts sector was undertaken by the National Council of Applied Economic Research, New Delhi in 1995-96. The results of the census, finalized in 1999, in respect of number of units, number of artisans, and value of production in 1999, are shown in Table 11.1.

Table 11.1 presents key data for all States. In the 24 States the total units of handicrafts production were 12.66 lakh. The artisans working in these units were 41.03 lakh. The Table 8.1 indicates the estimated value of production to have been Rs. 26,213.13 crore. The average scale of a unit in these 24 States was 3.24 artisans. Uttar Pradesh, by itself, accounted for a share of 22.41 per cent of units and 28.79 per cent of artisans; the average scale per unit in U.P. was 4.14 artisans. Among the remaining States, the ones that accounted for impressive shares of the aggregate were, in descending order, West Bengal, Rajasthan, Manipur, Tripura, Bihar, Andhra Pradesh and Maharashtra. These States accounted for a share of 57.02 per cent of the aggregate units and 49.75 per cent of the number of artisans.

Table 11.1: State-wise Status of Handicrafts Industry in India (1995-96)

States	*Number of Units*		*Number of Artisans*		*Value of Production (Rs. In Crores)*	
(1)	*(2)*		*(3)*		*(4)*	
Andhra Pradesh	76283	(602)	121880	(2.98)	379.41	(1.44)
Assam	30360	(2.39)	100482	(2.45)	7820.94	(29.72)
Arunachal Pradesh	4044	(0.31)	15735	(0.38)	855.56	(3.25)
Bihar	70533	(5.57)	213115	(5.21)	91.52	(0.34)
Delhi	17021	(1.34)	44904	(1.09)	74.65	(0.28)
Goa	572	(0.04)	1122	(0.02)	107.2	(0.40)
Gujarat	32697	(2.58)	131970	(2.81)	72.25	(0.27)
Himachal Pradesh	26058	(2.05)	49015	(1.19)	45.6	(0.17)
Haryana	16222	(1.28)	117933	(2.88)	776.58	(2.95)
Karnataka	12383	(0.97)	21779	(0.53)	41.37	(0.15)
Kerala	7395	(0.58)	15258	(0.37)	1748.26	(6.64)
Madhya Pradesh	21954	(1.73)	51123	(1.25)	65.46	(0.24)
Maharashtra	52449	(4.14)	112816	(2.76)	139.62	(0.53)
Mizoram	2213	(0.17)	5260	(0.12)	5.93	(0.02)
Manipur	98051	(7.74)	379988	(9.29)	147.6	(0.56)
Meghalaya	11512	(0.90)	53564	(1.31)	2580.67	(9.80)
Nagaland	17603	(1.39)	79878	(1.95)	9463.99	(35.98)
Orissa	25968	(2.05)	69356	(1.69)	56.71	(0.21)
Rajasthan	128871	(10.17)	407700	(9.97)	278.4	(1.05)
Sikkim	2198	(0.17)	9768	(0.23)	5.59	(0.02)
Tamil Nadu	31746	(2.50)	125342	(3.06)	63.1	(0.23)
Tripura	77375	(6.11)	244495	(5.98)	60.8	(0.23)
Uttar Pradesh	283804	(22.41)	1176529	(28.79)	1004.5	(3.81)
West Bengal	218697	(17.27)	554281	(13.56)	426.42	(1.62)
Total	1266009		4103293		26312.13	

Note: Figures in parentheses are percentages to total.

Source: Census Survey of Handicrafts Sector (State-wise Report), NCAER, New Delhi, 1999.

Table 11.2 has data in terms of craft groups as per the basic material/medium. It is observed by the census that textile crafts accounted for a big share of the handicrafts sector; with 50.57 per cent of units and 54.35 per cent of artisans. The next largest group was cane and bamboo crafts followed by straw/grass/fibre group. These groups account for 74.10 per cent of units and 77.88 per cent of artisans. The major craft groups vary from State to State. This obviously follows the natural resource endowment of each State. But what is striking is that textile crafts are omnipresent, practically every State reports is to be the top-ranking craft group. Similarly, Cane and Bamboo, straw/grass/fibre craft, Clay and Ceramics are present in numerous States. Woodcrafts rank highest in Karnataka, while Cane and Bamboo crafts are top-ranking group in Tripura, Orissa, Meghalaya, whereas Straw, Grass handicrafts are at the top in Kerala.

Table 11.2: Craft-wise Status of Handicrafts Industry in India

Craft Group	*Number of Units*		*Number of Artisans*		*Est. of Production (Rs. In Crores)*	
(1)	*(2)*		*(3)*		*(4)*	
Textiles	640247	(50.57)	2230343	(54.35)	12832.41	(48.76)
Cane and Bamboo	176556	(13.94)	494844	(12.05)	6287.13	(23.89)
Wood	86474	(6.83)	261387	(6.37)	4161.9	(15.81)
Metal	54507	(4.30)	179996	(4.38)	1323.95	(5.03)
Stone	11553	(0.91)	35593	(0.86)	106.06	(0.40)
Straw, Grass	121529	(9.59)	305876	(7.45)	541.76	(2.05)
Fibre and Leaf Leather	36246	(2.86)	122704	(2.99)	152.73	(0.58)
Glass	12136	(0.96)	65619	(1.59)	48.14	(0.18)
Clay and Ceramics	73966	(5.84)	257714	(6.28)	498.86	(1.89)
Ivory, Bone, Horn and Shells	8797	(0.69)	28123	(0.68)	91.39	(0.34)
Miscellaneous	43998	(3.47)	121094	(2.95)	267.8	(1.01)
Total	1266009	(100.00)	4103293	(100.00)	26312.13	(100.00)

Note: Figures in parentheses are percentages to total.

Source: Compiled from source of Table 11.2.

Table 11.3: State-wise Major Craft Groups

States	*Major Craft Groups*
1	*2*
Andhra Pradesh	Textile crafts
Assam	Textile crafts; cane and bamboo
Arunachal Pradesh	Textile crafts; cane and bamboo
Bihar	Textile crafts; straw/grass/fibre crafts; Cane and bamboo; clay and ceramics
Delhi	Textile crafts; metal-based crafts
Goa	Textile crafts; cane and bamboo
Gujarat	Textile crafts; cane and bamboo
Himachal Pradesh	Textile crafts; straw/grass/fibre; wood
Haryana	Textile crafts; leather; clay and ceramics
Karnataka	Wood crafts; cane and bamboo; textile and crafts
Kerala	Straw/grass/fibre; textile crafts
Madhya Pradesh	Textile crafts; cane and bamboo; clay and ceramics; metal crafts; wood crafts
Maharashtra	Textile crafts; cane and bamboo; leather; clay and ceramics; wood
Mizoram	Textile crafts; cane and bamboo
Manipur	Textile crafts; cane and bamboo
Meghalaya	Cane and bamboo; Textile crafts
Nagaland	Textile crafts; cane and bamboo; wood
Orissa	Cane and bamboo; textile crafts; metal craft; clay and ceramics; straw/grass/fibre crafts
Rajasthan	Textile crafts; art metalware; wood
Sikkim	Textile crafts; cane and bamboo
Tamil Nadu	Textile crafts; straw/grass/fibre
Tripura	Cane and bamboo; textile crafts; wood
Uttar Pradesh	Textile crafts; clay and ceramics; straw/grass/fibre crafts; glass crafts; metal; wood; leather; cane and bamboo
West Bengal	Textile crafts; cane and bamboo; straw/grass/ fibre crafts; wood; clay and ceramics

Source: Census Survey of Handicrafts Sector, NCAFR, New Delhi, 1999.

Locations of Handicrafts Industries

Handicrafts units exist in locational concentrations. The prominent locations in India for various craft groups are given below:

Art Metalware	:	Moradabad, Sambhal, Aligarh, Jodhpur, Jaipur, Delhi, Revari, Thanjavur, Chennai, Manpad, Beedar, Jagadhri, Jaleshar, Hyderabad
Wooden Artwares	:	Saharanpur, Nagina, Hoshiarpur, Srinagar, Amritsar, Jaipur, Jodhpur, Jagdalpur, Bangalore, Mysore, Chennapatina, Chennai, Manpad, Behrampur
Handprinted Textiles	:	Amroha, Jodhpur, Jaipur, Farrukhabad, Bagru, Sanganer
Embroidered Textiles	:	Kutch, Jaisalmer, Baroda, Lucknow, Jodhpur, Agra, Amritsar, Kullu, Narasapur, Dharamshala, Chamba, Srinagar
Marble and Soft Stone Crafts	:	Agra, Chennai, Jodhpur, Bastar
Papier Machine Crafts	:	Jaipur, Kashmir
Terracotta	:	Rajasthan, Chennai, Bastar
Zari and Zari Goods	:	Surat, Amritsar, Agra, Varanasi
Imitation Jewellery	:	Delhi, Moradabad, Machilipatnam, Jaipur, Kohima., Sambhal
Carpet	:	Bhadoi, Mirzapur, Srinagar, Jaipur, Panipat, Warangal.

From the standpoint of exports, the key locations are: Moradabad, Saharanpur, Jodhpur, Jaipur, Narsapur, Bhadoi and Mirzapur.

Trends in Handicrafts Exports

In the span of five years since 1994-95, exports of handicrafts grew by 89.15 per cent in rupee terms and 41 per cent in dollar terms. The resultant growth rate averaged 17.27 per cent per annum in rupee terms and 9.02 per cent per annum in dollar terms. The most remarkable performance has been registered by embroidered goods, exports of which in the above five years grew by eight times from US $ 32.57 million crore in 1994-95 to US $ 275.58 million crore in 1998-99. Hand-printed textiles, art metalware, carpets and woodware saw doubling of their export turnover in the five year period.

The principal destinations for handicrafts are Germany, France, U.K., Japan, Italy, Canada and Netherlands. Over 30 per cent of export value in 1998-99 was accounted for by U.SA. alone. The prominent E.U. countries together accounted for nearly 30 per cent of the export value.

Thus, between U.S.A., and the major countries in E.U. market, nearly 65 per cent of export of handicrafts is accounted for by these two major markets. In terms of various handicrafts categories, while U.S.A. remains, by and large, the leading handicrafts export destination, other significant countries vary from group to group.

India's exports of handicrafts have been dominated by a few items. In 1997-98, out of 441 items in the H.S. system, 403 items recorded exports to the value of Rs. 7015 crore. Ninety per cent of the export value was accounted for by 79 items, each of which over Rs.10 crore of exports. 20 items of handicrafts and carpets contributed 75 per cent of export value, each item recording well over Rs.50 crore of exports. Going even further, 9 items accounted for nearly 63 per cent of export turnover. Thus it is evident that a very limited number of items form the core bread-basket of handicraft exports from India. 90 per cent of the export value was accounted for by 79 items, each with over Rs. 10 crore of exports.

The main principle of Gandhian approach is to set up a system of village self-sufficiency. In this regard, the hypothesis of M.K. Gandhi was establishment of 'Gram Swaraj' in the country side which means the complete independence of the Indian villages. The ultimate goal of Gandhian planning was to make Indian villages fully independent. Mahatma Gandhi often used to say that the real India was to be found in the villages, not in the cities and towns. This sector has not only continued to play a vital role in fulfilment of socio-economic objectives but also offers an excellent opportunity for industrial self-employment.

It was Mahatma Gandhi, who pioneered the revival of the age-old self-sufficiency (*Gram Swavalamban*) and leased a new life and extinct glory to the concept of Swadeshi. According to Gandhi, the law of Swadeshi was the *swardharma* of the *Gita* interpreted in terms of one's physical environment. Gandhi advocated Khadi as the necessary and most important corollary of the principle of *Swadeshi* in its application to society, he warned that "it is the greatest delusion to suppose that the duty of Swadeshi begins and ends with merely spinning some yarn and wearing Khadi made from it. In Swadeshi there is no for ill-will. It is a doctrine of selfless service and has its roots in the purest *ahimsa*, love". (R. Chowdhury, *Gandhi's Ethical Ideas*, 2007).

Rural industrialization is important not as a means of generating employment opportunities in the rural areas with low capital cost and raising the real income of the people, but because it contributes to the development of agriculture and urban industries. Without rural industrialization, it would be considerably more difficult to solve the problem of agricultural unemployment and widespread underemployment. Rural industrialization promotes rural industry.

The definition of village industry has been recently modified by the government so as to enlarge its scope. Accordingly, any industry located in rural areas, village or town with a population of 20,000 and below and an investment of Rs. 10 million in plant and machinery, is classified as a village industry.

Rural industry embraces different kinds of village and small industries. All the village industries have been grouped into seven major categories as follows:

(i) Mineral based industry
(ii) Forest based industry
(iii) Agro based industry
(iv) Polymer and Chemical based industry
(v) Engineering and non-Conventional industry
(vi) Textile industry (excluding khadi) and
(vii) Service industry.

Need for Rural Industrialization

Developing industries in the rural areas is essential because:

1. Rural industries are labour intensive.
2. By providing employment, these industries have also high potential for income generation in the rural areas.
3. These industries encourage dispersal of economic activities in the rural areas and thus, promote balanced regional development.
4. Rural industries also help protect and promote art and

creativity i.e., the age-old rich heritage of the country. Rural industries being environment-friendly lead to development without destruction.

Programmes: The Government has taken a number of policy initiatives through various Central Ministries for over-all promotion of village and small scale industries. Some of the important policies are:

1. Progressive allocations made in the Five Year Plans.
2. Policy of reservation.
3. Price preference (up to 15 per cent) and purchase preference policy for marketing small scale industrial products.
4. Technical assistance through industrial extension service centres.
5. Provision of built up factory accommodation in industrial estates.
6. Supply of machines under the hire purchase system.
7. Subsidy on power consumption.
8. Provision of raw material.
9. Policy of priority credit, and
10. Entrepreneurship Development Programmes conducted by various National Institutes and support to state level Institutes.

The Centre and State Governments in India have sponsored various employment generation and poverty alleviation programmes for development of rural industries. Some of them are as follows:

1. Prime Minister's Rozgar Yojana (PMRY),
2. Swarnjayanti Gram Swarozgar Yojana (SGSY),
3. Rural Employment Generation Programme (REGP),
4. District Rural Industrial Project (DRIP).

State Scenario

During the colonial period, large parts of the region of the North-Eastern States were "Excluded Areas" or "Partially Excluded Areas". Further, under the Inner Line Regulation Act, Arunachal Pradesh remained secluded and restricted to outsiders. The entries as such were permitted based on administrative necessity otherwise outsiders were strictly prohibited entry in the tribal territorial area beyond the inner line. The British, through such measures, sought to protect the tribal culture from so-called exploitation by others (the non-tribal). Tribes were thus left to themselves to pursue their traditional methods of livelihood and manage their affairs in accordance with their traditional/ancestral customs.

The most of the tribes inhabiting the state are ethnically similar; but their geographical isolation from each other has brought about distinctive characteristics in language, dress and custom amongst themselves. They have a tradition of artistic craftsmanship and a sense of aesthetics manifested through a variety of crafts such as weaving, painting, basketry etc. The design of weaving varies from tribe to tribe. No attempts have been made to blend these variations which may result in developing a vivid colour and exquisite patterns generating high demands due to blending of the patterns. Patent right for the different patterns exquisite to each group of tribe has not been initiated till date.

The tribal communities were extremely self-reliant; they constructed their own intervillage path, build their own cane bridge, devised their own indigenous equipments to husk or grind rice and millets, weaving their own cloths, ornaments and jewels, hats, cooking vessels, weapons. This shows the exceptional similarities of Gandhian concept of self-reliance in the tribal Communities of the state. However, there was hardly any development. The economy and the society at the dawn of independence were primitive. But, now the days are fast moving far from culture of self-sufficiency in this tribal soil.

This territory is proud of her traditional and fantastic indigenous handicrafts and most colourful handloom products. In the past years, the role conceived for the Industries Department in Arunachal Pradesh was one of the revival and revitalization of the traditional handloom and handicrafts. The notable activities have been the establishment of craft centres, production centres in the board areas, extension of sericulture programme and setting up of small scale industrial units.

The Adis are excellent in the production of useful eye-catching handicrafts. Their handicrafts products and textile bear ample testimony to the rich heritage. Their nimble fingers weave excellent designs on the textiles and carpets. The intricately executed woodcrafts, cane and bamboo works, blacksmithy, leather working, pottery making, paper making and weaving bear eloquent testimony to the fine artistic temperament and poetic imagination of the hardworking tribesmen of these areas.

Weaving is very common craft in this district. Every woman and girl is expert in weaving. The Gallong weave cloth is of highly artistic design and the finest product is a beautiful skirt with a central pattern of black year netted in regular design of black and white Galuk, Jese Kore etc. Vivid colours and exquisite pattern of weaving designs in the area are almost exclusively of an angular geometric type, though they vary from a formal arrangement of line and bands to elaborate patterns of diamonds and logenges, enhanced by internal repeatation, hachur and other decoration The Padam and Miniyong are also expert and active in weaving. Magnificent carpets are woven by the Membas and Khambas of northern Siang.

Bamboo and cane are the main raw materials for making baskets and utensils which are one of the most important items of their daily household purpose. The Adis are very skilful in cane and bamboo works. It is much more widely distributed than any the wood working, pottery making, blacksmithy etc. They make various types of baskets for domestic use and the designs are always of high quality. The most beautiful and artistic cane work is noticed in the making of varieties of hats. The hat which they call 'Balup' is made up of good variety of cane. The hat is made up and bound together with strips of fine cane woven vertically and so closely as to cover the ring foundation. The knitting of the hat is so fine and compact that it does not allow water to pass through it, and it is strongly made as to be 'sword proof'. The another most skilful engineering work as well as labour shown is in the construction of cane and bamboo suspension bridges Besides these they also make various baskets for daily use. The Adi baskets are meant to render vigorous and hard services and to stand rough use and weather so durability and strength are more conspicuous in them.

The Adi have considerable proficiency in blacksmithy. They make various types of things like forging knives, daos, swords, spears, arrowheads, metal pipes, brass bracelets, girdle disc, bayop plates etc. Carpentry and pottery making is almost absent among them.

In the field of handicrafts, its tribal background is mainly helpful. The people of Arunachal Pradesh are artistically minded and gifted with deft hands and skilled fingers. Various arts and crafts are in their very blood. Handloom, for instance, offer wide scope to produce a variety of artistically blended and beautifully designed clothings. Weaving is a very common craft in Arunachal Pradesh. Magnificent carpets are woven in West Kameng and in northern Siang, while beautiful rugs are woven in the Adi area. Vivid colours and exquisite patterns, sometimes geometrical, sometimes abstract and at other floral; are the hallmark of the weaving wool, cotton and silk throughout the territory. There is a steady export market for these Monpa carpet, Adi skirts, the Mishmi bags and shawls.

Beautiful wood carving and grass necklace is practised by the Wanchus. The wood carving which decorates the communal house and funerary images are also subjects of carvings. Among the Monpas, the speciality is the carving of musks and these are fine examples of craftsmanship. The carving of mithun and hornbill are often realistic, though a little conventionalized. The art of wood carving in Arunachal Pradesh is now undergoing a change as the traditional skills of the craftsmen now being trained at the craft centres acquired aesthetic sophistication. The same vigorous aesthetication occurs in the intricate jewellery worn by the Monpa, Miji, Hrusso, Mishmi and Nocte ladies and is mostly the products of the local Craftsmen. Our tribal handicrafts were well known and greatly prized not only in the territory but outside the country also. The old art are losing in utility as the pattern of life changes. Now due to modernization the traditional dress and arts and crafts are replaced by the new one. It is the Industry Department which has to look after to save the traditional arts and crafts from extinction, otherwise ultimately it will be vanished. As for example the making of cane hat (BALUP) is gradually vanishing due to limited number of skilled craftsmen.

Small Scale Industry

Small scale and cottage industries are the second largest and most potential source of economy for this territory and is the mainstay of economic progress of the people. These are even more important from the point of view of providing gainful employment to the people. As more than 60% of the area of Arunachal Pradesh is under forest having varieties of resources, the development of the forestry and forest based industries, such as paper mills, match wood factory, card board factory, plywood factory, timber treatment and seasoning plant, resin and turpentine factory have been found feasible, all having growth potential. Our plywood is one of the best quality plywood which has been exported to other places. There is an equal scope for agro based industries including fruit preservation, small engineering, electronic, chemical and such other industries also offer scope.

The numbers of measures have been taken by the Arunachal Government to promote growth of the small industries as the territory has abundant natural resources. The Science and Technology Council has been constituted to formulate appropriate plan for growth of these industries utilizing local natural resources and also to suggest suitable technology for harnessing such resources.

Although the Khadi and Village Industries sector is a very important and integral part of the inclusive socio-economic development of the state specially the rural areas, there are very few literatures available regarding this in the state. The state has 3,863 villages with about 80 per cent of its population living in rural area. It virtually appears that no serious thought or extensive studies have been made on Khadi and Village Industries pertaining to the state of Arunachal Pradesh. One hardly finds any mention of this priority sector in the developmental plan documents of the State Government.

The State Khadi and Village Industries Boards have come into existence in response to advice of the All India Khadi and Village Industries Board which was required by the Government Resolution of January 14, 1953 to work "in close cooperation with the State Government". Today there are 33 States and Union Territories Khadi and Village Industries Boards in the country. The Arunachal Pradesh Khadi and Village Industries Board (APKVIB) was created by a state Act. The Board is a promotional body with no income of its own as it does not undertake any commercial operation but generally channelizes and monitors utilization of central sector

Table 11.4: Physical Achievement of Craft/ Weaving Centres in Arunachal Pradesh during 2003-04

Sl. No.	Particulars	Unit	2001-2002	2002-2003	2003-2004
1	2	3	4	5	6
1.	Craft/ Weaving Centres	No.	88	88	88
2.	Trainees in Craft Weaving Centres	No.	247	302	303
3.	Handloom Development Centre and Quality Dyeing Units	No.	6	6	6
4.	Value of Production of Cloth/ Craft	Rs. in lakh	NA	NA	28.59
5.	Emporium	No.	15	15	18
6.	Show Room-Cum Sale Counter	No.	3	3	5
7.	Annual sale proceed of Emporium and Show Room cum Sales Counter	Rs. in lakh	39.80	40.09	
	Cash				6.72
	Credit				38.26

Source : Directorate of Textile and Handicraft, Itanagar.

developmental funds provided by KVIC. The broad objectives are similar to that of the KVIC within the jurisdiction of the state of Arunachal Pradesh. However, the State Government has to bear its establishment and administrative expenses. The APKVIB Act was amended in 1998 and also framed its Rules and Regulations in this year. The Board got its first developmental fund from the KVIC in year 1991-92.

Development of Khadi and Village Industries and Employment Scenario

The nodal agency for implementation of KVI programmes in the state is APKVIB. The Arunachal Pradesh Seva Sangh runs HRD Programme in the MDTC including Khadi spinning and weaving. The KVIC's state office headed by Assistant Director with 9 other supporting staff has been implementing REGP and other Programme. The APKVIB is in a shocking position. It devoids the attention of the authority. The Chairman is appointed casually. There is no regular or full time CEO. The post of vice-chairman is non-functional and creates unnecessary strains on hard earn resources. State Government's funding is abysmally meagre with no long term plan on anvil. Indifference of the state authorities coupled with lack of institutional in-built capacity has resulted *inter alia* a low treatment by KVIC in sharing developmental funds. The Board has ended up by distributing KVIC funds without further follow-up/monitoring. The KAVIRC observes, 'although these Boards were supposed to be replicas of the KVIC at the state level, but in reality they have not gone beyond the disbursement of KVIC funds. The Boards have even not efficiently and properly performed their primary functions' (Report of KAVIRC, 1987). 'Organizational weakness, lack of trained manpower and technical expertise, inadequate support from the State Government are some of the reasons for inability of the Board in making any significant impact' (Majumdar, 2000). The number of units of KVI established in different years is shown in Table 11.5.

Table 11.5: No. of Unit of KVI Established in Different Years

Year	*No. of units*
1999-2000	9
2000-01	60
2001-02	23
2002-03	16
2003-04	14
2004-05	20
2005-06	19
2006-07	30
Total	191

Source: The Arunachal Pradesh Khadi and Village Industries Board.

The year-wise employment generation, total investment and per capita investment are shown in Table 11.6.

Table 11.6: Year-wise Employment generation

(Rs. in Lakhs and employment in No.)

Year	*Employment*	*Total investment*	*PCI*
1991-92	107	26.70	0.250
1992-93	98	24.62	0.251
1993-95	222	55.48	0.250
1995-97	160	132.79	0.830
1999-2000	100	41.52	0.415
2000-01	378	187.21	0.495
2001-02	168	95.79	0.570
2002-03	190	103.83	0.546
2003-04	78	67.78	0.869
2004-05	137	99.64	0.727

Source: The Arunachal Pradesh Khadi and Village Industries Board.

Per Capita Investment (PCI) low and almost fixed then sudden high in 1995-97. The PCI has been near stabilized from 1999-2000 to 2002-03. Then sudden jump and again in 2004-05 fall considerably. Industry-wise employment generations in different industries are shown in Table 11.7.

With the impact of globalization and development of education the number of job-seeker is increasing drastically. The Khadi and Village Industries in the state are playing a significant role in employment generation.

Problems

The Small Scale Industries are not commercially viable due to (i) lack of interest of workers, (ii) lack of raw materials, (iii) lack of working capital or timely finance, (iv) lack of marketing facilities, (v) lack of capacity utilization, (vi) lack of technical know-how, (vii) devoid of organizational strength, (viii) competition on Khadi (hand spun and hand woven) from power loom (machine spun and machine woven) and handloom (machine spun and hand woven), (ix) lack of entrepreneurial knowledge, (x) lack of power, (xi) lack of transport facilities, etc. Let us discuss some major constraints.

Table 11.7: Industry-wise Employment generation

Year	*Khadi*	*Mineral based*	*Agro based*	*Chemical based*	*Engineering & NCE*	*Textile*	*Forest based*	*Service industry*	*Total*
1991-92	10	-	2	-	33	42	20	-	107
1992-93	10	-	23	-	24	36	2	3	98
1993-95	2	16	52	8	37	18	89	-	222
1995-96	-	-	19	38	46	18	39	-	160
1997-99	-	-	-	-	-	-	-	-	Nil
1999-2000	-	22	16	-	34	-	22	6	100
2000-01	-	-	79	-	98	66	57	78	378
2001-02	-	24	48	-	46	-	32	18	168
2002-03	-	36	14	-	78	18	20	24	190
2003-04	-	-	-	-	38	26	14	-	78
Total	22	98	253	46	434	224	295	129	1,501

Source: The Arunachal Pradesh Khadi and Village Industries Board.

Marketing Facility

The industry does not end with production of goods. These have to be marketed quickly and a sustained demand has to be ensured. In this process lack of transport facilities is an impediment. For the prosperity of the state it is essential that goods produced in the territory find increasing market in other states and abroad. Marketing of handicrafts produced by the local artisans is done through ten emporia and other agencies at various places like Gauhati, Shillong and New Delhi by providing all facilities to the bulk buyers and traders. The participation in the National Small Industries Fair at New Delhi and such other events is also aimed to secure this end. Development of tourism is also increasing the marketing outlets for our handicrafts. The government also encourages entrepreneurs, specially the local people, and provides training facilities to produce more skilled men and women. Efforts have been made by the government for improving the technique of production. Design is very important in handloom industry. A research design centre has since been established in the territory for revival and revitalization of local arts and crafts and to conduct research on scientific line with an aim to preserve the local arts and crafts without losing their originality.

The product of small scale industries is not accessible to the modern means of marketing. In modern market economy, the buyer and seller are able to get in touch with one another so that the exchange of goods and services for money takes place between them. This can also be done through E-mail, internet, telephone, courier, speed post and ordinary mails. It is undisputedly accepted that success of an industry depends on market of its products. It has no well organized market outside this state and even inside the state. It has no worldwide Website and no advertisements through electronic or print media. Only entrepreneurs are given opportunities to participate to various exhibitions etc. which are also due to intrinsic reasons not availed to full extent.

Inner-Line System: Inner-line System that was introduced in 1873 still exists even in the present changed scenario. This restricts the free movement of Non-Arunachalees to the state. A Non-Arunachalee who wants to cross beyond the Inner-line has to get the IL Pass issued for a limited period with certain conditionality as it is viewed that the territory is located at strategic-point from the standpoint of defense. Besides, the Government of India feels it necessary to protect the tribal and their land and forest, who has a vivid socio-economic and cultural dimension, from the Non-Arunachalees' hunger of grabbing.

Globalization refers to a process of increasing economic integration and growing economic interdependence between the contemporary world economies. It is associated not only with increasing cross-border movement of goods, services, capital, IT, and people but also with an organization of economic activities which crosses national boundary. To get the good effect of globalization in the state it needs first cross state flows among the states of India. In fact the Inner-line System posing as a major hindrances for free flow industrial environment.

The N.E. Region is isolated, landlocked which shares only 2% of its border with the rest of the country and rest with Bhutan, Bangladesh, Myanmar and the Tibetan region of China. For most of this international border has been artificially created. The result has been the elimination of the region's trade, commerce and other linkages, which existed in the pre-independence days. These N.E. states are very close to the dynamic South-East and East Asian economics. It is imperative to develop a coherent policy linking this area. (Dr. G. Sachdeva, JNU).

Entrepreneurial Lack: In the N. E. Region, the unemployment problem has become a paradox because the unemployment in the region is growing, not because there is lack of opportunities, but because the unemployed youths have failed to take advantage of the opportunities available. It is an accepted fact that the availability of entrepreneurship is the most important determinant in the process of industrialization. The government in its efforts to create entrepreneurship provides for various monetary and non-monetary incentives like the development of an infrastructure, assistance in marketing and procuring raw-materials, providing finance or granting subsidies on investment. Various State and Central Organizations have accordingly been created to cater to the needs of entrepreneurs.

It can be argued that lack of entrepreneurial skill of the local people and their deficient interest to invest and innovate has contributed in preventing the evolution of modern economic system in the state. One example of their lacking interest in setting up enterprises is that the those tribal boys/girls who go for craft training do not want to have their own business but like to join as craft teachers in government organizations (Krishna, 2000). The mindset of the tribal is not to establish their own enterprise but to venture either in politics, contract business, or government services to earn "*easy money*". This mindset can be termed as **psychological barrier** which has emerged very strongly in the present socio-economic context of the state. Some tribal people within a very short period of time have experienced income and wealth inequalities to a high degree. Very few of them have been found to become very rich overnight and enjoy luxurious life and prefer conspicuous consumption which has been adversely affecting the rest of the society. The income inequalities in the tribal society are very strong. Some are very rich and some are stark poor. The presence of high degree of corruption at all levels and existence of underground economy is also a deterrent to state's economy (Mandal, 2006).

License Issuing System: The outsiders who want to venture business in the state are to obtain license in the name of some Arunachalees who get rent from the concern businessman for the license. These trading people earn money and mostly siphon off in their respective home because they don't get the right to buy property for independent business. This status largely refrain the private investors in coming and opening up ventures in A.P. Institutional credit for trade and industries are available to the local people but they lack entrepreneurial skills and show hardly any interest in industrial activities. Therefore, like IL permit, the **License issuing system of the government has discouraged** the opening up of KVI units in the state.

Lack of Dignity of Labour: The contemporary Arunachalee, mostly, oblivious of their age-old pride of dignity of labour and even for petty household works they depend on migrated labour. This has quietly uprooting the habit of doing productive works on self-help basis and making them dependent on others. This is contrary to the entrepreneurial trait.

Power: Power is one of the major infrastructures for the growth of industrial activities of any size. 'Arunachal has a huge potential for the development of hydroelectric power because of its many rivers. The state has the potential to supply a third of total hydroelectric requirement of the country. The per capita consumption of electricity in Arunachal was 86.9 kWh in 2001-02 against the all-India average of 335 kWh (APHDR, 2005, p. 45). In addition to water resource, the state has oil, natural gas and coal resources that can be used in the production of electricity. The Government of India has taken initiative for large scale production of hydropower. Such initiative will also have the spin-off benefits like employment avenues, increase in consumption of industrial products, roads, schools, banks, health care, postal facilities, and training centres etc. In 1971-72 only 37 villages were electrified. By March, 2001 this has rose to 2506 out of 3649 villages. The state having untapped estimated hydropower potential of 49,000 MW, may emerge as powerhouse of India when this potential is fully harnessed (**Source:** Dept. of Power, GoAP).

Transportation: The service of transportation is a prerequisite for economic development. The road density in the state is very low. In 2001, the road density was 17.36 km per 100 sq. km of area as against the national average of 82 km per 100 sq. km. The main reasons for this low density are: the difficult topography and undulating terrain, the late start of development process, and the high cost of construction in the inaccessible and remote areas (APHDR, 2005, p. 44). The states does not have lateral roads connecting districts, since roads run vertically connecting places in Assam with districts or sub-divisions in A.P. This has not only resulted in high transportation costs but also affected by disturbed law and order situation and insurgency problem of Assam. The state at all has no railways except 1.26 km. metre gauge railway line laid in 1989 connecting Bhalukpong with Indian railway map. This is a major handicap.

Banking Scenario: KVI comes under the priority sector *vide* RBI's circular No.RPCD.PLNFS.BC.84/06.0612/93-94 (Source RBI). The REGP is only scheme in common to be offered as rural industrialization tool. Under this major assistance has to come from bank as loan. In 2000-01, there were only 99 bank offices with an average of 9.07 offices per 1,00,000 population and availability of finance is not widespread in Arunachal yet. The credit-deposit ratio is only 17.25 per cent, which is lowest among the N.E. states and is considerably lower than the national level (58.53 per cent) (APHDR, 2005). There are vast areas where either there is no any bank or is a single man branch which is obviously not equipped to go beyond the normal banking transactions.

Vocational Training / Education: The State Government has a network of 88 craft centres, earlier called Cottage Industries Training and Production Centres (CITPC). Lack of modern tools, equipments, poor physical infrastructure, shortage of competent training instructors, outmoded curriculum and training methods, neglect of skill upgradation, low stipend offered to trainees etc. are some of the reasons for the suboptimal performance of the craft centres (Majumdar, 2000).

The dropout rates in Arunachal at the primary and upper primary level in 2003 were 20 per cent and 36 per cent respectively (APHDR, 2005). After primary school, vocational streams should be available to train the boys and girls in the local context so that they find education is relevant and employment oriented. A. P. is below the National level of female literacy (NHDR, 2001). This is a case of Gender disparity contrasting women empowerment.

Probable Solutions

The following may be few suggestions to consider in order to strengthening the Small Scale Industries in the state:

1. The sector needs advertisement for its product through all modern media. Initially, the free web-space provided by the KVIC in their website (www.kvic.org.in) for the state KVIBs should be filled with information.
2. The State Government and the KVIC should implement the good recommendations made in the Anindo Majumdar Report, 2000.
3. Priority to develop border trades with Bhutan, China and Myanmar to be given.
4. A comprehensive techno-economic survey of the entire territory of the state should be done to find out potential area of activities under this sector.
5. Modernizing the government run craft centres is needworthy. Incorporation of innovative training streams on the basis of

potentiality study. Setting up of interface with existing good technical and managerial institutes like SFRI, NERIST, IIE may be considered.

6. Complete financial support and its proper utilization in any probable unit should be shouldered by the government. Identification of non-REGP villages and devising alternative scheme for these localities will be generous step in this direction.
7. Implementation and execution of KVI schemes and programmes should be left to APKVIB. The local KVIC may perform mainly the supervisory and liaisoning role with GoI, KVIC head office etc.
8. The flow of relevant information relating to village and small industries should be regularly circulated to keep the entrepreneurial world abreast with the recent trends. The department of Industries may launch a periodical bulletin.
9. The bank should play more constructive role in lending credit support to good proposals. The A. P. Industrial Development and Financial Corporation needs to be revived. The monitoring machinery needs to be strengthened including detection of sick of industrial units and draw up a nursing plan for their rehabilitation.
10. Tourism/eco-tourism may be encouraged which will have ripple effect on the village and small industries . Nearing to the Eco-tourist spot, Gramodyog Darshan Park may be established to showcase the treasure trove.
11. The state should strive hard to be self-sufficient in raw material, technical know-how, machines/tools and a well-knitted marketing network.
12. A single item can be identified which could be synonymous with the name of the state. Escort services should be given to village industry unit in graduating it to a SSI unit.
13. The existence of Inner Line System appears to be irrelevant in present global scenario and therefore authority may contemplate twice on its continuation.
14. Sustainability of any project depends upon fulfilment of certain basic requirements. Systematic approach, training to entrepreneurs, technology, Quality Control and marketing

support etc. if all these will be taken care adequately, the village and small industries can play an exemplary role in the process of Socio-Economic Development in Arunachal Pradesh.

Conclusion

In the improvement and preservation of traditional tribal dresses cannot be forgotten. Dr. V. Elwin, the Advisor of Tribal Affairs of the then NEFA, who pleaded and stressed through his writing for preservation of fashionable dresses of the tribal people in Arunachal Pradesh. With his advice and suggestions some fashionable local dresses were once introduced as school dresses and official dresses during the fifties. The present Government should also revive this spirit to encourage preservation of traditional dresses and the people should cultivate the spirit of inter-exchange of fashionable dresses among themselves for emotional integration. The people must learn to love self-respect and to preserve self-identity through traditional dresses and costumes. More facility and encouragement should be given to interested individual by the Government to export local fashionable dresses to outside. To do this, network of production centres of weaving and crafts in the village level should he opened by the departments concerned. Thus, a new incentive programme for cultural development and revitalization should be taken up.

To bring about industrial development this territory should be self-sufficient in raw materials, technical knowledge, machine and machine tools, skilled labour and technicians. Therefore, our efforts for development of industries in the territory have been to get concentration of those industries, for which raw materials are locally available. Arunachal Pradesh has rich natural resources for rapid industrialization. In course of time, in the near future this territory will occupy a place in the industrial map of India which will meet the needs and demands of the people. But in the process of industrial development the importance of cottage industries should not be ignored. Of course, top priority must be given to those small scale industries which are essential for the manufacture of light machine tools and other equipments because today a country's progress is measured by the quality of goods it produces.

Employment is the surest way to enable the vast numbers of people living below the poverty level to raise them above it. The village and small industries is capable of offering employment opportunities at the place of residence to a large section of population. This has the capacity to correct regional imbalances by initiating industrial activities on dispersed basis in the most neglected, backward inaccessible areas like most of the areas of North-East States where perhaps large scale sector is unable to penetrate. The village and small industries is a key to rural development and rural prosperity.

NOTES AND REFERENCES

Borgohain, H. (1997), "Development of Industries and Handicrafts in Siang Region" in Pandey, B.B. (ed) "Patterns of Change and Potential for Development in Arunachal Pradesh", Himalayan Publishers, Itanagar, New Delhi.

Information from various records of Department of Industries, GoAP. Various issues of *Jagriti*, a monthly journal of KVIC.

Kamalakannan, K. (2008), "Rural Industrialistion and Poverty Alleviation", Kurukshetra, *A Journal of Rural Development*, Ministry of Rural Development, May,Vol. 54, No. 52, New Delhi.

Majumdar (2000), *The Khadi and V.I. Sector in Arunachal Pradesh*, published by KVIC, Govt. of India.

Mandal, R.K. (2005), "Emergence of Marketing of Handloom and Handicrafts Products of A.P." Paper presented in the Annual Conference of NEEA, Oct. 2005.

Mandal, R.K. (2006), "Arunachal Economy as Emerging Power House", *Journal of Global Economy*, Vol. I, No. 4, Oct-Dec., p. 223.

Mandal, R.K. (2006), "Constraint of Economic Development in Arunachal Pradesh with special reference to Globalization and Inner Line System", Artha Beekshan,Vol. 15, No. 3, Kolkata.

Mandal, R.K. (2005), "Arunachal Economy: Socio-Economic Transformation", Champion Publisher and Distributor, Itanagar, pp. 90-91.

Samiran Das, Amal Prava Das (1986), A biography translated by Hiranmoyee Devi, Publisher H. Devi.

Verma, D.Y.N. (2010), "Role of Village and Cottage Industries in Economic Transformation: A Study on Handicraft Industry" in Ahmed, Jaynal Uddin(Ed): Development Vision of North East India, Concept Publishing Company, New Delhi, pp. 126-49.

Report

Arunachal Pradesh Human Development Report, 2005, Deptt. of Planning, GoAP.

Human Development Report, 2005 of UNDP.

National Human Development Report, 2001.

Report of High Power Committee on KVI, 1994 under the Chairmanship of Lt P.V. Narasimha Rao.

Report of NIRD on Rural Industrialization, 1999, NE Regional Centre, Guwahati.

Report of the Khadi and V. I. Review Committee, under the Chairmanship of M. Ramkrishnayya, Ex-Chairman, NABARD and Ex-Dy. Governor, RBI, 1987.

Reports of A. P. Khadi and V. I. Board, Itanagar.

SECTION - III

Empirical Study

12

Traditional Handicrafts of Assam: Challenges and Opportunities in Bamboo and Cane Crafts

MANOJ KUMAR PAUL

Introduction

North-Eastern Region (NER) is a land of beautiful handicrafts with a wide range in variety of crafts. The people of the region have a tradition of artistic craftsmanship. Crafts such as weaving painting, pottery, basketry, woodcarving, bamboo and cane crafts, smithywork, etc. are widely practiced in NER as the tradition of their art of living and culture. Among these crafts, bamboo and cane crafts are the important traditional handicrafts. The people of this region are practicing this craft from time immemorial. It includes a variety of household and decorative items which are used by the people of the state irrespective of their social or economic class. It is one of the important industries of the state of Assam next to tea. Due to its artistic look and beauty, the bamboo and cane products have gained much popularity in recent period both within the state as well as outside the state. Thus the state of Assam is now not only known for its tea but for its bamboo and cane crafts also.

Importance of the Traditional Crafts in the Present Context

The importance of these crafts in the socio-economic life of Assam can be understood from the following facts:

- These Crafts represent our rich heritage in arts and crafts. The products produced by the craftsmen have both their use value and artistic value. Therefore, they are acceptable to almost all classes of people of the society. Hence, these crafts need to be preserved, protected and promoted.

- The products are produced by using traditional and indigenous techniques and hence put no burden on our import bill for import of machinery and technical know-how. Rather, these products have good demand in export market and therefore can earn foreign exchange for the country.
- The technique of production being capital light in nature, these crafts play a special role in socio-economic development in capital scarce states like Assam and other states of North-Eastern Region.
- The industry being labour-intensive in nature, has vast potential in generating both full-time and part-time employment opportunities in rural, suburban as well as in urban areas.
- These crafts can reduce the dependence of rural people on agriculture as their exclusive source of livelihood by providing gainful subsidiary employment. Thus, it can play a positive role in reducing the level and extent of poverty in the region and uplift the social status of the downtrodden people living in rural areas of the region.
- Further, these industries can accommodate all types of workers viz., skilled, semi-skilled as well as unskilled and therefore have great potential to reduce the problem of unemployment in both rural and urban areas. Not only this, it can provide self-employment for educated youths also.
- These crafts can play a positive role in the process of political socialization of the rural people and can be an important step towards social inclusion in the process of economic development as well as for women's empowerment in rural and suburban areas.
- The traditional crafts like **cane and bamboo crafts** of the region are of special importance from the viewpoint of environmental issues also. The plastic pollution is now a bigger threat to the society. Because of its durability, portability light-weight, attractive colour and cost effectiveness, at present plastic furniture are widely used. But as they are not bio-degradable, the plastic wastes are causing environment pollution. If the

cane and bamboo products (such as, furniture and other household items) are popularized then it would, at least to some extent reduce the use of plastic and thereby reduce the plastic pollution.

On the other hand, popularization of wooden furniture has a negative impact on environment as it leads to deforestation. But cane has a number of advantages. Its maturity period being much lesser than that of trees (timber) and it can be renewed quickly. Further, the climate in north-eastern region being favourable for easy growth of cane, therefore, it can be cultivated successfully. Thus, even with the growth of this industry, there is less possibility of deforestation.

Objectives of the Paper

In spite of its vast natural resources, Assam is industrially backward. A number of reasons are cited for slow growth of industries in Assam as well as in the North-Eastern region as a whole. While, some of these reasons are geographical, some others are infrastructural and the rest are purely political in character. The reasons like geographical isolation, infrastructural bottlenecks, scarcity of capital, smaller size of market, lack of skilled labour, etc. might be responsible for slow growth of big or large scale industries in the state (as well as for the NER as a whole) to a large extent. But, the same set of factors cannot be held accountable for the slow growth of small scale and cottage industries based on its traditional handicrafts like cane and bamboo crafts of the region. The region is blessed with natural abundance of Cane and Bamboo; the basic raw materials used for the industry and at the same time the highly skilled manpower for these crafts are also available in the region. Therefore, there is ample scope of development of the traditional crafts like cane and bamboo crafts of the region. These crafts could be an engine for economic growth of the region, if adequate measures are taken at different levels to boost up these crafts.

With a view to highlight the above fact, the study has been carried out with the following objectives:

- To explore the prospect of the cane and bamboo industry in particular in the state of Assam.

- To identify the current problems faced by this industry on its way of development.
- To suggest adequate policy measures that are needed to develop the industry.
- To generate academic interest among the scholars for further study in the similar field.

Review of Literature

Cane and Bamboo Craft is one of the traditional tribal crafts in India. The North-Eastern States of India in general and Assam in particular are famous for their handicrafts based on cane and bamboo. Cane and bamboo products happen to be the two most commonly used items in daily life and have remained inseparable parts of life in Assam.

However, the existing literature on cane and bamboo industry is limited. Further, no study of high magnitude has so far been made either at government level or at institutional level. As a result it is not possible to analyse and compare the views of different scholars on the issue. However, the SISI[1] gives great importance of cane and bamboo crafts in the economic development of the region. So far as the importance of this industry is concerned, Mali[2] , Eupen[3] and others have highlighted these crafts as the most important crafts of Assam from the viewpoint of employment generation, utilization of latent resources, both human and natural; as micro-enterprise and for overall economic improvement of the rural poor. Further, they pointed out the role of these crafts in reducing the dependence of rural people on agriculture as the exclusive source of their livelihood and suggested for adequate support to this industry by the government.

---

1. "Modernization guide on Cane and Bamboo Industries"(1992): Small Industries Service Institute, Guwahati, under the Ministry of Industries, Government of India, 16th Sept, 1992.
2. Mali, D.D. (1989): *Economic Problems of Assam*, OMSONS Publications, New Delhi, p. 99.
3. Eupen Mridul (1996): "Rural Non-Farm Employment: Some reflections on Petty Production", *EPW*, Vol. 31, No. 26, June 29, 1996, p. 1673.

Assam is rich in forest resources and most of its forests are richly stocked with bamboos and canes of various species. Assam has probably the maximum resources for cane and bamboo industry in India, comparable with Canada and the Scandinavian countries—Sweden, Norway and Finland.

Bamboo is a raw material of great versatility and forms an integral part of the lifestyle and economy of Assam. Special mention may however be made of the forests of Mizo Hills, Cachar, Mikir and North Cachar Hills, Nowgong and Lakhimpur districts. The important species of bamboos of economic value are the **Muli** (Melocanna Bambusoides), **Dalu** (Teinostachyum dalloa), **Khang** (Dendrocalmus longispatnus), **Kaligoda** (Oxytenanthera nigrociliata) and **Pecha** (Dendrocalamus Hamilton-II). The **Muli** and the **Dalu** have great commercial importance, the former for pulping, constructional and fencing purposes, and the latter for the mat and basket industry.

Rattans (the prickly palms more commonly referred to as cane) are one of the most important non-timber forest produces found in the tropical countries of South East Asia, Africa and America. India has a good representation of rattans with their concentration mainly in Western Ghats, Andaman and Northeast India. Out of 5 genera and 60 species found in India, North-Eastern states alone accounts for 4 genera and more than 25 species. Each state has different number of species of cane, the highest being in Arunachal Pradesh followed by Assam. The varieties of cane which are available in the NE states are presented in Table 12.1.

The main commercially important species of cane, used in handicraft and furniture industries are: Jati (Calamus tenuis), Tita (Calamus leptesadix), Lejai (Calamus floribundus), Sundi (Calamus garuba), Golla (Calamus erectus) and Raidang (Calamus flagellum). 'Murta' (Clinogyne Dichotoma), a plant of the reed family, locally known as *patidai*, is required for making the famous "Sital Pati" (cool-mat). The other cane species like Calamus Nambariensis, Calamus inermis, Calamus Khasianus, Plectocomia Himalayana are also considered good for furniture.

So far as cane and bamboo crafts are concerned, no definite records are available to establish the antiquity, history and origin of these crafts in Assam. However, it can be safely assumed that

Table 12.1 Availability of Cane varieties in North-Eastern Region

Sl.No.	*Name of species*	*Assam*	*Arunachal Pradesh*	*Nagaland*	*Manipur*	*Meghalaya*	*Mizoram*	*Tripura*	*Sikkim*
1.	Calamus Leptospadix	✓	✓	✓	✓	✓	✓	✓	✓
2.	Calamus.Tenuis	✓	✓	✓	✓	✓	✓	✓	✓
3.	Calamus. Inemis		✓						✓
4.	Calamus latifolius	✓	✓	✓		✓		✓	✓
5.	Calamus.latifolius var. mormoratus								✓
6.	Calamus nambariensis	✓	✓						
7.	Calamus khasianus	✓	✓	✓	✓	✓	✓		
8.	Calamus gracilis	✓	✓			✓			
9.	Calamus flagellum	✓	✓	✓	✓	✓	✓	✓	✓
10.	Calamus erectus	✓	✓	✓	✓	✓	✓		
11.	Calamus floribundus	✓	✓	✓	✓	✓			
12.	Calamus floribundus var. depauperatus					✓			

13. Calamus acanthospathus	✓	✓		✓	✓	✓		✓
14. Calamus guniba	✓	✓			✓	✓		
15. Calamuskingianus	✓				✓			
16. Calamus masterstianus	✓							
17. Calamus viminalis								✓
18. Calamus arunachalensis	✓	✓						
19. Daemonorops jenkinsiana		✓	✓					
20. Plectocomia himalayana	✓	✓						
21. Plectocomia assamica	✓	✓						
22. Plectocomia bractealis	✓	✓						
23. Plectocomia khasianus					✓			
24. Zalacca secunda	✓	✓						

Source: State Forest Research Institute, Department of Environment and Forests, Government of Arunachal Pradesh, Itanagar-791 111 (2002).

these crafts have been practiced since the misty past with the very dawn of civilization. Early literature refers to the well-decorated and coloured *'SITAL PATIS'* (cool mats) used by the rich people. Mats were usually made of cane. The classical writers testify the abundance of cane in the forests of Assam. An idea about the cane and bamboo products of Assam was found even during the time of Bhaskara Varman, the king of Assam[4] (*early part of the 7th century A.D*). Evidence of the production of other cane articles is also available in the ***'Harshacharita'***, which mentions stools of cane. All these prove that various industrial arts were developed in Assam at an early period and are continued to be practiced till recent times.

Methodology

Area of Study: The area of the present study is Barak Valley of South Assam, comprising the three districts namely, Cachar, Karimganj and Hailakandi which are well known for their cane and bamboo crafts.

- **Population and Sample:** Reliable data on exact number of units engaged in the production of cane and bamboo goods is neither available at the state level nor at the district level as no such survey has so far been conducted by any organization/ institution. However, on the basis of information received from District Industrial Centres (DICs), Small Industries Service Institute (SISI), North-Eastern Handloom and Handicrafts Development Corporation (NHHDC), District Rural Development Authority (DRDA), Khadi and Village Industries Board (KVIB), Khadi and Village Industries Commission (KVIC), and the Department of Economics and Statistics, Government of Assam, it can safely be said that more than 2000 units of this industry, either at tiny level or at cottage level or at small scale level are operating in the study area. From this population, a sample of 120 units, taking 40 from each district, has been selected purposively for the study.
- **Period of data Collection, Statistical Tools Used and the Method Adopted:** The data for the study was collected through

4. "The History of Civilization of the People of Assam" by Dr. P.C. Choudhury.

the personal interviews with the entrepreneurs during the period 2008-09. A specially designed questionnaire was filled in on the spot based on the replies of the respondents. Common statistical tools have been used for interpretation of results and SPSS software has been applied for analyzing the data set.

- **The Products Included Under Study:** The making of cane and bamboo products is perhaps the most universal of all the crafts practiced by a large number of artisans scattered throughout the North-Eastern region. The magnificent skill of artisans of Assam is reflected in the production of a wide range of more than 100 exquisite products produced out of cane and bamboo. These products are used for a wide range of purposes and extensively used in every household. The products vary in size, shape, design and delicacy depending on their purpose of use, market demand and craftsmanship.

The common items made out of cane and bamboo includes furniture like sofa sets, 'Murhas' (stool), mats, chairs, tables, various types of baskets, cradle; room-partitions, Dharia (one type of mat made of bamboo), office trays, bottle carriers, sieves, *japi* or *chatta,* caps, cane belts, Lamp Shades, flower vase, etc.

Besides these, various kinds of fishing implements locally known as *'Polo', 'Jakai', 'Khalai' 'Dori', 'Chepa', 'Jhuti', 'Hoga', 'Patrans'* are generally used in catching fishes in shallow water. Apart from these contrivances, there are some other implements made of bamboo and cane used for catching fishes in deep waters. These are locally known as 'Gut', 'Dingaru', 'Thupa', etc.

Cane baskets of various types are produced in different parts of the State. These baskets are used for various purposes such as, for carrying sand, soil, stones, vegetables and other goods; for storing grains and keeping valuables. Extensive manufacture of 'plucking baskets' is found in all the three districts under study on a commercial basis. Generally, the tea planters purchase these baskets which are used by the tea-pluckers in the gardens.

However, there are inter-enterprise product differences as well as intra product differences in terms of size, shape, design, and quality. Therefore, it becomes very difficult to compare the products produced by one entrepreneur with that of another. Nevertheless, the products produced by the cane and bamboo industry can be categorized into following four broad categories: (a) Furniture items, (b) Decorative items, (c) Articles of domestic use and (d) Shital Pati (the Cool Mat).

The different items of these categories of products, included in the study are:

(a) The **furniture items** included in the study are: (i) Chair, (ii) Table, (iii) 'Morah' (the Stool), (iv) Sofa set, (v) Cradle, (vi) Baby Cot, (vii) Dressing Table, (viii) Dining Table, (ix) Kitchen Shelf, (x) Shoe rack, (xi) Book Shelf, (xii) Telephone stand, (xiii) Light Stand (xiv) Corner stand and (xv) Room partitions.

(b) The **Decorative items** taken into account are: (i) Flower Vases, (ii) Model House, (iii) ***'Kalash'*** (Pitcher), (iv) Ash tray, (v) ***'Gamla'*** (basin), (vi) Ornament Box, (vii) Milk Container, (viii) Lamp shades, (ix) Lantern, (x) Utensil Models, etc.

(c) **Other articles of domestic use** included in the study are: (i) Bamboo brooms (ii) Baskets, (iii) Fishing implements, (iv) ***'Dharia'***, ***'jharia'*** or ***'darma'*** (Bamboo mat), (v) Waste paper basket, (vi) ***'Chalani'*** (Sieves), (vii) ***'Dala'*** (bamboo tray) (viii) ***'Kula'*** (winnowing tray), (ix) ***'Japi'*** or ***'Chhatta'*** (umbrella), (x) Caps.

(d) **Shital Pati** (the Cool Mat): This is another popular product of cane. It has been kept under separate category considering the fact that it is produced by a separate group of craftsmen with a separate technique of production and with a special variety of cane.

Analysis of data and observations of the study

Investment size and Investment structure

(i) The study observed that the amount of capital investment varies widely from Rs. 700 to more than Rs. 4 lakh. However the distribution of units as per their size of capital investment, shown in Table 12.2, clearly depicts the fact that the industry can accommodate both tiny enterprises as well as the big enterprises.

(ii) However, it is interesting to note that the tiny producers are generally engaged in the production of the articles of domestic

Table 12.2: Distribution of units as per the size of their capital investment

Size of investment (in Rs.)*	*Mid-value*	*No. of units under the sample*	*Category of items produced***	*Percentage to the total*	*Cumulative percentage (less than)*	*Cumulative percentage (more than)*
700-1000	850	7	C	5.83	5.83	100.00
1000-5000	3000	5	C,D	4.17	10.00	94.17
5000-10000	7500	5	A,C,D	4.17	14.17	89.99
10000-20000	15000	13	A,B,C	10.83	25.00	85.82
20000-40000	30000	9	A,B,C,D	7.50	32.50	74.99
40000-60000	50000	10	A,B,C,D	8.33	40.83	67.49
60000-80000	70000	13	A,B,C,D	10.83	51.66	59.16
80000-100000	90000	11	A,B,C,D	9.17	60.83	48.33
100000-150000	125000	22	A,B,C	18.33	79.16	39.16
150000-200000	175000	9	A,B,C,D	7.50	86.66	20.83
200000-250000	225000	7	A,B,C	5.83	92.50	13.33
250000-300000	275000	5	A,B,C,D	4.17	96.67	7.5
300000-400000	350000	3	A,B,C	2.50	99.17	3.33
above 400000	425000	1	A,B,C,D	0.83	100.00	0.83
Total	—	120	—	100.00	—	—

Source: Field Survey.

use such as bamboo brooms, bamboo fans, various types of baskets, different fishing implements, 'Dharia', 'Dala', etc. and a few of them are also engaged in production of Shital Patis.

(iii) Further, all the tiny entrepreneurs (with investment size less than Rs. 40,000) are running their productive activities at the cottage level using family labour.

(iv) On the other hand, although the units with investment of Rs. 1 lakh or more are found to produce all categories of items, i.e., furniture items, decorative items, articles for domestic use, and 'Shital Pati', yet the number of varieties of each category of product produced by them is less than that of the units with investment size Rs. 2 lakh or more. Thus the study observed that size of capital investment is an important factor determining the number of varieties that an entrepreneur can produce under each category of products.

Note: * Size of investment includes the value of tools and implements, value of raw materials, circulating capital and value of inventories, if any.
** A = Furniture items, B = Decorative items, C= Other Articles for Domestic use, D = Shital Pati.

Sources of Finance: The study observed that the industry is yet to achieve confidence of the financial institutions to receive financial assistance from them. The sources from which the units manage their finance are given in Table 12.3.

(i) It has been observed that only 5.83 per cent of the sample units are benefited from financial assistance by commercial banks and the role of cooperatives in this regard is quite discouraging as no unit was found as a beneficiary from cooperative societies or cooperative banks in the selected sample.

(ii) However, the regional rural bank provided loans to 10 per cent of the sample units and the rest 84.17 per cent didn't receive any assistance from financial institutions. This depicts the reluctance of institutional sources to provide finance so far as the traditional crafts like cane and bamboo are concerned. As a result, the entrepreneurs are to depend on the traders, businessmen, agents, moneylenders, relatives and friends for finance and as usual, they have no other option but to pay high interest rate and get exploited. The rate of interest from non-institutional sources varies from 120 per cent to 180 per cent per annum (*10% to 15% per month*).

(iii) The study also observed that because of poor financial strength, the artisans and craftsmen, in most of the cases, are not in a position to start their own production units. As a result, either they work at cottage level as a subsidiary occupation to supplement their family income or get employed under an employer either on daily wage basis or on job contract basis.

Table 12.3: Sources of Finance

Sources of Finance	*No. of units*	*Percentage to the total*
Institutional	**19**	**15.83**
(a) Commercial Banks	7	5.83
(b) Cooperative	0	0.00
(c) Regional rural banks	12	10.00
Non-institutional	**101**	**84.17**
(a) Traders/businessmen	17	14.17
(b) Agents	5	4.17
(c) Moneylenders	34	28.33
(d) Relatives and friends (with interest)	9	7.50
(e) Relatives and friends (without interest)	12	10.00
(f) Own fund	24	20.00
Total	**120**	**100.00**

Source: Field Survey.

Product designing: The product designs are totally indigenous which are traditionally developed by the craftsmen themselves and evolved to the present form gradually through generations. However, these craftsmen are not trained by any organization or institution, rather, they gathered the particular skill through learning by doing process under the guidance of some skilled craftsmen or the skill is passed from father to son and from one generation to the other. The product designs are not patented by any body. As a result different craftsmen are free to adopt any design of their products as they like and they adopt the designs following the buyers' craze towards a few designs and costing of the product design. However, the entrepreneurs try to invent newer designs and also imitate the product designs from others.

Supply of raw materials

(i) So far as the bamboos are concerned, there is till now no crises for this raw material. But it is not so easy for cane. However, there is neither any agency nor any mechanism for an uninterrupted supply of cane to the entrepreneurs by the government. As a result the prices of the raw materials fluctuate very much depending on the market demand for finished product and availability of raw materials.

(ii) Further, the supply of cane is mainly under the control of a few 'Mahaldars'[5] who are the authorized persons to extract cane from forests. As a consequence, its prices are under their control. It is worth mentioning that the prices of bamboo and cane vary depending on the variety of species, its diameter, its length and maturity.

(iii) Further, the big units are in a position to keep a sufficient stock of cane to overcome the irregularity in supply particularly in the rainy and winter season and to avoid the loss due to price hike. But this is beyond the capacity of the smaller units and they are to buy cane at higher prices from the stockists or from the big firms.

(iv) However, in most of the cases, irrespective of the size of the firm, bamboo and cane, the two primary raw materials are procured through illegal means without approval from forest departments. This is causing a huge loss of revenue of the government in one hand and encouraging illegal and unplanned extraction of cane and bamboo from forests.

(v) At present the insurgency/militancy problem is posing a threat to the 'Mahaldars' who are subject to extortion by them and because of this problem, regular supply of raw materials is frequently disturbed and the prices of bamboo and cane have increased enormously in recent times.

---

5. The Mahaldar is a person who takes lease of a forest area from the Government to extract cane and other forest products.

Marketing of products

(i) The marketing system of different items of cane and bamboo crafts produced by the craftsmen and different units is totally unorganized.

(ii) Only 29 per cent of the sample units were found to have their own shops or selling outlets and 71 per cent of the units sell their products to the big enterprises, traders, agents supplying these products to other states, government suppliers, export agencies, or sell their products carrying them door to door by themselves.

(iii) The study observed that because of existence of a class of intermediary in between the producers and the end users, both the producer as well as the customers are exploited and the major chunk of profit are appropriated by these intermediaries. In the absence of their adequate financial strength and support from institutional finance, the craftsmen are worst hit as the major share of their profit is eaten by the intermediaries.

Cost of production

(i) The firms used to produce a number of items and each item has a number of varieties and therefore, there is a wide range of variation in the cost of production per unit of a product and also in their unit prices.

(ii) The wide variation in the cost of production across the firms is due to the difference in the quality of raw materials used, differences in procurement prices of raw materials, differences in establishment costs; efficiency skill and dexterity of craftsmen; product design, artistic look or excellence of the product, size of the product, transportation cost, etc.

(iii) Further, as the market is imperfect, the prices of the same product of the same variety, design and quality vary from firm to firm and from one place to another. The wide range of variation in unit costs and unit prices of some common products is shown in Table 12.4.

Table 12.4: Variation in Cost of Production and Price (per unit)

Sl. No.	*Name of the product*	*Range of variation of*	
		Unit cost	*Unit price*
A. Furniture items			
1.	Sofa set	5000-25000	8000-35000
2.	Dressing Table	2000-3000	3000-4500
3.	Dining Table	1500-3000	2000-5500
4.	Chair	150-550	200-850
5.	Table	300-1200	450-1800
6.	Easy chair	1000-1500	1300-3500
7.	'DOLNA' (Cradle)	800-2500	1000-3500
8.	'Singhashan' (Throne for God/ Goddess)	400-2000	450-5000
9.	Baby Cot	550-1500	1200-4000
10.	Book Shelf	250-750	450-1000
11.	'Morah' (the Stool),	120-350	150-750
12.	Kitchen Shelf	300-1250	400-2000
13.	Shoe rack	200-750	250-1200
14.	Telephone stand	200-300	250-500
15.	Light Stand	120-200	200-300
16.	Corner stand	120-200	150-300
17.	Room partitions	1200-2500	2500-7500
B. Decorative items			
18.	Flower Vases	200-500	400-700
19.	'Kalash' (Pitcher)	150-750	200-3000
20.	Model House	300-1000	500-1500
21.	Ornament Box	200-750	500-1000
22.	Lantern	80-150	150-250
23.	Milk Container	75-200	100-300
24.	Lamp shades	50-175	80-250
25.	Decorative baskets	110-200	200-500
26.	'Gamla' (basin)	100-120	250-400
C. Articles of Domestic use			
27.	Bamboo Brooms	2-3	5-10
28.	Bamboo baskets	5-20	10-40
29.	Cane baskets	30-70	40-100

contd...

30. Tray	25-120	40-175
31. Ash tray	10-15	20-50
32. Waste paper basket	40-60	50-200
33. POLO (fishing implements)	80-150	125-200
34. DORI (fishing implement)	120-300	150-400
35. 'Chalani' (Sieves)	10-25	20-40
36. 'Dala' (bamboo tray)	10-25	15-40
37. 'Kula' (winnowing tray)	10-25	15-40
38. 'Japi' or 'Chhatta' (umbrella)	30-100	75-200
39. Caps.	15-100	25-200
40. CHATAI (Bamboo mat used for sitting purposes)	30-75	40-100
41. 'Dharia', or 'Darma' (Bamboo mat used in construction, partition, etc.)	7-10	12-20
D. SHITAL PATI		
42. Ordinary quality single size	65-80	125-200
43. Fine quality (single size)	150-200	200-400
44. Ordinary Quality (Double size)	100-150	200-400
45. Fine Quality (Double size)	225-400	350-800

Source: Field Survey.

(iii) The cost of production of small firms are less than those of the bigger firms primarily because of the fact that (i) they use mainly family labour, (ii) use low quality of materials, (iii) have zero or negligible establishment cost, (iv) collect bamboo and cane directly from forest or through illegal way which is unnoticed by the concerned authorities as their scale of operation is small.

(iv) The price of the products produced by the small firms or sold by the craftsmen themselves are low because they normally do not employ any hired labour and they consider the price of the products as good as their wage added with the cost of raw materials. Further they do not have the capacity to bargain for a better price of their produce or wait for a better buyer because of their poverty. Further, there is lack of information relating to the prices of products and their market avenues.

(v) The craftsmen and tiny producers are forced to sell their products at predetermined prices to the agents or big businessmen as per their agreed terms and conditions of finance or supply of raw material or for repayment of loan taken from moneylenders (termed as Mahajans).

(vi) In some cases the big firms engage craftsmen on job-contract basis. In such cases, the craftsmen are provided with the necessary raw materials and the craftsmen are to supply the finished articles as per the requisition of the big firms on piece rate basis. In such cases, the labour cost of production becomes comparatively low than in case of wage employment.

(vii) In case of bamboo products like 'Dharia' or 'Darma' labour cost is the major cost of production and these are produced by a special type of skilled labour who are not skilled in doing other cane or bamboo products.

(viii) 'Shital Pati' is a special cane product which needs a completely separate skill and found to be produced in few locations of the valley whereas the other items are found to be produced in almost everywhere throughout the valley. The price of Shital Pati depends on the fineness of weaving works, quality of cane used and obviously on their size. The range of variation in prices of Shital Pati is from Rs. 65 to Rs. 800.

Profitability: Profitability of a firm depends on a number of factors. The important factors influencing the rate of profit earned by a firm under cane and bamboo industry, as observed by the study, are: (i) the volume of capital investment, (ii) total turnover, (iii) the ratio of hired labour to total labour, (iv) source of finance, (v) location of the selling outlet of the firm, (vi) marketing channels used by the firm, (vii) skill and efficiency of the workers employed, (viii) the waiting capacity of the firm for a better price of the product, and so on. With a view to formulate a profit function, a regression equation of the form

$\pi_j = \alpha_j + \Sigma\beta_i X_{ij} + u_j$; ($i = 1, 2, 3, 4$ and $j = 1, 2, 3\ldots120$) was fitted, wherein,

π_j = Profit per unit of Capital (i.e., Total Profit to Total Capital ratio) of the jth firm, ($j = 1, 2, \ldots 120$).

α_j = intercept,

X_{ij}'s ($i = 1, 2, 3, 4$ and $j = 1, 2, \ldots 120$) are the independent variables influencing π_j

u_j = the other random factors not included in the function,

β_{ij}'s (i = 1, 2, 3, 4 and j = 1, 2, ... 120) are the coefficient of respective X_{ij}'s.

The independent variables considered for the function are:

X_1 = Total turnover,

X_2 = No. of items produced,

X_3 = Hired labour to total labour ratio.

X_4 = the Dummy Variable representing the sources of finance *(0 for non-institutional sources and 1 for institutional sources)*

The observations of the regression analysis are represented as under:

Model Summary#

R	*R Square*	*Adjusted R Square*	*Std. Error of the Estimate*	*Change Statistics*				
				R Square Change	*F Change*	*df1*	*df2*	*Sig. F Change*
0.807*	0.651	0.639	7.26158	0.651	53.71	4	115	0.00

Predictors: (Constant), no. of items produced, total turnover, hired labour to total labour ratio, source of finance.

* Dependent Variable: profit per unit of capital.

The *R* value (0.807) depicts a stronger relationship between the dependent variable and the regressors and R^2 (0.651), the multiple coefficient of determination, depicts that 65.1% of total variation in the dependent variable is jointly explained by the explanatory variables included in the regression model. Thus it justifies the goodness of fit of the model.

ANOVA

	Sum of Sqares	*df*	*Mean Square*	*F*	*Sig.*
Regression	3369.352	4	842.338	53.710	0.00
Residual	1803.563	115	15.683		
Total	5172.915	119			

The goodness of fit of the model is further confirmed by the ANOVA table with statistically significant *F*-value [$F_{(4,115)} = 53.71$; $p = 0.00$).

The estimated values of the coefficients of the explanatory variables ($X_i s$) are as under:

Coefficients[∈]

	Unstandardized Coefficients		*Standardized Coefficients*	*t*	*Sig.*
	B	*Std. Error*	*Beta*		
(Constant)	$\alpha' = -0.0713$	0.010		0.820	0.414
Total turnover (X_1)	$\beta'_1 = 0.191$	0.000	0.198	2.176	0.032
No. of items produced (X_2)	$\beta'_2 = 0.003$	0.001	0.029	2.480	0.015
Hired labour to total labour ratio(X_3)	$\beta'_3 = -0.011$	0.021	– 0.046	2.295	0.024
Source of finance (X_4)	$\beta'_4 = 0.024$	0.016	0.143	2.044	0.043

• Dependent Variable: profit per unit of capital.

Thus the estimated equation for profit per unit of capital becomes as:

$$\pi' = -0.0713 + 0.191X_1 + 0.003\,X_2 - 0.011\,X_3 + 0.024\,X_4$$

i.e., Profit per unit of capital = – 0.0713 + 0.191 (Total annual turnover) + 0.003 (No. of items produced) – 0.011 (Hired labour to total labour ratio) + 0.024 (Sources of Finance).

The results of the regression analysis reveal the following:

- The regression equation has a negative intercept (– 0.0713) which is not statistically significant ($t = 0.820$, $p = 0.414$).
- The variables (i) *Total annual turnover* (X_1), (ii) *No. of items produced* (X_2) and (iii) *Source of finance* (X_4) have positive and statistically significant impact on the profitability of a firm under study, as reflected by the *t*-values of the coefficients ($p < 0.05$).
- However, the study depicts that the *sources of finance* can be considered as the second important factor in the model determining of rate of profit per unit of capital, next to *Total annual turnover* of the firm, followed by the *No. of items produced* (i.e. *variety of products*).

- The study observes, as it can also be expected normally, a positive significant relationship between *total annual turnover* (X_1) and rate of profit per unit capital investment ($t = 2.176$, $p = 0.032$). This divulges the importance of marketing in profitability of the firms also.
- The *number of items produced* (X_2) has also a significant positive impact on the profit rate ($t = 2.480$, $p = 0.015$). This illustrates that the firms producing more variety of product items have higher profitability. This significant positive impact may be because of the fact that the firms enjoy economies of scale when they produce more varieties of products and this possibly increase their turnover by increasing the volume of sales by attracting more customers. It may also be due to optimum utilization of raw materials and workforce when a number of varieties of a product are produced.
- *The ratio of hired labour to total labour* (X_3) has a significant negative influence on the profitability of a firm ($\beta'_3 = -0.011$, $t = 2.295$, $p = 0.024$). The negative impact of *hired labour to total labour ratio* on the profitability may be because of the fact that higher is the ratio, higher is the wage bill which reduces the volume of profit and profitability. Further, with the increase in the number of hired labour, after a certain level, the law of diminishing returns might start operating in the event of existence of some fixed factors, such as, workshed, commonly used working tools, etc.
- The positive coefficient ($\beta'_4 = 0.024$, $t = 2.044$, $p = 0.043$) of the *dummy variable* (X_4: Source of finance) highlights the fact that institutional sources of finance contribute positively to the profitability of the firms under the study. This result implies that, an arrangement of easy access of institutional sources of finance would lead to an improvement in the profitability of the firms and thereby would act as a booster to these traditional crafts of the region. At the same time this would improve the economic conditions of the artisans and craftsmen and encourage new entry to the industry.

7. The major obstacles before the cane and bamboo industry:

The industry faces almost all the common problems of a small scale and cottage industry such as, low volume of capital, low capacity level, illiteracy of the artisans and craftsmen, lack of training facilities, dominance of intermediaries, traditional methods of production, inadequate loan facilities, problems of marketing, irregularity in supply of raw materials, and others. However, the study identified the following specific problems encountered by the industry:

1. There is no agency to assist the firms or to suggest the firms with regard to the optimal size of investment and guide the entrepreneurs regarding their product design, marketing of finished products, portfolio management, etc.
2. There is no organization to provide any technical assistance to improve the process of production and liberate the industry from its traditional techniques.
3. The study observed that the small firms are run by the poor artisans themselves at the cottage level and they are badly in need of finance for carrying out the production purposes and even for consumption purposes during the time lag between production and sell. But the institutional sources of finance being almost unavailable, they depend either on money-lenders or traders or agents for financial assistance at a very high rate of interest or with a contract to sell the products to them at predetermined lower prices. In some cases the rate of interest is as high as 120 per cent to 180 per cent per annum (10% to 15% per month).
4. Cooperative societies in the region are not giving adequate importance to these crafts and do not come forward to provide any financial or marketing assistance to the industry. However, in some cases, NGOs have come forward and they are providing moral, technical and financial support to this industry.
5. The benefits of government marketing agencies are enjoyed by a few big firms only and the small firms and the artisans are totally unaware about the existence of any government agency that assists the craftsmen and entrepreneurs in any form.

6. The unemployed youths are not motivated towards this industry. The wards of the craftsmen and artisans are discouraged to learn this art and craft because of the poverty of their parents. Therefore, the skill of this craft is not passing from one generation to another as it is used to happen earlier. As a result there is a possibility of extinction of these crafts within next few generations because of the lack of craftsmen.
7. There is no organization/centre in the region to impart education and training to the workers and modernization of these crafts. As a result it is still running in traditional and age old mode with almost no use of modern science and technology.
8. Because of voluminous nature of the products, the industry is facing problems in transporting its products.
9. There is scarcity of raw cane as a result of bulk purchase made by the big firms from the Mahaldars. Further, due to continuous deforestation and unscientific or unplanned extraction of cane from the forest, there is gradual depletion of cane from forests of this region. As a result, the industry is likely to face severe crisis of raw material if adequate steps are not taken immediately.

Suggestions and Policy Recommendations

In view of the above findings about the problems of the industry, the study comes out with the following suggestions and policy recommendations:

1. A specialized agency should be set up for proper guidance to the entrepreneurs of bamboo and cane products about the optimal size of investment, portfolio management, product designing and technological upgradation. The firms may set up a 'Research and Development Wing' on cooperative basis for modernization of production techniques, product designing, exploring new market in both home and abroad, etc.
2. The government should arrange adequate training facilities for the workers engaged in this industry for their skill development. Training for cane and bamboo crafts may be included in the vocational courses for the region also. The NGOs and SHGs can play a major role in this regard.

3. There should be proper coordination among the agencies like DIC, SISI, KVIC, NEHHDC, KVIB and they should come forward to assist cane and bamboo industry by providing various techno-economic support to all the firms irrespective their size and scale of operation.
4. Considering the financial needs of the craftsmen and entrepreneurs, a subsidized loan facility on easy terms and conditions needs to be provided to them. Therefore, necessary instructions are to be given by the government to all financial institutions for the same. There is also an urgent need of simplification of procedural complexities of the banks and other financial institutions to avail loan facilities from them. This would emancipate the poor and illiterate craftsmen from the clutches of moneylenders.
5. A market information centre should be set up at district level to provide market related information and assistance for both raw materials and finished products.
6. It has been observed that with the establishment of paper mills, the illegal extraction of bamboo has increased many times to meet the demand of raw materials to these mills. Adequate measures are to be taken to stop illegal and unscientific extraction of bamboo and cane from the forests.
7. Steps are to be taken to assure the supply of raw materials to this industry, especially cane. Considering the future needs, the forest department should start plantation of cane in suitable locations of forests and encourage villagers for the same for plantation on commercial basis. Setting up of an organization like 'Cane Board' may be considered by the government for this purpose.
8. In order to increase the durability of the products, firms should adopt scientific methods of seasoning of cane and bamboo before their utilization in order to increase the durability of the products. Chemical treatment of bamboo and cane may also be done to make the articles fire and termite proof.
9. Different technical institutes may be requested to develop appropriate technology for the industry.
10. To give a boost to the industry, Indian Railways should extend its helping hand by providing subsidies in freight charges of cane and bamboo products.

REFERENCES

Books and Journals

Chander Sheikhar, P. (1989), *Arunachal Pradesh, Religion, Culture and Society*, Konark Publishers Pvt. Ltd., New Delhi.

Choudhury R.K. (1989), *Economic Problems of Assam*, Kitapghar, Guwahati.

Dr. Das A. K.(1979), *Tribal Art and Crafts*, Agam Kala Prakashan, New Delhi.

Eupen M.(1996), *Rural Non-Farm Employment: Some reflections on Petty Production*, EPW, Vol.31, No. 26, June 29.

Goeal, C. L. (1992), *Tips on Cultivation and Harvesting Techniques of Canes (Rattans) in India in Rattan Management and Utilization*. Karnataka Forest Research Institute (KFRI), Trichur.

Gustov, R. and Stewart F. (1993) "Rural Non-Agricultural Activities in Development – Theory and Application", *Journal of Development Economics*, Vol. 40, No. 1, Feb., 1993

Isabella, S. Rani and Krishnamoorthy, S. (1993), "Rural Industrialisation – Case for Coir Industry", *Journal of Rural Development*, Vol. 12, No. 5.

Jain, L.C. (1986), "A heritage to Keep: The Handicrafts Industry 1955-85"; *E.P.W*, Vol. 21, May 17.

Lakhsmana, A. C. (1993), *Rattans of South India*, Evergreen Publishers, Bangalore.

Mali, D.D. (1989), *Economic Problems of Assam*, Omsons Publications, New Delhi.

Sachdeva, Gulshan (2000), *Economy of the North East: Policy, Present Condition and Future Possibilities*, Konark Publishers, New Delhi.

Saraf, D.N.(1991), *In the Journey of Craft Development, 1941-1994, (The Panorama crafts in States)*; Sampark (Publication Division), New Delhi.

Seethalakshmi, K. K. (1992), *Propagation of Clustering Rattans Using Suckers in Rattan.*

Management and Utilization, Karnataka Forest Research Institute (KFRI), Trichur.

Surveys/Reports

Government of Assam, Directorate of Economics and Statistics, Assam, *Economic Survey and Annual Plans* of different years.

Government of Assam, Directorate of Economics and Statistics, *Statistical Hand Book, Assam, various issues.*

Haridasan, K., Sarmah, A., Hegde, S. N., and Bhuyan, L.R. (2002), SFRI Information Bulletin No. 15, *Field Manual for Propagation and Plantation of Canes in Arunachal Pradesh*, State Forest Research Institute, Department of Environment and Forests, Government of Arunachal Pradesh, Itanagar -791 111.

Nath, T.K., *A study on Bamboo cane and Assam*, Sponsored by Industrial Development Bank of India, Small Industries Development Bank of India, Guwahati, Assam.

Ranjan, M.P., Iyer, N. and Pandya, G., National Institute of Design, *Bamboo and Cane Crafts of North East India.*

Shukla, S.P. Commission (1997), *Report of the High Level Commission, Transforming the North-East-Tackling Backlogs in Basic Minimum Services and Infrastructural Needs, Part I*, Planning Commission, Government of India.

Small Industries Service Institute (Ministry of Industries, Govt. of India) (1992) *Modernisation Guide on Cane and Bamboo Industries – A Report.*

Society for Socio Economic Studies and Services, Kolkata (1997-98), *Diagnostic study on status potential and expansion of marketing for handicrafts, West Bengal.*

Vaikunth Mehta National Institute of Cooperative Management, Pune 1997-98, *Study of women contribution towards handicrafts sector in general and handicrafts cooperatives in particular in Maharashtra and Gujarat.*

Websites

http://www.arunachalpradesh.nic.in/

http://www.assam.nic.in/

http://databank.nedfi.com/

http://www.ignca.gov.in/

http://crafts.indianetzone.com/

http://www.necouncil.nic.in/

http://www.nedfi.com/

http://northeast.nic.in/

http://www.tripura.nic.in/

13

Human and Social Capital in Forming Financial Capital: An Empirical Study

CHIMUN KUMAR NATH

Introduction

This is a paper about how the past can influence the present. The present researcher tackles the question of how peoples' prior work experiences, affiliations, and status may help or hinder them in subsequent career decisions. The present researcher analyzes this question in the context of organizational founding, which requires the gathering of people and resources to create a new legal entity. Originally blank slates; the early identities of these start-up firms are molded by their founders' decisions and abilities to acquire resources. What resources organizations gather—and how quickly they obtain them—will depend in part on the combined characteristics of their founders' industry exposer (status), entrepreneurially relevant demographic features, and social capital.

Inherent to these relationships is the degree to which path dependence impinges on firms. Some researchers argue that founders have an imprinting effect on their firms, setting them on trajectories from which it is difficult to depart (Boeker, 1988), while others suggest that founders have no enduring influence on their firms because organizations are malleable, sensing and reacting to changes in the environment (Teece, Pisano, and Shuen, 1997). Rather than pose the question as either/or, the present researcher considers the extent to which founders may have lasting effects on their firms. To be sure, there are always charismatic leaders who have the ability to change the course of a firm (Ensley, Pearce, and Hmieleski, 2006), but who the entrepreneurial team is and the decisions that they make in the early years of an organization may both shape its subsequent characteristics and constrain its range of future options (Kimberly, 1980; Miles and Randolph, 1980). As Boeker (1988, p. 34) stresses, "while organizations undergo modifications and display varying degrees of flexibility, they are cast at birth into a mold that is discernible in all subsequent stages of their lifecycle."

The present researcher also aim to augment our current understanding of the ways in which founders can use their pasts to gain legitimacy for their firms. Legitimacy—that is, being seen as desirable and appropriate (Berger and Luckmann, 1966)—is "often a critical ingredient for new venture success" (Starr and MacMillan, 1990). Organizations deemed legitimate are better able to attract the resources that they need (Stinchcombe, 1965). Yet where does an organization's initial legitimacy come from? Are all organizations judged to be legitimate based on the same criteria? The present researcher argues that initial legitimacy is transferred to the organization from the founding team. Moreover, the present researcher suggests that which features of the founding team's biography are used to determine an organization's legitimacy will depend primarily on the industry status of the founding team.

In sum, the present researcher formulate a framework that considers how an organization's initial legitimacy, and thus ability to obtain resources, is derived from the interaction between three main facets of its founders' backgrounds: industry status, entrepreneurially relevant demographic features, and social capital. As the arguments and illustrations suggest, the presence of one type of capital may reduce the dependence on or need for others. The framework has applicability to a variety of industries with uncertain outcomes resulting from high risk and/or long product cycles (e.g., Jetrofa Cultivation, Silk, etc.) or subjective quality (e.g., restaurants or movie parlours).

The Challenge: Making the Best Bet on a Highly Uncertain Future

High-growth new ventures, particularly those based on novel unproven technologies, face significant hurdles in getting started (Aldrich and Fiol, 1994). These individuals—and most are teams or partners (Kamm, Shuman, Seeger, and Nurick, 1990)—must overcome the skepticism of outside resource providers in order to gain legitimacy and thus access to resources that are essential to building and growing a corporation (Singh, Tucker, and House, 1986). Of those attempting to found organizations, approximately half succeed in getting their companies started, and fewer than one in 10 grow their organizations (Reynolds and White, 1997). Companies founded on the commercialization of early stage technology are among those high-risk, high-reward firms most dependent on external sources for resources, such as employees, strategic alliances, and financial investments necessary for growth.

Unfortunately, nascent ventures usually lack track records providing evidence that their products and/or services are marketable and/or that they have the right management experience for their companies (Ostgaard and Birley, 1996). Thus, absent established predictors of success, outsiders must depend on "symbolic signals of competence" when deciding whether to invest in new organizations (Sine, Mitsuhashi, and Kirsch, 2006). Often included in their evaluations are characteristics of the external environment, the market and industry, the technology, the type of business, and founding team (Muzyka, Birley, and Leleux, 1996). Of these, "venture capitalists' strongest belief is that it is the founding entrepreneur who determines much (though not all) of a venture's prospects for success" (Sandberg and Hofer, 1987, p. 25). As such, the remainder of this paper focuses on the role of the founders in securing resources, with the caveat that any empirical test of the proposed framework should include controls for the other variables.

The Framework: Experience Leads to Opportunities

Why do some organizational founders receive resources when others do not? To answer this question, the present researcher develop a framework that teases apart the relationships between three facets of the founder's prior experience—namely, industry status, entrepreneurially relevant demographic features, and social capital—and its organization's ability to gain legitimacy and thus resources. As demonstrated in propositions 1, 2a, and 3a in Figure 13.1, the present researcher follow previous studies and suggest that each of these factors is positively related to organizational legitimacy and thus resource obtainment. In the framework, initial organizational legitimacy, which cannot be tested directly, fully mediates the relationship between the characteristics of the founding team and the initial obtainment of organizational resources.

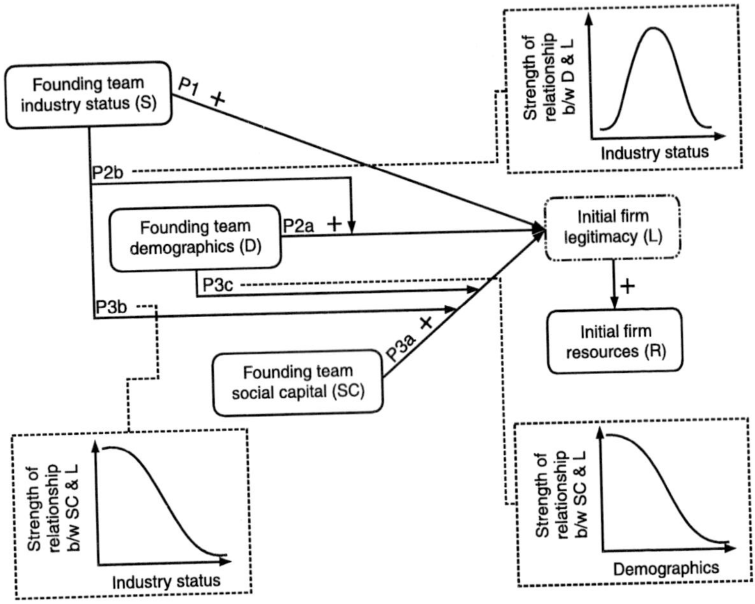

Fig. 13.1: Relationship between Industry Status, Demographic Features, and Social Capital of the Founder and its Ability to Gain Organizational Legitimacy and Thus Resources

This framework differs from prior research, however, in two important ways. First, the present researcher considers industry status, entrepreneurially relevant demographic features, and social capital in conjunction with one another because of the special intention to explore the KVI financing in Assam, whereas researchers in the past have primarily studied these factors in isolation or in pairs. Second, and more importantly, the present researcher argues that it is the combination of the three main factors that is critical. The focus on different types of factors as partial substitutes for one another differs from prior work that, with few exceptions (e.g., Boxman, de Graaf, and Flap, 1991), presumes different factors are additive. These key interaction effects are highlighted as propositions 2b, 3b, and 3c in Figure 13.1. Interactions 2b and 3b indicate that the strength of the positive relationships between the entrepreneurially relevant demographic features or social capital of the founding team and legitimacy is moderated by the team's level of industry status. Proposition 3c indicates that the strength of the positive relationship between social capital and organizational legitimacy is also moderated by the team's entrepreneurially relevant demographic features.

Legitimacy

Legitimacy is a somewhat elusive, but widely used, concept in organizational research. Organizations that are legitimate are considered to have established their competency and the value of their business and its offerings, thus having an easier time securing needed resources (Meyer and Rowan, 1977; Pfeffer and Salancik, 1978). This relationship is highlighted in Figure 13.1 by the arrow and positive sign between organizational legitimacy and organizational resources. The box surrounding legitimacy is dashed to indicate that legitimacy cannot be tested directly and instead is most easily inferred through resource acquisition. The greater the initial resources obtained, the greater the initial legitimacy of the organization.

Building on Suchman (1995), Zimmerman and Zeitz (2002) focus specifically on the role of legitimacy in entrepreneurial firms. They identify four strategies—conformance, selection, manipulation, and creation—that organizations can use to build their regulatory, normative, and cognitive legitimacy. Among these, they identify conformity, with a focus on developing cognitive legitimacy, as the strategy that may be most beneficial to the newest of organizations. An organization can gain cognitive legitimacy by putting "forward the impression that its identity is such that it provides what is needed or desired and will be successful in the business domain in which it purports to operate" (Zimmerman and Zeitz, 2002, p. 421). As depicted in Figure 13.1, in the beginning an organization's identity, and therefore its legitimacy, is primarily based on the characteristics of its founding team. The present researcher investigates the relationship between each type of characteristic and organizational legitimacy in more detail below.

Status

Status is the "esteem, respect, or approval that is granted by an individual or a collectivity for performances or qualities they consider above the average" (Goode, 1978, p. 7). There are three types of status. First, ascribed status refers to characteristics that cannot be changed, such as ethnicity and gender. Many studies that have contrasted large populations of self-employed to employed workers have considered the benefits or limitations of ascribed characteristics (Constant and Zimmerman, 2006).

The second type of status is affiliative, which is the benefit people receive from being connected with high-status institutions. Citing Domhoff (1967) and Mills (1958), D'Aveni (1989, p. 1127) argued that the inclusion of such a measure was based on the presumption "that association with elite universities creates more credibility and prestige than does association with less visible schools." He found that teams with higher status were less likely to face bankruptcy when compared with financially similar, but lower-status, firms.

Finally, the third type of status is achieved status, which results primarily from education and prior occupations. Riley (1979) found that employees of employers who knew their educational credentials were paid more than similarly skilled and educated employees whose employers did not know their educational credentials. In other words, employers paid a premium for education that exceeded the true productivity value gained from that education.

Regardless of whether the status is ascribed, affiliative, or achieved, the rewards to people with status are clear. Those with high status receive overt deference, gifts, hospitality, and services from others who have lower status. A high level of status also brings an "aura" of legitimacy and morality, the expectation of high performance, and a greater confidence in the abilities of those involved (Giordano, 1983).

Organizations can also both have and benefit from status. For example, young biotechnology firms that gained affiliative status from the "endorsement" of prominent strategic alliance partners and organizational equity investors went to initial public offering faster and earned greater valuations than firms that lacked such connections (Finkle, 1998; Stuart, Hoang, and Hybels, 1999). Similarly, Certo, Daily, and Dalton (2001) studied the initial public offerings of 748 companies across more than 50 different industries and found that the greater the achieved status of the boards of directors, the less underpricing that occurred in the initial public offering. In Finkle's (1998) study, status was based on the presence of a sample generated list of the most active venture capitalists and lead underwriters, while in Stuart *et al.*'s (1999) study, it was based on the presence of a highly cited portfolio of biotechnology patents, and an established track record of working with and evaluating young companies in the industry. Certo *et al.* (2001) measured the achieved status of the board of directors as the total number of additional board seats held by the outside directors of the organization.

These studies, along with others, share an important feature, namely, they take as given that some firms have high-status partners, while others do not and simply compare the results between the groups. There is an implicit assumption that nascent firms are too young to develop their own status and therefore rely on the status of others to serve as a proxy for their own organizational legitimacy. Yet it is equally important to know which organizations are able to secure these high-status affiliations that serve as valuable corporate resources. Ruef, Aldrich, and Carter (2003) found that entrepreneurs with generally preferred ascribed characteristics had a greater ability to attract other team members when compared to those without these characteristics. If we extend this argument to the organization, it would suggest that the firms perceived to be of high status will be the most successful in attracting resources perceived to be the most valuable. Thus,

Proposition 1: As the status of the founding team increases, the firm's initial cognitive legitimacy and thus its initial likelihood of obtaining outside resources will increase.

Proposition 1 is displayed graphically in Figure 13.1.

Source of Organizational Status

There are many ways in which an organization's status can be determined. Higgins and Gulati (2006) used the affiliative status of the top management team (based on the financial success of their past employers) to serve as a proxy for organizational legitimacy. Burton, Sorensen, and Beckman (2002) used the founding team's biographical background as proxy for the expected success of the new enterprise. Thus, the affiliative status of the founding team was transferred from the individual- to firm-level at the time of founding and served as the initial status for the organization. Burton *et al*. (2002) inductively measured the status of the founding teams in their geographically bounded, but multi-industry, sample. Organizations that "generated" many entrepreneurs were considered more prominent.

To gauge an organization's initial status, the present researcher argue that the most relevant measure is industry-specific and based on the features of the founder that are deemed critical to expected success in the industry. These features may be the result of prior or current affiliations of founding team members to particular institutions, specific achievements that they have demonstrated, and/or ascribed characteristics of the team itself. Outside observers initially use the perceived quality of the industry-essential characteristics to attribute a level of status to the founding team. This categorization is particularly crucial where the uncertainty of the product, and thus the firm, is high.

The key point is that these factors will differ depending on the industry. For example, a law firm's success, in terms of both recruiting clients and future associates, is dependent on the affiliative status of the institutions from which its recent hires obtained their law degrees (Kim and Laumann, 2003). Among investment services firms, those companies that are viewed most favourably are those with the greatest number of analysts who have obtained achieved status by making the peer-nominated Institutional Investor's "All American Research Team" (Phillips and Zuckerman, 2001). Finally, in science-driven fields, achieved status is also important as the perceived scientific capability of the organization's employees and research partners is crucial to gaining resources (Darby, Liu, and Zucker, 1999). In each of these examples, the measure of status is highly specific to the industry and is of little relevance to the other industries highlighted. A founding team that is classified as high-status in one industry may be considered low-status in another industry.

In summary, one way that founding teams can gain organizational legitimacy is to highlight the industry-relevant status of their founding teams. Team-level industry status acts as a proxy for initial organizational-level industry status, and organizations with greater levels of industry status are expected to attract greater levels of resources. In the next two sections, the present researcher elaborate how lower-status organizations can also be successful in obtaining resources. To do so, they must capitalize on other features of their founding teams in order to augment the legitimacy of their firms.

Demographic Features

The second method by which founding teams can increase the legitimacy of their organizations and thus the ability to gain resources is to conform to investors' mental models of what attributes are held by effective founding teams. In essence, the teams, through highlighting their entrepreneurially relevant demographic features, increase their organizations' cognitive legitimacy. Following Beckman, Burton, and O'Reilly (2007, pp. 149–155), the present researcher utilizes the term demographic features instead of human capital because "demography theorizes about team composition and diversity in addition to the existence of any particular experience."

Previous industrial, management, and entrepreneurial experience are all important demographic determinants in one's success as an entrepreneur. Investors consistently consider industry experience to be a key predictor of new venture success (Hall and Hofer, 1993). Those with industry experience bring detailed knowledge about how the industry works, likely have a better understanding of customer demand, and may have previous experience growing a company in the industry (Boeker and Karichalil, 2002). Numerous studies have found support for the link between the founding team's prior industry experience and organizational performance. Examining a sample of high-technology firms founded in the Silicon Valley region of California, Cooper and Bruno (1977) showed that 80 per cent of high-growth firms were in a similar market as the founder had been in previously. Feeser and Willard (1990) found similar results for a mostly California-based sample of computer firms.

Prior management experience is a second demographic feature viewed by venture capitalists as an important component of the founding team (MacMillan, Siegel, and Subba Narishma, 1985). Also important is having a diverse or complete skill set. An experienced CEO adds diversity to a technology-based team and conveys confidence to stakeholders that administrative tasks will be completed and organizational demands will be managed (Wasserman, 2003). More broadly, diverse teams have been found to have improved strategic decisions, increased ability to handle complex situations, and better long-term firm performance (Gartner, 1985; Kamm and Nurick, 1993; Murray, 1989).

Prior founding experience is a fourth demographic feature considered beneficial to entrepreneurial teams. Many tasks associated with starting a new venture are unique to start-ups, tacit in nature, and can only be learned by doing (Shepherd, Douglas, and Shanley, 2000). The likelihood that inventors at the Massachusetts Institute of Technology founded a company based on their invention was greater when they had prior founding experience (Shane and Khurana, 2003), and the number of prior new ventures started by the CEOs of young technical ventures in the New York and New England region was significantly related to firm performance (Stuart and Abetti, 1990). Looking outside of the United States, Colombo and Grilli (2005) demonstrated that superior growth was correlated with prior entrepreneurial experiences among Italian firms.

A fifth demographic feature that potential resource providers view positively is prior joint work experience. Nahapiet and Ghoshal (1998) suggest that the creation of intellectual capital is increased through the shared language and vocabulary that comes from prior joint experience. In a study of work groups at a Midwestern contract research and development organization, teams with members who had previously worked on projects together completed their current projects faster than teams that did not have prior co-workers (Reagans, Zuckerman, and McEvily, 2004). Similarly, Eisenhardt and Schoonhoven (1990) demonstrated that joint work experience was positively related to organization growth in a sample of semi-conductor companies. More generally, individuals who have worked together in the past and are willing to work together again probably have stable relationships. Therefore, it is less likely a key member of the group will leave because of personal conflicts.

In short, having a diverse skill set, and prior industry, management, founding, and joint work experience can all positively influence firms' early abilities to gain resources, form strategic alliances, and succeed in the long term. Taken together, the present researcher refers to this set of characteristics as entrepreneurially relevant demographic features because the highlighted qualities are important to entrepreneurship irrespective of industry. Further, while having more features is advantageous for the team, the added value of one factor versus another is difficult to discern. For example, it is beneficial to have a founding team with business, technical and financial experience—or a diverse skill set—regardless of whether the team is starting a biotechnology company or a semiconductor firm. In the same way, people who have gone through the process of founding a company in the past will have a better idea of what is involved and will be beneficial in any founding situation. A team that has both a diverse skill set and prior founding experience should be better prepared than a team with just one of these skills. The added value of one factor versus another however is difficult to discern *a priori*. Thus,

Proposition 2a: The greater the number of entrepreneurially relevant demographic features among founding team members, the greater the firm's initial cognitive legitimacy and thus its initial likelihood of obtaining outside resources.

Proposition 2a is illustrated in Figure 13.1. While the present researcher expect there to be a generally positive relationship between a higher number of entrepreneurially relevant demographic features and an organization's overall legitimacy, the present researcher also expect the founding team's level of industry status to play an important moderating role.

Following the norm is most beneficial to those in the middle. To explain the relationship between status and entrepreneurially relevant demographic features of founding teams, the present researcher draw on the work of Phillips and Zuckerman (2001), which advances a long-standing theory that there is an inverted 'U'-shaped relationship between status and conformity. Conformity may entail certain behaviours, appearances, or attributes. For example, a teenager's peers will judge the coolness of his or her fashion choice, or firms will be scrutinized on the appropriateness of their service offerings. In turn, the present researcher argue that founding teams will be judged on the degree to which they appear to possess the characteristics required to successfully lead their new ventures.

Phillips and Zuckerman's key point is that the position on the status curve a person or organization occupies is not as important as the group to which she or he belongs. The institutions at the top of the hierarchy are secure in their spots and enjoy freedom to break the rules if they choose to do so. At the other end of the spectrum, the lowest-status individuals are also free to break the rules because they have little chance of advancement. In contrast, organizations in the middle find that competition is fierce, and must manage the fine balance between accepted and deviant activities or appearances. Thus, conformity to what is expected is most important for those who fall in the middle range of the status hierarchy. For example, Phillips and Zuckerman (2001) demonstrated that among law firms that introduced the low status practice of family law, only middle-status firms had a subsequent decrease in the quality of their new hires.

In the world of new venture creation, the highest industry status teams live off of their reputations, while the lowest industry status teams are deemed illegitimate from the beginning. Those middling in industry status, however, are scrutinized on the extent to which they look like a successful founding team. The more entrepreneurially relevant features they have the more likely they are to obtain resources. Thus,

Proposition 2b: Industry status will moderate the relationship between entrepreneurially relevant demographic features and the firm's initial cognitive legitimacy in an inverted 'U'-shaped such that the positive relationship between the two will be weaker at the lowest and highest levels of status.

Proposition 2b is displayed graphically in Fig. 13.1. The pop-out box in the top right corner shows how the strength of the relationship between demographic features and organizational legitimacy varies as status increases. The flat tails at the lowest and highest levels of status reflect Phillips and Zuckerman's (2001) comment about those at the top and the bottom being secure in their place and therefore not gaining any advantage from conforming. For certain, there will be demographically strong highest and lowest industry-status founding teams, but the presence of these features will not significantly increase their organizational legitimacy.

In summary, a second way that founder can gain organizational legitimacy is to highlight the entrepreneurially relevant demographic features of their founding teams. Teams that resemble perceived successful teams would establish greater cognitive legitimacy and thus resources for their organizations. Moreover, this relationship will be most important for founding teams who fall in the middle of the industry status hierarchy. Thus, an organization with a moderate level of industry status, but a demographically strong founder, is expected to obtain resources at a level comparable to higher industry status organizations, while one with a demographically weak founding team will face resource constraints similar to lower industry status teams. In the next section, the present researcher concludes the discussion of the framework depicted in Fig. 13.1.

Social Capital

The third aspect of a founding team's background that influences its ability to obtain resources is its prior social connections, or social capital. Social connections are widely recognized as an important means through which organizations can acquire legitimacy (Aldrich and Fiol, 1994). For example, in a study of start-ups in Indiana, the main source of help in assembling resources was the entrepreneur's social networks (Birley, 1985). Similarly, among Russian entrepreneurs in the post-Soviet era, those with greater revenues and profits had numerous acquaintances and were able to use rich and powerful contacts to gather financial resources (Batjargal, 2003). All else being equal, the person who is socially connected to the community from which he or she wants to gain resources will more easily be able to obtain the desired goods. In short, personal social networks are often the most valuable assets that founders can provide for their emerging firms (Hansen, 1995).

Since a firm does not start with its own network, during the initial founding stages the social network of the founding team is analogous to the firm's network (Hite and Hesterly, 2001). Powell *et al.* (1999) observed that intellectual and social ties formed as early as graduate school linked scientists across different organizational forms and facilitated collaboration. In addition, Burton *et al.* (2002) showed that founders who were formerly employed in well-connected firms were more successful at generating outside funding. Therefore, individuals may be able to directly capitalize on their prior work experiences to gain substantial economic benefits, measured by rates of growth, profitability, or survival (Podolny, 1993). Specifically,

Proposition 3a: As the number of organizations affiliated with members of the founding team increases, the firm's initial cognitive legitimacy and thus its initial likelihood of obtaining outside resources will increase.

Proposition 3a is also illustrated in Figure 13.1. While the present researcher expect there to be a generally positive relationship between the increasing social capital of the founding team and its overall legitimacy, the present researcher also expect both the founding team's level of industry status and number of entrepreneurially relevant demographic features to play important moderating roles.

Relying on friends is most beneficial to those at the bottom. Although all people and organizations benefit from having social connections, Boxman *et al.* (1991) found that only when human capital was low did social capital play an important role in the income attainment of Dutch employees. In other words, "actors can sometimes compensate for a lack of financial or human capital by superior 'connections' " (Adler and Kwon, 2002, p. 21). For example, Starr and MacMillan (1990) highlighted how a Cuban-American entrepreneur who lacked a reputation in the U.S. fashion industry was able to capitalize on the resources and strategic location of a college classmate to establish legitimacy through association. Similarly, Kalnins and Chung (2006) found that the least prosperous immigrant entrepreneurs in the Texas lodging business benefited the most from their connections to better-established ethnic peers. Turning to the social capital of founding teams the present researcher suggest,

Proposition 3b: Industry status will moderate the relationship between social capital and the firm's initial cognitive legitimacy such that the strength of positive relationship between the two will diminish as the level of status increases.

Proposition 3c: The entrepreneurially relevant demographic features of the founding team will moderate the relationship between social capital and the firm's initial cognitive legitimacy such that the strength of the positive relationship between the two will diminish with a higher number of demographic features.

As with the other propositions, these relationships are graphically illustrated in Figure 13.1. The two pop-out boxes at the bottom of the diagram show the changing strength of the relationship between the variables mentioned. The same argument about diminishing returns (and thus flattened tails) that was utilized in proposition 2b applies here. In addition, the same argument about the benefit versus the presence of these factors applies for social capital as it did for entrepreneurially relevant demographic features. Higher industry status and demographically strong founding teams are not precluded from relying on past social relations and likely do so, particularly if those prior affiliations are the most appropriate organizations with which to partner.

Taken together, the three sets of propositions provide a refined way of considering how industry status, entrepreneurially relevant demographic features, and social capital work in concert. The present researcher argue that organizations, along the industry status continuum, capitalize on different types of features of their founding teams' biographies in order to establish cognitive legitimacy and thus resources. Overall teams at the upper end of the status spectrum live off their reputations or great expectations for success, and obtain more outside resources than middle or low industry-status teams. While the venture teams that fall in the middle range of the status hierarchy are not taken for granted, they can augment their overall legitimacy by highlighting the entrepreneurially relevant demographic features of their founding teams. Those who are most successful should establish a level of legitimacy that is comparable to higher-status organizations. Finally, the lowest-status organizations as well as the demographically weak, middle-status organizations will use their social networks to build their organizations' legitimacy either through the process of endorsement or the direct solicitation of resources from members of their networks. In summary, an organization's initial "stock" of legitimacy may be composed of industry status alone, or industry status augmented by entrepreneurially relevant demographic features and/or social capital of the founding team.

Examples from the KVIC Units

Founder that understand the expectations for their industries and then play to their appropriate strengths will increase their probability of obtaining resources. Figure 13.2, which is meant to be illustrative, highlights the likelihood of firms obtaining resources based on the characteristics of their founder/founding teams. In this stylized version, as applicable to KVIC Schemes, decisions are black and white. If the founding team meets the criteria, they obtain their desired goods; if they do not, then they also do not secure sufficient resources. In reality, of course, decisions are rarely black and white. Thus, landing in either box should be seen as increasing or decreasing one's probability of resource obtainment rather than guaranteeing it. To connect this figure more clearly to Figure 13.1, the present researcher indicate which proposition has been used to determine the outcome at each decision point that leads to a final yes/no answer. For example, if a founder has a high level of industry status, then the decision to invest may be made on that basis alone, supporting proposition 1. Put differently, financial facilitators make up their minds to invest before they have evaluated the demographic features and social connections of the promoter, thus highlighting the interactions between status and the other variables described in propositions 2b and 3b. If the promoter is not among the highest status organizations in its industry, potential resource providers will evaluate the feasibility on its entrepreneurially relevant demographic features and/or its social connections.

To further build on this stylized portrait, the present researcher draw on several founding stories that illustrate the resource acquisition abilities of KVI unit backed founders with different types of career histories. KVI unit is an excellent business proposition in which to test this framework because of the general lack of objective criteria (e.g., a prototype) on which to judge a company at the time of founding. The stories and quotes that are described anonymously come from confidential interviews that the present researcher conducted with a small number of KVI unit founders in the Dibrugarh district area in June 2008 and the Tinsukia district area in December 2008. A total of 38 units were interviewed. These examples were selected because each succinctly describes a different pathway through the flowchart.

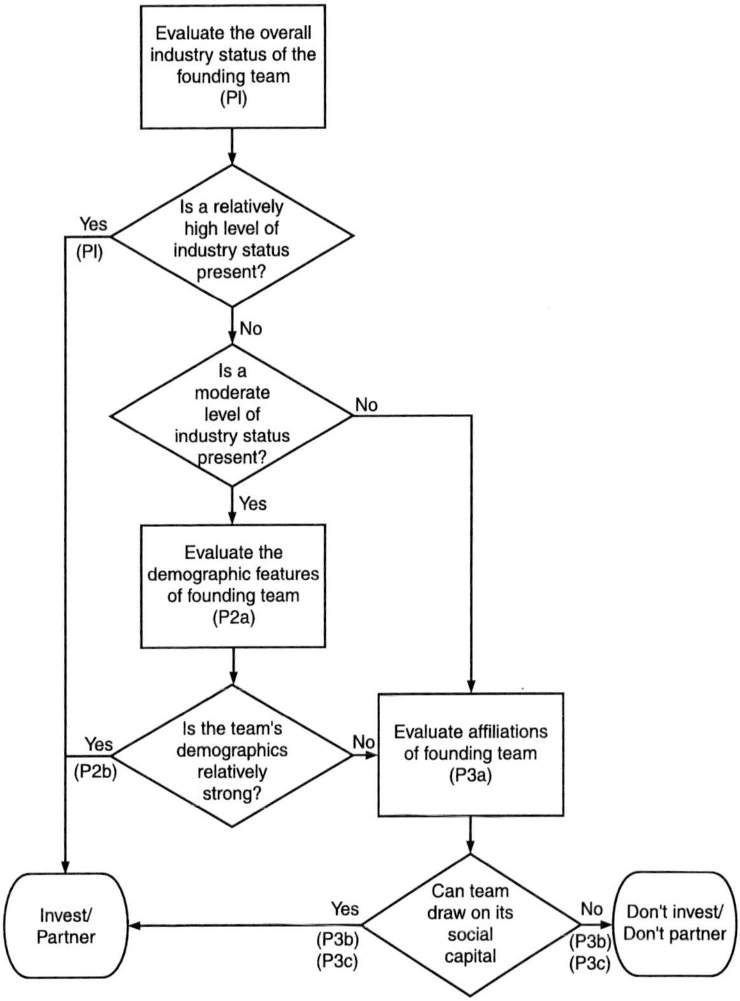

Fig. 13.2: Likelihood of Firms Obtaining Resources Based on the Characteristics of Its Founding Team.

In the first example, a founder, who was passed BA from a college in Dibrugarh district, described how he was financed through KVIC:

In the late 1980s . . . it seemed that the KVIC people, having satisfied itself that jute could be the basis for a company, discovered the jute bag industry in Assam. And I, and probably many other people who work on the industry, began to be visited by KVIC people. 'How would like to have a company?' I had never thought about it and I really had no experience with it.

Similarly, in 1986, a young enthusiastic employee at the tea estate firm, to found out a new concept in the Tinsukia area named Dolomite Spray. He may be treated as one of the researchers behind this innovative idea in this area. Mapping these scenarios onto Figure 13.2, the founders met the hurdle of having a high level of industry status. Therefore, the decision to invest and collaborate was clear, despite the overall lack of management and industry experience in each of the two cases described. This process of KVI actively recruiting the high-status researcher occurs in other technology-based industries as well (Timmons and Bygrave, 1986).

In contrast to the aforementioned businessmen, one founder of silk-based industry started her firm at the bottom end of the industry status spectrum. Not only did she lack an established track record of scientific achievements, she did not have an advanced scientific degree. She did, however, have close ties to KVIC and silk consulting firms with whom she had worked previously. In Figure 13.2 she failed the first two checkpoints, but was able to capitalize on her former relations to secure early financing for her firm (Conte, 1997; Glater and Barnum, 1992).

In-between the first two examples are business firms whose founding teams have some level of scientific ability, but the perceived quality of this ability is more difficult to determine as compared to their higher-status counterparts. As a result, groups that fall in the middle-level or low-level of the industry-status hierarchy are scrutinized on the extent to which they conform to the demographic features of generically successful founding teams. To that end, it is not surprising that a career aspirant attempting to found a firm on his own experienced substantial difficulty in searching for funds.

I spent the latter half of '98 and the first part of '99 developing the idea, writing a business plan, filing applications, and then going out and talking to various financers in the traditional sense. . . . I had one consultant who was helping me with a business plan, with financer's introductions, and presentations. I did that through the first quarter of '99. At that point, we had no success with the financer. So, I decided to back off from raising money, and basically did consulting work through [the firm he had founded] . . . [In early 2002 I] finished going through 30 or 40 firms, . . . who I identified as probably being interested in this kind of stuff. Unfortunately, again, no investors came out at the other end.

This middle industry-status founder was a career economist who held a MA (Economics), but his abilities were not taken for granted. Furthermore, he lacked almost all of the demographic features thought to be associated with winning founders. He also did not have a set of social connections that he could capitalize on to overcome his lack of entrepreneurially relevant demographic features. Therefore, he was unsuccessful in his initial attempts to secure resources for his firm.

Contrast to this person's lack of success, to another person who paired up with a friend who had previously founded two firms, *albeit* in different industries. As the friend explains, "I said, 'Sure I'll help you with this', I'll lend my expertise, my consulting expertise and everything to this project, and so we started the firm with help of KVI funding. Right away I put the manager in place, and the accountants, and kind of built the structure that I was used to building." The pair was successful in closing a seed round of financing through a financing of KVI. The KVIC and Bank people judged the team on the combination of their industry status and entrepreneurially relevant demographic features (one member had industry experience, the other had founding experience, and there was a diversity of skills between the two).

Discussion and Implications

The framework advanced in this article contributes to the field of entrepreneurship by taking three commonly studied aspects of entrepreneurial teams and consolidating them into a single argument. The dependent variable in the framework proposed is the acquisition of resources, whether it is employees, strategic partners, and/or financial assistance. Further, it is these types of resources that are particularly important to the survival and growth of KVI/new ventures, as opposed to other types of start-ups, which tend to be more commonly bootstrapped. The independent variables have all been used in prior research, thus many opportunities exist to empirically test this model against a variety of resources, such as initial funding, acquisition of employees, and formation of strategic partnerships. Of course, any empirical test of the model should control for other factors, such as technology and type of business, that also influence organizational legitimacy.

In recent years, organization theorists have devoted substantial effort to studying the role that top management teams play in firm outcomes and to companies' increased abilities to attract desired resources when they have prestigious partners (Davis and Greve, 1997; Michel and Hambrick, 1992). Few studies, however, have stepped back and asked whether there are events that lead to a diverse management team or the ability to attract high status partners. The present researcher would like to suggest here that much of what is known about firms in the present can be traced back to the characteristics of their founders. Specifically, the present researcher draw on sociological literature to demonstrate how something as simple as the transfer of founding team biographies to an organization's initial level of legitimacy can have an enduring effect on a firm's ability to obtain resources by utilizing the KVI experiences.

Once formed, first impressions are often difficult to change (Dougherty, Turban and Callender, 1994). For example, Merton (1968) showed that rewards and recognition accrue more rapidly in academic science to renowned researchers than to less well-known scientists doing similar work. Furthermore, the process was one of accumulative advantage: a young entrepreneur would get a break, perhaps in form of sponsorship from a pre-eminent entrepreneur. Freed to do more research, because grants allowed the entrepreneur to buy out teaching time, the young entrepreneur was able to progress more rapidly than his peer who did not receive sponsorship. In the corporate world, high-status organizations frequently maintain their high ranking because people want to work for these corporations. Thus, they are able to recruit abler and more productive employees than their lower-status counterparts (Goode, 1978). Previous research has found ample support for this pattern of "the rich getting richer" at the individual, university, and even national levels (Allison and Stewart, 1974; Bentley and Blackburn, 1990; Bonitz, Bruckner, and Scharnhorst, 1997; Owen-Smith, 2003).

Organizations that begin their lives resource-rich may also experience an extended period of adolescence (Fichman and Levinthal, 1991). Br derl and Schussler (1990) use the term "liability of adolescence" to suggest that just as children are evaluated less critically than adults, new organizations may also be given the benefit of the doubt with respect to performance. Moreover, they found that in a sample of German companies the length of an organization's adolescence was positively correlated to its initial endowment of resources.

These points emphasize how the initial composition of the founding team can set the organization on a particular trajectory that will have long-term benefits. Organizations with strong founding teams will be born with greater levels of legitimacy, which will allow them to gain larger initial endowments. Armed with these resources, they will be able to attract talented employees and partners, and use their extended period of adolescence to solve complex problems and develop saleable products or services. When the time comes for them to return to the market for resources, the progress that they have made may be greater than their lower industry status counterparts and they once again will be rewarded accordingly. Thus, characteristics of the founding team were important predictors of initial investment, which in turn was an important predictor of whether the company had an initial public offering.

Conclusion

Despite the importance of history in determining an organization's level of legitimacy (Suchman, 1995), few researchers have considered the existence of important underlying factors. In this paper, the present researcher would like to suggest that a company's legitimacy originates in large part from the past accomplishments and achievements of its founding team. This is particularly true for companies based on early stage methodologies, where both the technical and commercial successes of their products are largely unknown/unpopular at the time of founding.

The unquestioned legitimacy of the highest industry-status teams implies that they are able to draw on their prior reputations, while those lacking this benefit must either capitalize on different features of their group or demonstrate their abilities anew. The lowest industry-status firms are deemed illegitimate from the outset and therefore have difficulty securing resources. Freed from expectations, however, low industry status groups may choose novel or unconventional strategies, or depend on references (their social capital) to speak of their abilities. Finally, in addition to low and high industry status firms, some organizations are neither part of the "in" nor "out" group. Phillips and Zuckerman (2001) suggest that these companies are "middling in status" because they are located in a zone where competition is fierce and legitimacy cannot be taken for granted. For this group, increasing their legitimacy may mean highlighting their entrepreneurially relevant demographic features and if that is not sufficient, also emphasizing their social connections. Thus, it is the combination of the founding team's industry status, entrepreneurially relevant demographic features, and social capital that determines its initial level of cognitive legitimacy.

More broadly, the framework developed here builds upon the existing literature and addresses two issues important to entrepreneurial research: the transfer of individual-level characteristics to the firm level and the potential short- and long-term benefits of that initial transfer of legitimacy with the utilization of KVI experience.

REFERENCES

Adler, P.S. and Kwon, S. (2002). Social capital: Prospects for a new concept. *Academy of Management Review*, 27, 17–40.

Aldrich, H.E. and Fiol, C.M. (1994). Fools rush in? The institutional context of industry creation. *Academy of Management Review*, 19, 645–670.

Allison, P.D. and Stewart, J.A. (1974). Productivity differences among scientists: Evidence for accumulative advantage. *American Sociological Review*, 39, 596–606.

Audretsch, D.B. and Stephan, P.E. (1996). Company-scientist locational links: The case of biotechnology. *American Economic Review*, 86, 641–652.

Batjargal, B. (2003). Social capital and entrepreneurial performance in Russia: A longitudinal study. *Organization Studies*, 24, 535–556.

Beckman, C.M., Burton, M.D., and O'Reilly, C. (2007). Early teams: The impact of team demography on VC financing and going public. *Journal of Business Venturing*, 22, 147–173.

Bentley, R. and Blackburn, R. (1990). Changes in academic research over time: A study of institutional accumulative advantage. *Research in Higher Education*, 31, 327–353.

Berger, P.L. and Luckmann, T. (1966). *The social construction of reality*. New York: Doubleday.

Birley, S. (1985). The role of networks in the entrepreneurial process. *Journal of Business Venturing*, 1, 107–111.

Boeker, W.P. (1988). Organizational origins: Entrepreneurial and environmental imprinting at the time of founding. In G.R. Carroll (Ed.), *Ecological models of organizations* (pp. 33–51). Cambridge, MA: Ballinger Publishing Company.

Boeker, W.P. and Karichalil, R. (2002). Entrepreneurial transitions: Factors influencing success. *Organization Science*, 14, 149–172.

Bonitz, M., Bruckner, E., and Scharnhorst, A. (1997). Characteristics and impact of the Matthew effect for countries. *Scientometrics*, 40, 407–422.

Boxman, E.A.W., de Graaf, P.M., and Flap, H.D. (1991). The impact of social and human capital on the income attainment of Dutch managers. *Social Networks*, 13, 51–73.

Brüderl, J. and Schussler, R. (1990). Organizational mortality: The liabilities of newness and adolescence. *Administrative Science Quarterly*, 35, 530–548.

Burton, M.D., Sorensen, J.B., and Beckman, C. (2002). Coming from good stock: Career histories and new venture formation. In M. Lounsbury and M.J. Ventresca (Eds.), *Research in the sociology of organizations* (Vol. 19, pp. 231–264). Oxford: JAI Press.

Certo, S.T., Daily, C.M., and Dalton, D.R. (2001). Signaling firm value through board structure: An investigation of initial public offerings. Entrepreneurship Theory and Practice, 26(2), 33–51.

Colombo, M.G. and Grilli, L. (2005). Founders' human capital and the growth of new technology: A competence-based view. *Research Policy*, 34, 795–816.

Constant, A. and Zimmermann, K.F. (2006). The making of entrepreneurs in Germany: Are native men and immigrants alike? *Small Business Economics*, 26, 279–300.

Conte, L.A. (1997). *Shaman Pharmaceuticals* [SEC 10-K Form]. South San Francisco. Available at http://www.sec.gov/edgar.shtml.

Cooper, A.C. and Bruno, A.V. (1977). Success among high-technology firms. *Business Horizons*, 20, 16–22.

D'Aveni, R.A. (1989). Dependability and organizational bankruptcy: An application of agency and prospect theory. *Management Science*, 35, 1120–1138.

Darby, M.R., Liu, Q., and Zucker, L.G. (1999). Stakes and stars: The effect of intellectual human capital on the level and variability of high-tech firms' market values. *National Bureau of Economic Research Working Paper* 7201. Cambridge, MA: NBER. Available at http://www.nber.org/papers/w7201, accessed 11 May 2007.

Davis, G.F. and Greve, H.R. (1997). Corporate elite networks and governance changes in the 1980s. *American Journal of Sociology*, 103, 1–37.

Domhoff, G.W. (1967). *Who rules America*? Englewood Cliffs, NJ: Prentice-Hall.

Dougherty, T.W., Turban, D.B., and Callender, J.C. (1994). Confirming first impressions in the employment interview: A field study of interviewer behaviour. *Journal of Applied Psychology*, 79, 659–665.

Eisenhardt, K.M. and Schoonhoven, C.B. (1990). Organizational growth: Linking founding team, strategy, environment, and growth among U.S. semi-conductor ventures, 1978–1988. *Administrative Science Quarterly*, 35, 504–529.

Eisenhardt, K.M. and Schoonhoven, C.B. (1996). Resource-based view of strategic alliance formation: Strategic and social effects in entrepreneurial firms. *Organization Science*, 7, 136–150.

Ensley, M.D., Pearce, C.L., and Hmieleski, K.M. (2006). The moderating effect of environmental dynamism on the linkage between entrepreneur leadership behaviour and new venture performance. *Journal of Business Venturing*, 21, 243–263.

Feeser, H.R. and Willard, G.E. (1990). Founding strategy and performance: A comparison of high and low growth high tech firms. *Strategic Management Journal*, 11, 87–98.

Fichman, M. and Levinthal, D. (1991). Honeymoons and the liability of adolescence: A new perspective on duration dependence in social and organizational relationships. *Academy of Management Review*, 18, 442–468.

Finkle, T.A. (1998). The relationship between boards of directors and initial public offerings in the biotechnology industry. *Entrepreneurship Theory and Practice*, 22(3), 5–30.

Gartner, W.B. (1985). A conceptual framework for describing the phenomenon of new venture creation. *Academy of Management Review*, 10, 696–706.

Giordano, P.G. (1983). Sanctioning the high-status deviant: An attributional analysis. *Social Psychology Quarterly*, 46, 329–342.

Glater, J. and Barnum, A. (1992, June 17). A walk in woods for biotech San Carlos firm enlists rain forest medicine men in drug search. *The San Francisco Chronicle* (San Francisco), B1.

Goode, W.J. (1978). *The celebration of heroes: Prestige as a control system*. Berkeley, CA: University of California Press.

Hall, J. and Hofer, C. (1993). Venture capitalists' decision criteria in new venture evaluation. *Journal of Business Venturing*, 8, 25–42.

Hansen, E.L. (1995). Entrepreneurial networks and new organization growth. *Entrepreneurship Theory and Practice*, 19, 7–20.

Higgins, M.C. and Gulati, R. (2006). Stacking the deck: The effects of top management backgrounds on investor decisions. *Strategic Management Journal*, 27, 1–25.

Hite, J.M. and Hesterly, W.S. (2001). The evolution of firm networks: From emergence to early growth of the firm. *Strategic Management Journal*, 22, 275–286.

Kalnins, A. and Chung, W. (2006). Social capital, geography, and survival: Gujarati immigrant entrepreneurs in the U.S. lodging industry. *Management Science*, 52, 233–247.

Kamm, J.B. and Nurick, A.J. (1993). The stages of team venture formation: A decision making model. *Entrepreneurship Theory and Practice*, 17, 17–25.

Kamm, J.B., Shuman, J.C., Seeger, J.A., and Nurick, A.J. (1990). Entrepreneurial teams in new venture creation: A research agenda. *Entrepreneurship Theory and Practice*, 14, 7–17.

Kim, H.H. and Laumann, E.O. (2003). Network endorsement and social stratification in the legal profession. *Research in the Sociology of Organizations*, 20, 243–266.

Kimberly, J.R. (1980). *The lifecycle analogy and the study of organizations: Introduction*. In J.R. Kimberly, R.H. Miles and Associates (Eds.), The organizational lifecycle: Issues in the creation, transformation, and decline of organizations (pp. 1–14). San Francisco: Jossey-Bass Publishers.

MacMillan, I.C., Siegel, R., and Subba Narishma, P.N. (1985). Criteria used by venture capitalists to evaluate new venture proposals. *Journal of Business Venturing*, 1, 119–128.

Merton, R.K. (1968). The Matthew effect in science. *Science*, 159, 56–63.

Meyer, J.W. and Rowan, B. (1977). Institutional organizations: Structure as myth and ceremony. *American Journal of Sociology*, 83, 340–363.

Michel, J.G. and Hambrick, D.G. (1992). Diversification posture and top management team characteristics. *Academy of Management of Journal*, 35, 9–37.

Miles, R.E. and Randolph, W.A. (1980). *Influence of organizational learning styles on early development*. In J.R. Kimberly, R.H. Miles, and Associates (Eds.), The organizational lifecycle: Issues in the creation, transformation, and decline of organizations (pp. 44–82). San Francisco: Jossey-Bass Publishers.

Mills, C.W. (1958). *The power elite*. New York: Oxford University Press.

Murray, A. the present researcher. (1989). Top management group heterogeneity and firm performance. *Strategic Management Journal*, 10, 107–114.

Muzyka, D., Birley, S., and Leleux, B. (1996). Trade-offs in the investment decisions of European venture capitalists. *Journal of Business Venturing*, 11, 273–288.

Nahapiet, J. and Ghoshal, S. (1998). Social capital, intellectual capital, and the organizational advantage. *Academy of Management Review*, 23, 242–266.

Ostgaard, T.A. and Birley, S. (1996). New venture growth and personal networks. *Journal of Business Research*, 36, 37–50.

Owen-Smith, J. (2003). From separate systems to a hybrid order: Accumulative advantage across public and private science at research one universities. *Research Policy*, 32, 1081–1104.

Pfeffer, J. and Salancik, G. (1978). *The external control of organizations: A resource dependence perspective*. New York: Harper and Row.

Phillips, D.J. and Zuckerman, E.W. (2001). Middle-status conformity: Theoretical restatement and empirical demonstration in two markets. *American Journal of Sociology*, 107, 379–429.

Podolny, J.M. (1993). A status-based model of market competition. *American Journal of Sociology*, 98, 829–872.

Powell, W.W., Koput, K.W., Smith-Doerr, L., and Owen-Smith, J. (1999). Network position and firm performance: Organizational returns to collaboration in the biotechnology industry. *Research in the Sociology of Organizations*, 16, 129–159.

Reagans, R., Zuckerman, E., and McEvily, B. (2004). How to make the team: Social networks vs. demography as criteria for designing effective teams. *Administrative Science Quarterly*, 49, 101–133.

Reynolds, P.D. and White, S.B. (1997). *The entrepreneurial process: Economic growth, men, women and minorities*. Westport, CT: Quorum Books.

Riley, J. (1979). Testing the educational screening hypothesis. *Journal of Political Economy*, 87, 227–251.

Roure, J.B. and Madique, M.A. (1986). Linking prefunding factors and high-technology venture success: An exploratory study. *Journal of Business Venturing*, 1, 295–306.

Ruef, M., Aldrich, H.E., and Carter, N. (2003). The structure of founding teams: Homophily, strong ties, and isolation among U.S. entrepreneurs. *American Sociological Review*, 68, 195–222.

Sandberg, W.R. and Hofer, C.W. (1987). Improving new venture performance: The role of strategy, industry structure, and the entrepreneur. *Journal of Business Venturing*, 2, 5–28.

Schoonhoven, C.B., Eisenhardt, K.M., and Lyman, K. (1990). Speeding products to market: Waiting time to first product introduction in new firms. *Administrative Science Quarterly*, 35, 177–207.

Shane, S. and Khurana, R. (2003). Bringing individuals back in: The effects of career experience on new firm founding. *Industrial and Corporate Change*, 12, 519–543.

Shane, S. and Stuart, T. (2002). Organizational endowments and the performance of university start-ups. *Management Science*, 48, 154–170

Shepherd, D.A., Douglas, E.J., and Shanley, M. (2000). New venture survival: Ignorance, external shocks, and risk reduction strategies. *Journal of Business Venturing*, 15, 393–410.

Sine, W., Mitsuhashi, H., and Kirsch, D. (2006). Revising Burns and Stalker: Formal structure and new venture performance in emerging economic sectors. *Academy of Management Journal*, 49, 121–132.

Singh, J.V., Tucker, D.J., and House, R.J. (1986). Organizational legitimacy and the liability of newness. *Administrative Science Quarterly*, 31, 171–193.

Starr, J.A. and MacMillan, I.A. (1990). Resource cooptation via social contracting: Resource acquisition strategies for new ventures. *Strategic Management Journal*, 11, 79–92.

Stinchcombe, A.L. (1965). Social structure and organizations. In J.G. March (Ed.), *Handbook of organizations* (pp. 142–193). Chicago: Rand McNally and Company.

Stuart, R.W. and Abetti, P.A. (1990). Impact of entrepreneurial and management experience on early performance. *Journal of Business Venturing*, 5, 151–162.

Stuart, T.E., Hoang, H., and Hybels, R.C. (1999). Interorganizational endorsements and the performance of entrepreneurial ventures. *Administrative Science Quarterly*, 44(2), 315–349.

Suchman, M.C. (1995). Managing legitimacy: Strategic and institutional approaches. *Academy of Management Review*, 20, 571–610.

Teece, D.J., Pisano, G., and Shuen, A. (1997). Dynamic capabilities and strategic management. *Strategic Management Journal*, 18, 509–533.

Timmons, J.A. and Bygrave, W.D. (1986). Venture capital's role in financing innovation for economic growth. *Journal of Business Venturing*, 1, 161–176.

Wasserman, N. (2003). Founder-CEO succession and the paradox of entrepreneurial success. *Organization Science*, 14, 149–172.

Zimmerman, M.A. and Zeitz, G.J. (2002). Beyond survival: Achieving new venture growth by building legitimacy. *Academy of Management Review*, 27, 414–431.

14

Khadi and Village Industries in Assam : Problems and Prospects

P.C. DUTTA AND A. KHERKATARY

> In view of the meagreness of capital resources there is no possibility in the short run, for creating much employment through the factory industries. Now consider the household or cottage industries. They require very little capital with any given investment, employment possibilities would be ten or fifteen or even twenty times greater in comparison with corresponding factory industries.
>
> —*Gunnar Myrdal*

Introduction

Every effort towards the development of the country must begin with the development of villages. Every prosperity of a developing country like India is mainly dependent on integration of its agriculture with industry. It was recognized by the Government even at the time of the formulation of the First Plan which stated: Village industries have a central place in rural development programme. Diminishing opportunities for gainful employment account for the reduction of the standard of life of some sections of the rural population. Development outside the rural sector has not been rapid enough to arrest the increasing pressure of population on the land. The development of village industries should, therefore, be as much a matter of state action as the increase in agricultural production.

Consequently, the government has given priority to rural industries to create a healthy atmosphere for the all-round development of rural economy. More emphasis on rural development has been laid since the Fourth Plan and Slogan is, "If villages prosper, India prospers."

Industrial growth and development has been the much spoken phenomenon of the present day world. A country of a region can be said to be developed when both its primary and secondary sectors develop equally as well as simultaneously. It is said that the relationship between agricultural development and industrial progress is complementary to each other rather than competitive. Industrial growth in our country was not uniform throughout the plan period as it experienced a steady growth of nearly 8 per cent during first three plan periods with fluctuation subsequently.

Over the years, the production of khadi cloth has been on the decline. Hence employment in this area is also falling. However, production and employment in village industries have grown from Rs. 3,895 crore in 1997-98 to Rs. 7,140.52 crore in 2001-02 and new job creation has been reported. The main reasons for the poor performance in khadi production were (a) uncertainty over the continuation of the rebate policy for khadi, which upset the production schedule and output of khadi producers; (b) high stock of unsold khadi and mismatch in khadi production; (c) the project finance approach adopted in place of existing pattern approach for village industries units took the rural entrepreneurs sometime to get used to; and (d) there was a shortfall in availing funds from banks and budgetary resources.

The entire north-eastern region has been suffering from imbalance in industrial development which resulted in a widening gap between per capita income of the region and the country as a whole. Economic development of Assam as well as entire North East is not at all possible without an accelerated development in industrial sector as agriculture sector alone cannot make an impressive breakthrough. Handloom, Khadi and Village Industries of the state provide much scope for uplift of the rural economy. The state of Assam failed to attain its predominance in industrial background as it possesses less than 2 per cent of country's medium and large scale industries. Keen interest of investors from within and outside the state also throws light on significant improvement in industrial scenario of the State. A total of 2,7913 units of small scale industries in the State play a pivotal role in the network of industrialisation and generation of employment opportunities to solve the unemployment problem to some extent. For providing employment opportunities in rural areas and thereby strengthening the rural economy, Khadi and Village Industries (KVI) plays an important role. In order to have better implementation and monitoring of KVI programmes in NER, a zonal office of Khadi and Village Industries Commission (KVIC) has also been set up in Guwahati.

Jain (1975) advocates that rural industrialization is a weapon to minimize economic disparities between different population strata and different geographical areas. According to him, it is the best way to achieve balanced economic growth by which he meant, rural-urban development balance, agro-industrial development balance and regional development balance.

Dutta and Debnath (2009) emphasized that industry and agriculture are closely interrelated. They further emphasized the role of agro-industries in rural areas. They concluded that the establishment of agro-industries in rural areas may reduce the migration of people from rural areas to urban areas. These may also help in tackling the problem of exploitation of farming community by traders and middlemen. Further, income generation through agro-industries may improve the purchasing power of rural people, thereby creating potential for demand-based industries and increasing the standard of living of rural people. This will also help in generating employment opportunities.

Papola (1979) studied the structure, functioning and potential of rural industries covering 387 rural industrial units, belonging to 17 products categories in six blocks of Varanasi and Gorakhpur districts in eastern Uttar Pradesh. He found that the traditional activities requiring a negligible investment and yielding a very low income are undertaken by the landless backward caste people, whereas the new activities like oil products, food products, etc. which generate relatively high incomes and require a sizeable investment are shared by the intermediate and high caste people. He also found positive correlation between employment, investment and output not only in non-traditional manufacturing activities but also in traditional activities.

The state of Assam is predominantly rural and hilly in some areas. The topography of the region has largely shaped its economy. The State comprises of 27 districts and is situated in the north-east corner of India. Except for a narrow corridor running through the foothills of the Himalayas that connects the state with West Bengal, Assam is almost entirely isolated from India. According to 2001 census, the state has a total population of 26,638,407 with a density of 340 persons per sq. km. The literacy rate is comparatively high at 64.28 per cent with males constituting 71.93 per cent and females comprising of 56.03 per cent. The sex ratio is 932 females per thousand males. The state economy is primarily based on agriculture and oil. The state produces a significant part of the total tea production of the world and more than half of India's petroleum. It is ranked 14th in the Human Development Index which is the lowest among all the sub-project states. The performance of manufacturing and processing sector of the State has not been much encouraging in the scenario of State's economy. The contribution of this sector to the total NSDP has been estimated at 7.4 per cent at current prices and 7.2 per cent at Constant (1993-94) prices during 2003-04 (Quick Estimates). The Index of Industrial Production has moved up to 141.45 in 2003-04 from 132.37 in 2002-03.

The development of the region is intimately associated with the question of rural development. The rural-urban dualism may essentially be seen as the product of the failure of market mechanism. State intervention in favour of the rural sector is thus seen as a *sine-qua-non* for rural development. Rural Development has today become the most popular slogan of the policy-makers as well as the academic community. It is very complex phenomenon comprising myriad activities. The term Rural Development has been used differently at different times and in different contexts, so it is very difficult to give a universally acceptable definition of the term. Rural Development has two words – Rural and Development. Since the majority of population of Assam is living in rural areas therefore development of rural areas must receive much attention in the schemes designed for the development of State's economy. More precisely, economic policies of the state must be evaluated on their capacity to raise the economic condition of rural Assam.

In Assam where above 87 per cent of the total population live in rural areas and whose main source of livelihood is agriculture under such circumstances, from the strictly economic point of view, the most urgent problem of India in general and Assam in particular is the universal underemployment of the peasant. Integration of cottage industries with agriculture provides work to the farmers in their spare time and thus harnesses 'all the energies that at present run to waste.' In fact, these industries are best suited to the rhythm of rural life. These industries increase the income of the villagers and satisfy their basic requirements. They not only remove poverty and unemployment from the villages but also make the self-sufficient economic units.

Gupta (1982) studied the process of rural industrialization in the Punjab region comprising of Punjub and Haryana. His analysis covered almost all important categories of rural industries. He evaluated the programme and policies adopted by the governments of Haryana and Punjab to stimulate and bringing about a rapid growth of rural industries. The study also involved a case study of the achievement of the Rural Industries Projects Programme in Malerkotla in Sangrur district of the Punjab region. He analysed the performance of the project based on social benefit-cost ratios and Farell's index of technical efficiency and found that industries belonging to the "traditional sector" like wood products and agricultural implements show relatively high benefit-cost ratios but indicate low technical efficiency.

The common characteristic found in both - Khadi and Village Industries (KVI) is that they are labour intensive in nature. In the wake of industrialisation, and the mechanisation of almost all processes, Khadi and Village industries are suited like no other to a labour surplus country like India. Another advantage of Khadi and Village Industries is that they require little or no capital to set up, thereby making them an economically viable option for the rural poor. This is an important point with reference to India in view of its stark income, regional and rural-urban inequalities. The government has mustered courage to restructure the politically sensitive Khadi and Village Industries Commission (KVIC), through an amendment to the law to modernise the sector that provides over 76 lakh direct or indirect jobs.[1]

Khadi is Indian handspun and hand-woven cloth. The raw materials may be cotton, silk, or wool, which are spun into threads on a spinning wheel called a charkha. Khadi is a versatile fabric, cool in summers and warm in winters. Being a cruder form of material, it crumples much faster than other preparations of cotton. In order to improve the look, khadi is often starched to have a stiffer shape. It is widely accepted in fashion circles.

According to C.F. Andrews, the khadi industry does not claim to satisfy the economics of getting rich. "It offers an immediate, permanent and practicable solution of the problem of idleness." Regarding the same industry G.D.H. Cole observed—"Gandhi's campaign for the development of home-made cloth industry is no more mere fad of a romantic eager to revive the past, but a practical attempt to relieve the poverty; and uplift the standard of the village."

Mahatma Gandhi stressed the need for the development of khadi industry. Khadi to him was "the symbol of unity of Indian humanity, of its economic freedom and equality" and to Jawaharlal Nehru it was, "the livery of India's freedom." The khadi mentality means the decentralization of production and distribution of the necessaries of human life. Gandhi suggested a number of cottage industries that can be started in village. For example, gur making, basket making, rope making, broom making, oil pressing, etc. Above all, Gandhi gave priority to khadi industry. **Khadi is the sun of the village system.** Khadi, according to Gandhi, is the central industry on which all other village industries revolve. The employment of carpenters and blacksmiths engaged in the production of charkha or the spinning wheels, and of weavers, dyers and printers of the cloth depend upon the demand for khadi. Moreover, Gandhi related many religious and moral values to charkha.

The first Khadi Production Centre was established at Katiawad, Gujarat, Mahatma Gandhi used to refer to Khadi as "The livery of freedom". In fact, Khadi was introduced in 1920 as a political weapon and as the best instrument for giving concrete expression to the Swadeshi Spirit to boycott foreign goods. Khadi rendered an opportunity to every man, woman and child to cultivate self-discipline and self-sacrifice as a part of the non-cooperation movement.

India lives in its villages. Prosperity of India depends on the prosperity of its villages. Gandhiji gave the clarion call of Gram Swaraj and Antyodaya. Gram Swaraj is village self-sufficiency through strengthening and development of small cottage based industries. Antyodaya is economic prosperity and social upliftment of the people who are at the bottom of the social and economic pyramid.

After 1920, the events those contributed to the development of Khadi may be arranged chronologically. Development of All India Board under the Indian National Congress occurred in 1923. Gandhiji laid solid foundation for such initiative by establishing All India Spinners Association (Akhil Bharat Charkha Sangh) in 1925 and All India Village Industries Association in 1934.[2] Then in 1935, All India Village Industries Association (AIVIA) was formed. Govt. of Madras sought the advice of Gandhiji and set up a Department for Khadi in 1946. The post-independence period saw the Government of India and the Planning Commission assuring the responsibility of fitting Khadi and Village Industries within the framework. After the independence, in 1948, Govt. of India recognized the role of Rural Cottage Industries in the Industrial Policy Resolution, 1948. Constituent Assembly included Cottage Industries in Rural Areas among the directive Principles of the Constitution in Article 43. The post-independence period saw the Government of India and the Planning Commission assuring the responsibility of fitting Khadi and Village Industries within the framework of Five-Year Plans. Thus the ideas were elaborated in the First Five-Year Plan, which laid down the Policy framework for setting up of a body for Khadi and Village Industries. Central Govt. also recommended for setting up of a Board. In accordance with these recommendations, in 1953, Govt. of India set up All India Khadi and Village Industries Board (AIKVIB). It was decided, in the year 1955, that a statutory body should replace the Board. Accordingly, in 1956 Khadi and Village Industries Commission Act, 1956 was passed and as a result Khadi and Village Industries Commission came into being in the year 1957. Thus, Khadi and Village Industries Commission (KVIC) established under the Khadi and Village Industries Commission Act, 1956 (61 of 1956), is a statutory organisation engaged in promoting and developing khadi and village industries for providing employment opportunities in the rural areas, thereby strengthening the rural economy of the country. It took over the activities from the erstwhile All India Khadi and Village Industries Board with effect from 1st April, 1957. KVIC has been identified as one of the major organisations in the decentralised sector for generating non-farm employment opportunities in rural areas at low per capita investment.

Khadi and Village Industries Commission in its over 50 years of existence has helped in a remarkable way for the development of India particularly its rural populace. It has covered one-third villages of the country through various programmes providing earning avenues to millions of persons. Goods and services worth of Rs. 17,338 crore is being produced under KVI sector and its sales-turnover stood at Rs. 22,478 crore during 2008-09. The products of KVI sector are not only acclaimed in domestic market but also received tremendous response abroad as well. The natural eco-friendly products of KVI sector are most suitable for human consumption as these are totally organic and do not contain any harmful material.

The Jayanta Madhab Committee's Report looked into the causes of poor state of health for the enterprises under the Industries department.[3] The following were identified as the main causes :

1. Management failure in all fronts.
2. Inefficient financial management and control.
3. Lack of work culture and absence of systematic training programme.
4. Excessive overheads and overstaffing.
5. Inadequate/poor support system.
6. Non-availability of working capital.

Advantages of khadi and village industry:

1. It requires a very modest capital.
2. It is simple in operation.
3. It is a source of steady-income to agriculturists.
4. It is independent of monsoon conditions.
5. It is a perfect means of fighting famines.
6. It creates facilities for many allied industries.
7. It helps in the promotion of an equitable distribution of wealth.
8. It provides a solution to the problem of unemployment.

9. Through the development of KVI it is possible to reduce regional imbalance.

Need for development of KVI

1. The economic upliftment of the people of Assam especially in rural areas is possible only through the development of the KVI in these areas.
2. The development of KVI require not only for the mobilisation of local resources but also for creating adequate employment opportunities. These industries provide part-time and full-time employment to a large section of people.
3. Being labour intensive industries, it is highly necessary to develop in the state where there is paucity of capital and labour abundant.
4. These industries provide employment in workers' own place and their decentralized character has several advantages.
5. It helps in the promotion of an equitable distribution of wealth. We have, therefore, to support them on grounds of social welfare.
6. To reduce the regional imbalance it needs to establishment of KVI.

Keeping in view the importance of the subjects discussed above, the broad objective of the present study aims at examining the present status of Khadi and Village Industries of the state of Assam and its impact on over-all socio-economic development of the state. The study takes a special look at the development experiences of the khadi and village industries and their importance in rural economy of Assam and the various problems associated with these industries. However, special thrust has been given on government programmes and policies and their implementation. The study deserves the attention of the researchers, policy-makers and above all those who concern for the development of the state. The study is being made on the basis of published and unpublished statistical data and completed with viable suggestions.

Assam continue to make efforts for gearing up industrial activities with a view to create a strong industrial base by harnessing the un-tapped resources available in the State through various growth inducing factors besides taking steps for removal of existing infrastructure inadequacies. The Industries and Commerce

Department of the State as well as some other agencies like AIDC are closely associated with implementation of various promotional schemes meant for industrial development of the State. Despite various constraints a favourable industrial climate is gradually being created in the State as discernible from the increasing interest shown by investors of the State as well as from outside. The Index of Industrial Production in the State moved up to 141.45 in 2003-04 from 132.37 in 2002-03. The contribution of Manufacturing sector to the total economy was 7.4 per cent at current prices in 2003-04 which is however, not much encouraging. There are 55 Nos. of Khadi Production Centres, 57 Nos. of Sub-Khadi Production Centres in rural and remote areas of the both Plains and Hill Districts of the State.

Status of KVI

In the Tenth Plan, it was proposed to set up rural industrial estates and artisan clusters to provide necessary infrastructure and support services to the village industries. It was decided that developed land, power, water, common facility centres, training and skill upgradation centres, design and quality inputs and common packaging facilities would be provided at such clusters. The Common Facility Centres would be managed by the implementing agency for the industrial estate. Financial assistance would be provided to Common Facility Centres by KVIC or by agencies like the National Bank for Agriculture and Rural Development (NABARD), Small Industries Development Bank of India (SIDBI), Council for the Advancement of People's Action and Rural Technology (CAPART), etc.

The entire north-eastern region has been suffering from imbalance in industrial development which resulted in a widening gap between per capita income of the region and the country as a whole. Lack of development of North-East is experienced from apathy towards much publicised North-East Industrial Policy to which there was spontaneous response of entrepreneurs. So it is pertinent to review the industrial policy of the region which is trailing behind in all economic parameters. Economic development of Assam as well as entire North-East is not at all possible without an accelerated development in industrial sector as agriculture sector alone cannot make an impressive breakthrough.

The Khadi and Village Industries (KVI) sector has recorded a growth of 144.3 per cent over the period 1997-98 to 2003-04 as against the 71.6 per cent growth in total industrial production of the country for the same period. Production in this sector almost doubled to Rs. 9,682 crore in 2003-04 from Rs. 4,519 crore in 1997-98 as per Reserve Bank of India (RBI) estimates, Minister for Small Scale Industries, Govt. of India. As against the original Tenth Plan outlay of Rs. 2,950 crore for the Ministry of Agro and Rural Industries, an amount of Rs. 2,745.03 crore made available to it by the government in the first four years of the Tenth Plan (2002-03 to 2005-06) .

In order to extend the outreach of credit to this sector the government operated the Interest Eligibility Certificate Scheme (ISEC) through the Khadi and Village Industries Commission (KVIC). The Scheme provides bank loans to KVI units at subsidised rates of interest. In order that khadi products are able to compete with other products in the market, a Product Development Design Intervention and Packaging (PRODIP) scheme for improving designs and packaging has been launched by the government.

Present status of KVI in Assam

Khadi and Village Industries are an integral part of the economic life of an agriculturally-based poor state like Assam. As small industries take root, they go deeper in the life of people, extend work opportunities, raise income and standard of living of the people and bring about technical changes and a balanced and integrated rural economy. The Assam Khadi and Villages Industries Board has been given the responsibility to promote village and khadi industries in the state with a view to generate rural employment and to uplift the rural economy of the State. For this purpose, the board is financially supported by the Khadi and Village Industries Commission (KVIC), Government of India.

The Khadi and Village Industries Commission (KVIC) is a statutory body established by an Act of Parliament (No. 61 of 1956) as amended by Act No. 12 of 1987 and Act No.10 of 2006. In April 1957, it took over the work of former All India Khadi and Village Industries Board. As per information made available by the Khadi and Village Industries Board, Assam, a total of 56 bee-keeping centres, 521 oil extraction centres, 2184 pottery centres, 219 hand pounding centres and 1283 khandsari centres, 57 khadi production centres, 26 soap making centres, 5 cottage match factories, 189 footwear units, 15 hand made paper units, 832 cane and bamboo centres and 44 gobar gas plants were in operation in the state during 2002-03. These Khadi and Village Industries have always been a great source of employment, especially for the rural people in the state. But, during the last few years, downward trends have been observed in case of production and employment generation of these industries.

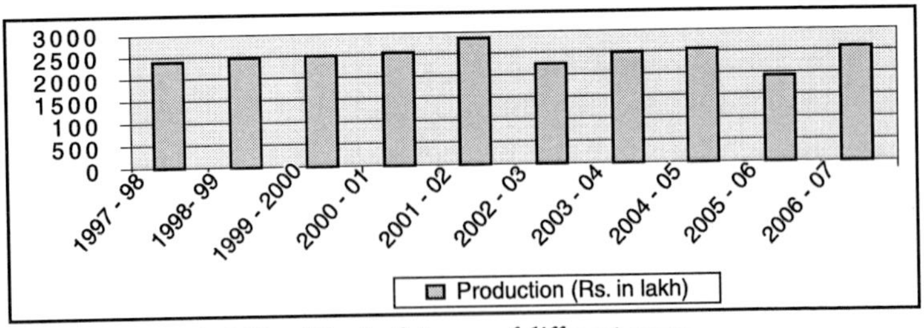

Source : Statistical Hand Book of Assam of different years.

Fig. 14.1: Khadi Production (Value in Rs. lakh) during the year 1997-2007

Fig. 14.1 shows the total value of production of Khadi and Village Industries achieved under Assam Khadi and Village Industries Board, Guwahati. The figure reveals the fact that the maximum production (Rs. 2,851 lakh) occurred in the year 2001-02 followed by Rs. 2,557 lakh and Rs. 2,521.96 lakh during the years 2006-07 and 2000-01 respectively while the lowest production of Rs. 1,935.65 lakh occurred in 2005-06.

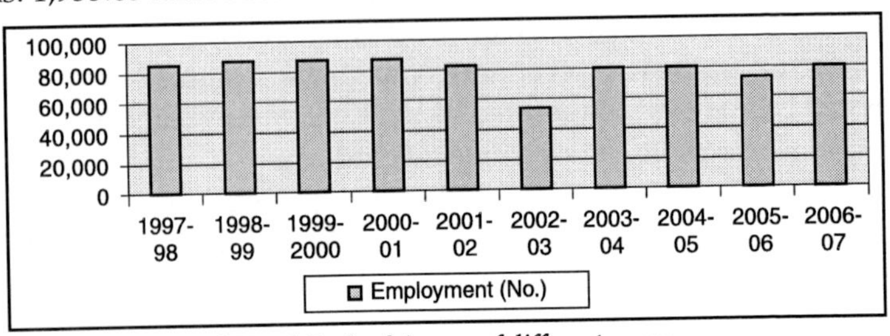

Source : Statistical Hand Book of Assam of different years.

Fig. 14.2: Employment in Khadi Production (Value in Rs. lakh) during the year 1997-2007

Total number of employment in Khadi production during the period 1997- 2007 is shown in Fig. 14.2. A close look at the figure reveals the fact that highest number of employment (88,360) occurred in the year 2000-01 followed by 87,440 and 86,900 in the years 1999-2000 and 1998-99 respectively and minimum (53,530) in the year 2002-03. It is important to note that the number of employment increased by 49.66 per cent in the year 2003-04 in comparison to its previous year (2002-03) while it decreased by 35.55 per cent in the year 2002-03 in comparison to 2001-02. However, the number of employment in the year 1997-98 was 85,630 which stood at 78,932 in the year 2006-07 showing a decrease by 7.82 per cent over the period 1997-2007.

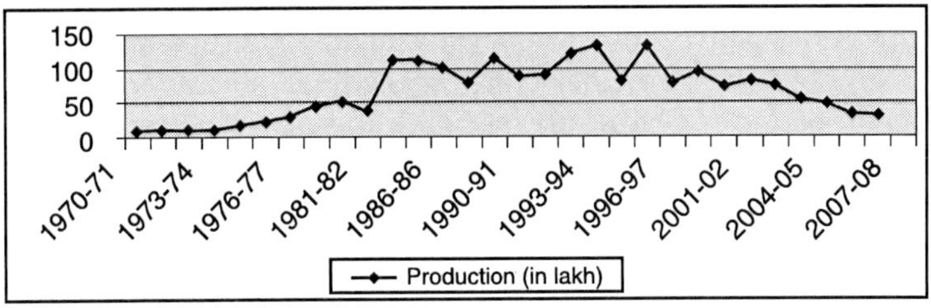

Source : Statistical Hand Book of Assam of different years.

Fig. 14.3: Total Production Value (Rs. in lakh) by Khadi Industries Board, Assam during the period 1970-2007.

Total Production Value (Rs. in lakh) by Khadi Industries Board, Assam over the periods 1970-2007 is shown in Fig. 14.3. It is striking to note that during the periods considered (1970-2007), production started with minimum value of Rs. 9.12 lakh in the year 1970-71 and reached the highest in the year 1993-94 (Rs.131.85 lakh) and 1995-96 (Rs.131.78 lakh) with ups and downs but after the year 2001-02 (Rs. 81.71 lakh), production gradually decreased and touched at Rs. 30.52 lakh in the year 2006-07. However, it is to be noted here that highest growth occurred in the year 1982-83 with 196.98 per cent over the previous year (1981-82). It is important to note that over the period of 37 years (1970-2007), total variation is of the tune of 59.49 per cent.

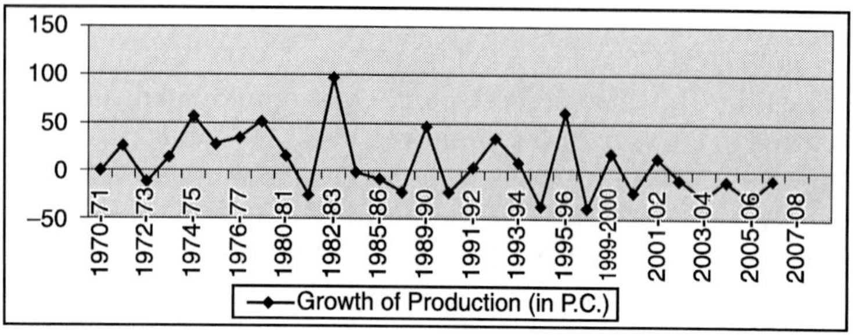

Fig. 14.4: Percentage Variation of Production over the years 1970-2007.

Thus, it can be seen that positive growth rate has been achieved in the State during the periods 1972-81 and 1990-94, so far as production is concerned while the periods 1982-88 and 2001-07 witnessed negative growth with many intermediate ups and downs.

Fig. 14.4 shows the percentage growth in value of production over the period of 37 years (1970 - 2007). The growth percentages are calculated from the secondary published data obtained from the Statistical Abstract and Statistical Hand Books of different years. A cursory view confirms the fact that during the period 1970-82, negative growth occurred only in the years 1972-73 (– 12.5%) and 1981-82 (– 25.61%) over the previous years. The figure reveals the fact that highest negative growth in production occurred in the years 1996-97 followed by 1994-95 and 2005-06 with (– 39.47%), (– 38.5%) and – 29.99 per cent respectively over the previous years. It is important to note that after 1995-96, the production value gradually decreased and reached at the level of Rs. 30.52 lakhs showing a total decrease of 76.84 per cent over the period 1995-2007.

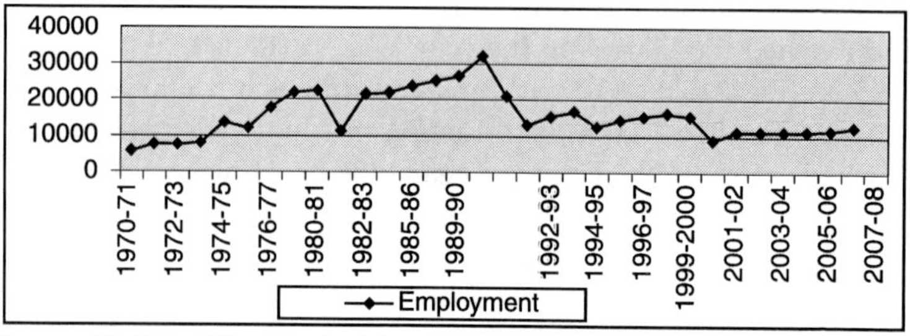

Source : Statistical Hand Book of Assam of different years and Statistical Abstract

Fig. 14.5: Total Number of Employment in Assam Khadi and Village Industries Board, during the period 1970-2007.

It is further to be noted here that highest positive growth in production (96.98%) occurred in the year 1982-83 followed by 61.34 per cent and 55.98 per cent in the years 1995-96 and 1974-75 respectively over the respective previous years. It is also to be noted here that the lowest positive growth occurred in the year 1991-92 (2.93%) and the lowest negative growth (– 2.23%) occurred in the year 1983-84 over the respective previous years. However, over the period 1970-2007, the production value increased by 234.65 per cent.

Fig. 14.5 shows the number of employment in Khadi industries under Khadi and Village Industries Commission in Assam for the periods 1970-2007. A close look at the figure confirms the fact that highest number of employment stood at 32,263 in the year 1989-90 followed by 26,358 and 25,223 in the years 1988-89 and 1987-88 respectively. It is remarkable to note that the number of employment in the base year 1970-71 was 5,363 which was the lowest strength of employment over the period 1970-2007. It is to be noted here that with respect to 1970-71, the number of employment increased by 501.58 per cent in the year 1989-90 and with respect to 1989-90, the number of employment decreased by 61.1 per cent in the year 2006-07 while over the total period of 37 years (1970-2007), the number of employment increased only by 134.03 per cent which is not a good sign.

Percentage growth of employment in Khadi Industries under Khadi and Village Industries, Assam for the periods 1970-2007 are shown in the Fig. 14.6.

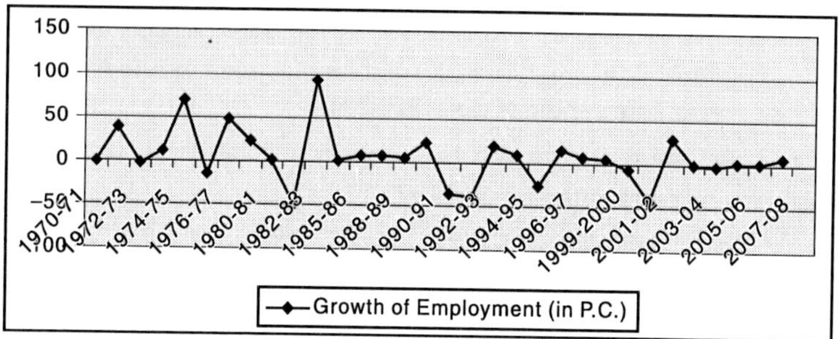

Fig. 14.6: Percentage Variation in Employment in Khadi Industries during the period 1970-2007.

With respect to the respective previous years, maximum growth in employment occurred in the year 1982-83 with 93.26 per cent followed by 69.57 per cent in 1974-75 and 48.98 per cent in 1976-77 while the minimum positive growth occurred in the years 1980-81 with 0.96 per cent followed by 1.66 per cent in 1983-84 and 2.18 per cent in 2005-06. It is to be pointed here that, with respect to previous years, negative growth occurred in the years 1981-82 with 50.19 per cent followed by – 42.4 per cent in 2000-01 and – 38.64 per cent in 1991-92. It is remarkable to note that during the period 1970-81, the number of employment increased by 315.77 per cent and decreased by 50.19 per cent in the following year (1981-82) but then again increased by 93.26 per cent in the year 1982-83 and it continued up to 1989-90 (highest peak) to reach the growth of 501.58 per cent with respect to 1970-71. A close look at the figure also reveals the fact that during the period 1989-2007, a negative growth occurred with 61.1 per cent and considering the whole period of 37 years (1970-2007), positive growth occurred with only 134.03 per cent.

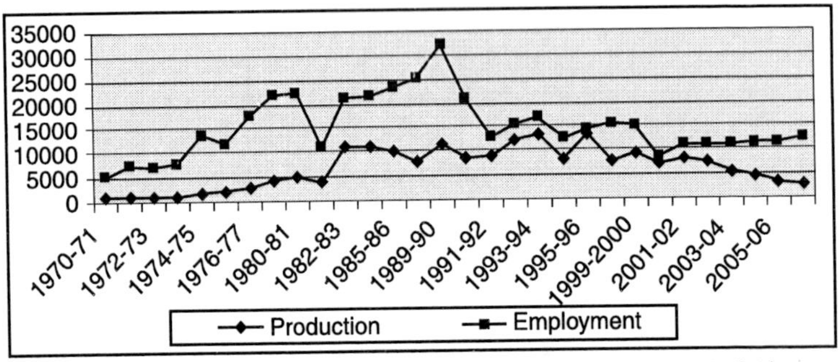

Source : Statistical Hand Book of Assam of different years and Statistical Abstract

Fig. 14.7 : Production (in '000) and Employment in Khadi during the period 1970-2007.

Fig. 14.7 shows both the production of Khadi (in '000) and Employment during the period 1970-71 to 2006-07.

A close look at the figure reveals that positive growth rates have been achieved in the years 1972-73 to 1980-81, 1991-92 so far as both production (in '000) and employment is concerned and witnessed negative growth during the period 2002-05.

Interestingly, negative growth rate has been achieved in the period 1980-90 so far as the employment is concerned while production (in '000) of Khadi witnessed positive growth during the same period.

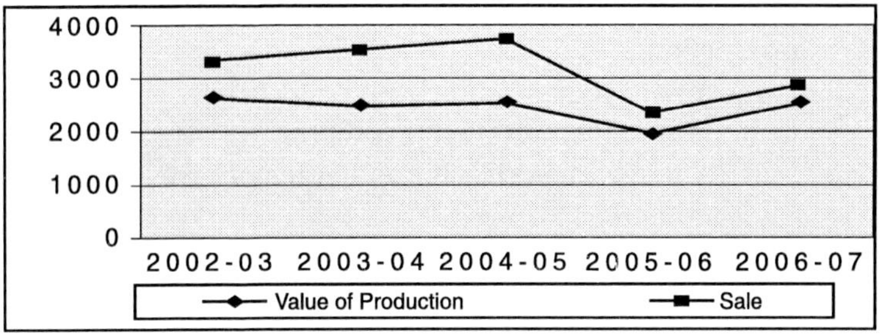

Source : Statistical Hand Book of Assam of different years.

Fig. 14.8: Achievement of Village Industries (Value of Total production and Total Sales) under Khadi and Village Industries Board, Assam during the period 2002-07.

The value of sales which was Rs. 3,314.6 lakh in the year 2002-03 increased to Rs. 3,738.43 lakh in the year 2004-05 and then gradually decreased in the subsequent years. On the other hand, the value of production was Rs. 2,651.66 lakh in the year 2002-03 which decreased in the year 2003-04 and then again increased in the year 2004-05 as shown in Fig. 14.8.

In recognition of the importance of traditional industries, since the era of planning in the country a series of measures were adopted. An industry which received highest official patronage all along these years is handloom industry as it is the oldest and largest traditional industries. Even in this era of liberalisation, the need to develop the industry is being articulated. The study is with reference to the handloom industry of Assam as the said industry in the state exhibits a high order performance compared to the rest of India. The Handloom Industry in the State of Assam has a long tradition in the socio-economic life of the people for supplementing the family income to a great extent and self-employment opportunities to lakhs of people of poor and downtrodden section of the society.

Problems

Despite its significant role Khadi and Village Industry in Assam is facing innumerable difficulties:

1. Due to ignorance and illiteracy, people connected with these

industries are using outdated tools and techniques of production.

2. For want of adequate and cheap finance these industries fail to modernize their production process.
3. Scarcity of raw materials is another major problem faced by these industries.
4. The absence of proper training facilities to the artisans compel them to adopt outdated methods of production.
5. Lack of proper marketing facilities also stand in the way of expansion of these industries in Assam.
6. Lastly these industries are facing tough competition from large scale industries.

Almost all types of industries are facing the problems in varying degrees. However, the main problems affecting KVI are infrastructural bottlenecks, underutilized capacity, shortage of raw materials, skilled artisans, low productivity and poor quality of products.

During the last 60 years, one important lesson has been learnt, i.e. Govt. cannot run industries profitably, except perhaps a few. The work culture and the motivation factors are different between Govt. and Private industries. Needless to say, Govt. machineries have not the mindset to work honestly and sincerely. Assam Khadi and Village Industries Board is in a severe financial crisis. It has 207 indigenous and 9,481 assisted production units, creating an employment potential about 1 lakh people. It is inefficiently managed even as it lacks appropriate support from Government and the Khadi Commission. The receivables are mounting. It has to professionalize its management with modern technology. With some financial input it could be turned around. On the other hand it can be treated as a welfare organization without having any powers of lending. Attention must be paid to recover the dues amounting to Rs. 26 crores. These recoveries can pay-off a major share of existing loan liabilities of Rs. 28 crores.[4]

Khadi and Village Industries Commission and its Role

The Khadi and Village Industries Commission is a statutory body formed by the Government of India, under the Khadi and Village Industries Commission Act of 1956. It is an apex organization, with regard to khadi and village industries within India, which seeks to "plan, promote, facilitate, organise and assist in the establishment and development of khadi and village industries in the rural areas in coordination with other agencies engaged in rural development wherever necessary." Its head office is based in Mumbai with its six zonal offices in Delhi, Bhopal, Bangalore, Kolkata, Mumbai and Guwahati. Other than its zonal offices, it has offices in 29 states for the implementation of its various programmes.

The Commission has **three main objectives** which guide its functioning. These are:

1. **The Social Objective**—to improve the living conditions of those engaged in this industry, especially the workers and manufacturers.
2. **The Economic Objective**—to help generate additional employment opportunities, encourage production of quality products acceptable to the export and domestic markets and facilitate reasonable returns to producers and exporters.
3. **The Wider Objective** — to create in active collaboration with all stakeholders, a self-reliant environment for healthy and sustainable growth of the industry.

One of the declarations in the National Common Minimum Programme of the Government was to revamp Khadi and Village Industries Commission (KVIC) through organisational restructuring of KVIC and initiation of measures to introduce modern management practices, in order to make khadi and village industry products competitive in the globalized economy while continuing to generate non-farm employment opportunities in rural areas.

Functions of the Commission

1. Subject to the provisions of this Act, the functions of the Commission shall generally be to plan, promote, organise and assist in the establishment and development of khadi and village industries in the rural area in coordination with other agencies engaged in rural development wherever necessary.
2. In particular, and without prejudice to the generality of the foregoing power, the Commission may take such other steps as it may think fit,— (a) to plan and organise training of persons employed or desirous of seeking employment in khadi

and village industries; (b) to build up reserves of raw materials and implements and supply them to persons engaged or likely to be engaged in production of handspun yarn or khadi or village industries at such rates as the Commission may decide; (c) to encourage and assist in the creation of common service facilities for the processing of raw materials or semi-finished goods and for otherwise facilitating production and marketing of khadi or products of village industries; (d) to promote the sale and marketing of khadi or products of village industries or handicrafts and for this purpose forge links with established marketing agencies wherever necessary and feasible; (e) to encourage and promote research in the technology used in khadi and village industries, including the use of non-conventional energy and electric power with a view to increasing productivity, eliminating drudgery and otherwise enhancing their competitive capacity and to arrange for dissemination of salient results obtained from such research; (f) to undertake directly or through other agencies studies of the problems of khadi or village industries; (g) to provide financial assistance to institutions or persons engaged in the development and operation of khadi and village industries and guide them through supply of designs, prototypes and other technical information for the purpose of producing goods and services for which there is effective demand in the opinion of the Commission; (h) to undertake experiments or pilot projects which in the opinion of the Commission are necessary for the development of khadi and village industries; (i) to establish and maintain separate organisations for the purpose of carrying out any or all of the above matters; (j) to promote and encourage cooperative efforts among the manufacturers of khadi or persons engaged in village industries; (k) to ensure genuineness and to set up standards of quality and ensure that products of khadi and village industries do conform to the said standards.

Khadi and Village Industries Board

With the liberalisation and globalisation of the economy and the removal of quantitative restrictions, the smaller units of the khadi and village industry sector are facing stiff competition. A large portion of India's population lives in the villages where illiteracy still prevails and large industry is not in a position to absorb the workforce from rural areas. In view of this, it is necessary to create more employment opportunities in villages by utilising local resources and skills so that rural people can get work in the villages itself.

Government of India has approved the introduction of a new credit linked subsidy programme called Prime Minister's Employment Generation Programme (PMEGP) by merging the two schemes that were in operation till 31.03.2008 namely Prime Minister's Rojgar Yojana (PMRY) and Rural Employment Generation Programme (REGP) for generation of employment opportunities through establishment of micro enterprises in rural as well as urban areas. PMEGP will be a central sector scheme to be administered by the Ministry of Micro, Small and Medium Enterprises (MoMSME). The Scheme will be implemented by Khadi and Village Industries Commission (KVIC), a statutory organization under the administrative control of the Ministry of MSME as the single nodal agency at the National level. At the State level, the Scheme will be implemented through State KVIC Directorates, State Khadi and Village Industries Boards (KVIBs) and District Industries Centres (DICs) and banks.

Rural industrial estates are proposed to be set up in the Tenth Plan to provide the required infrastructure and support services to village industries and artisan units. Growth of khadi cloth production was expected to be 8 per cent per annum in value terms during the Tenth Plan period. Employment in khadi industries was expected to increase at 3 per cent per annum and major efforts were taken to improve the quality and value of khadi production by focusing upon design inputs and improving the quality of khadi cloth. Anti-crease treatment for khadi cloth was achieved by technology tie-up with renowned laboratories and research institutions. Khadi institutions were strengthened to become economically viable by developing backward and forward linkages.

With a view to generating rural employment and developing rural economy, the Khadi and Village Industries (KVI) are promoted in the state by Khadi and Village Board with the financial support to Khadi and Village Industries Commission (KVIC) of India. The Assam Khadi and Village Industries Board has been implementing various village industries activities throughout the state through its 28 Departmental Training-cum-Production Centres and 73 Development-cum-Demonstration Centres in rural areas. The Board also has a marketing wing with 59 "Khadi Gramodyog Bhandars" located in various places of the state.

The Khadi and Village Industries Board have taken steps to liaise artisan and workmen to improve the quality and process of production. But considering the scope and necessity, the extension services have covered only a very small section of the weaves, artisans and craftsmen.

According to the Industrial Policy Statement of July 1980, "Government is determined to promote such a form of industrialization in the country as can generate economic viability in villages.... Handlooms, handicrafts, Khadi and other village industries will receive attention to achieve a faster rate of growth in the villages". The statement added that "while making all efforts towards integrated industrial development, it is proposed to promote the concept of economic federalism with the setting up of a few nucleus plants in each district, identified as industrially backward, to generate as many ancillaries and small and cottage units as possible". Also, "Policy regarding marketing support to the decentralized sector and reservation of items for small-scale industries, shall continue to be in force in the interest of growth of small-scale industries".

In the field of Khadi and Village Industries, various schemes are under implementation in the state. For the development of handicrafts industries in the state "Common facility centre" have been initiated for red glazed pottery at Barpeta, brass casting at Hajo, brass-bell metal at Sarthebary and dyeing of yarn at Sualkuchi. The Assam Khadi and Village Industries Board are running 20 training-cum-production centres in the state. Further, for the marketing of Khadi and Village Industries goods, the Board has been running 34 Khadi Bhandars in different commercial areas of the state.

It will thus be seen that so far as government policy is concerned, it covers practically every aspect of rural industries—

organizational, financing, imparting of training to artisans in modern skills, reservation of products, marketing and integration of rural industries development programmes with other programmes of rural development.

And yet it must be said that while a comprehensive policy covering practically every aspect of rural industries has been evolved over the years of various Five Year Plans, it is in the matter of effective implementation of well-defined policy that things are severely faulted.

The Union Government through the Ministry of Micro, Small and Medium Enterprises, provides funds to KVIC for undertaking its various activities under Plan and Non-Plan heads. The details of the funds provided from budgetary sources (both Plan and Non-plan) during the 10th Plan, are given in Table 14.1. The table reveals the fact that over the period under consideration, the amount of funds released has increased from 340.55 crore in 2002-03 to 589.82 crore in 2006-07 under 10th Plan showing an increase of 73.2 per cent over the plan period.

The total KVI production during 2007-08 (up to December 2007) is estimated at Rs.10,547.25 crore (Rs. 362.25 crore in Khadi and Rs. 10,185 in Village Industries) as compared to Rs. 10,325 crore (Rs. 339.50 crore in Khadi and Rs. 9,985.50 in Village Industries) in

Table 14.1: Budgetary Allocation and Funds Released During 10th Plan

(Rs. in Crore)

Year	*Budget Allocation (RE)*		*Funds Released*	
	Plan	*Non-Plan*	*Plan*	*Non-Plan*
2002-03	394.67	84.87	340.55	83.36
2003-04	444.75	83.75	423.60	63.70
2004-05	462.00	84.91	460.99	83.90
2005-06	560.82	84.82	558.56	84.76
2006-07	592.93	84.82	589.82	83.91
Total	2455.17	423.17	2373.52	399.63
2007-08*	650.40	84.82	479.59	62.10

Source: Annual Report of Khadi and Village Industries Commission, 2007-08.

2006-07 (up to December 2006), registering an overall growth of 2.15 per cent during the corresponding period. Sales also increased to Rs. 12,967.90 crore (Rs. 447 crore in Khadi and Rs. 12,520.90 crore in Village Industries) in 2007-08 (up to December 2007) as compared to Rs. 12,347.70 crore (Rs. 438.60 crore in Khadi and Rs. 11,909.10 crore in Village Industries) during the corresponding period of 2006-07, reflecting a growth of 5.02 per cent.

The total cumulative employment in the KVI sector is estimated to have increased to 88.92 lakh (8.84 lakh in Khadi and 80.08 lakh in Village Industries) during 2006-07 as against the previous year's level of 82.77 lakh (8.68 lakh in Khadi and 74.09 lakh in Village Industries), registering a growth of 7.43 per cent during the period. Further, the total cumulative employment in KVI sector is estimated to have increased to 94.85 lakh (9.00 lakh in Khadi and 85.85 lakh in Village Industries) during 2007-08 (up to December 2007) as compared to 85.22 lakh (8.77 lakh in Khadi and 76.45 lakh in Village Industries) persons during the corresponding period of 2006-07, thus registering a growth of 11.30 per cent.

The KVI sector recorded an improved performance during 2006-07 in comparison to the previous year. The total KVI production stood at Rs. 14,018.71 crore (Khadi - Rs. 491.52 crore and Village Industries – Rs. 13,527.19 crore) in 2006-07 as against Rs. 12,383.84 crore (Khadi - Rs. 468.30 crore and Village Industries – Rs. 11,915.54 crore) in 2005-06, registering an increase of 13.20 per cent. Similarly, sales of KVI products also increased to Rs. 17,562.40 crore (Khadi – Rs. 663.19 crore and Village Industries Rs. 16,899.21 crore) as compared to Rs. 15,276.02 crore (Khadi – Rs. 628.69 crore and Village Industries Rs. 14,647.33 crore), thus registering a growth of 14.97 per cent during 2006-07.[5]

Conclusions and Suggestions

Gandhi in his khadi scheme proposed the following measures to develop the khadi industry:

1. Compulsory introduction of spinning in all primary and secondary schools.
2. Cultivation of cotton in areas where it was not grown.
3. Organisation of weaving by the multipurpose cooperative societies.

4. All employees in the education and co-operative departments, municipal and district boards and gram panchayats should be required to pass a test in spinning, otherwise they may be disqualified.
5. Control of prices of handloom cloth woven of mill yarn.
6. Imposition of a ban on the use of mill cloth in areas where the handwoven cloth was in abundance.

Integration of the promotional programmes in the sector with other area development programmes and adoption of a cluster approach, particularly for the traditional industries.

Restructuring of the organizational base at the district level to make it more effective and result-oriented.

Development of appropriate technologies and skills; their effective extension and transmission.

Accelerated flow of institutional funds specially in favour of artisans, village industries and "tiny" units and rationalization of the interest rate structure;

Organisation of producer-oriented marketing both within and outside the country.

Selective reservation of items for exclusive production and purchase from the cottage and small industries;

Strengthening and extension of co-operative form of organisation, particularly for the cottage and tiny units;

Building up of a sound data base to facilitate proper policy formulation and evaluation.

Prospects for growth and expansion of KVI exists in Assam subject almost to removal of infrastructural problems.

As technology development in advanced industrialized countries may not be suitable for small KVI in poor countries, encouragement will have to be given to foster indigenous research and development. Technological improvement must aim at production of goods of basic necessities at the lowest cost. Because of the increased number of unemployed and underemployed, it may not be possible to go in for capital intensive technology. But nevertheless there is scope for adoption of low valued simple machine to improve efficiency of production.

Research is also necessary to evaluate market potentiality in the neighbourhood, within the state, in the country and abroad.

Through publicity and advertisement, exhibition, display , etc. the market for the products of KVI can be expanded.

"Modernisation Packages" will have to be evolved to suit the requirements of KVI including all aspects to raise productivity and reduce drudgery. It will be government's endeavour to ensure that the process of modernization percolates down to KVI.

Every effort is to be made for gearing up industrial activities by removing infrastructural inadequacies. Apart from these, improvement in credit delivery system is very crucial for the development of industrial sector of the state as finance is considered as the 'life force' of industry. Revival of sick industries of the country in general and the state of Assam in particular is also a crying need of the hour. Despite Government initiative to take over management of some industrial undertakings and to provide management support and financial assistance, sick industrial units of the country failed to revive effectively. Looking at this dismal scenario Industrial Reconstruction Bank of India was set up to revive potentially viable industries.

Village Industry clusters should be taken up under the NPRI to increase production as well as employment generation in these clusters. The cluster development programme will certainly visualize the establishment of backward and forward linkages, setting up of common facility centres and common service network support for satellite cluster units.

The State Government should naturally consider the social and economic advantages at the various methods of production and decide which of them will extend employment, raise the standard of living of the masses and bring about equitable distribution of our national economy. Having taken these decisions, we should protect these industries against machine competition. As the National Planning Committee observed "large-scale mechanized industries which compete with those cottage and rural industries which are specially selected by the state for support, must be owned to control by the state, so there may be proper co-ordination between the two."

NOTES

1. T.V. Sriram, April 01, 2009 , Economic Service, PTI.
2. Ruby T. Sharma, Khadi and Village Industries Commission – Popularising Khadi , Posted by NVO News on December 15th, 2009.
3. Report of the Advisory Committee on Industries, August 1996.
4. Recommendation of the COFR made in its report of December 2001.
5. Annual Report, 2007-08 , Khadi and Village Industries Commission.

Source of Data : Statistical Abstract-1978 and Statistical Hand Book of Assam of different Years, 1980-2008.

REFERENCES

Papola,T.S.(1979): Studies on Development of Uttar Pradesh, Rural Industrialisation: Issues and Evidences, Giri Institute of Development Studies, Lucknow, *GIDS Occasional Paper*, Vl.-I

Jain, O.P. (1975): *Rural Industrialisation*, Commercial Publication Bureau, New Delhi.

Dutta,P.C. and Debnath, A.(2009):Socio-Economic Development In Rural Assam: Problems And Prospects , in *Village Development in North East India (New Approaches)* (ed.) K. Singha, Concept Publishing Company, New Delhi.

Gupta,D.B.(1982): *Rural Industry in India—The Experiencing of the Punjab Region*.

15

Khadi and Village Industries in Assam

DULAL BISWAS AND BIMAN KUMAR NATH

Khadi and Village Industries (KVIs) are an integral part of the economic life of a poor state like Assam. Hand woven cloth from hand spun yarn is known as khadi. With a view to generate employment opportunities in rural areas KVIs are being implemented in eight states of north-eastern region under Rural Employment Generation Programme (REGP) for village industries. As KVIs take root, go deeper in life of the people, extent work opportunities and local initiatives and help in utilizing the idle manpower in rural areas for producing locally available raw materials by adoption of simple and primitive technology.

Sonitpur district at a glance: This paper deals with the present scenario of KVIs in Sonitpur district of Assam. Sonitpur district is situated in the north bank of Brahmaputra valley of Assam. According to 2001 census, total number of population of the district were 16,77,874 with 1693 villages. A good number of rural areas necessarily reveal the importance of khadi and village industries in the region.

Brief history of KVI: Indian economy is predominantly a rural economy since time immemorial. As per 2001 census, 72.2 per cent of the population lives in about 6,38,000 villages. This fact was well-understood by the freedom fighters in the first half of the 20th century. Consequently our father of nation, M.K. Gandhi cultivated the seeds of khadi industries in different parts of the nation. Gandhian technique of khadi (hand spun cotton cloth) and charkha (spinning wheel) got utmost importance when he visited the state in 1921. In those days Assamese women folk were vigorous with their art of weaving in leisure time. The preparation of 'kavach-kapor' during the days of Ahom rule proved the genius of Assamese weavers. There was a common belief that in case of person going to the battle field possessed this type of cloths, he would obviously win in the battle. The use of 'Aana-kata-kapor' by the bridegroom at the time of marriage is also associated with beliefs in the society. In due course of time khadi and village industries came into existence by the government effort to boost rural development.

Status of KVIs in Sonitpur district of Assam: The state of Assam has 57 numbers of khadi production centres and 59 numbers of sub-khadi production centres. They are located in rural areas of both plain and hill districts of the state. Sonitpur is a plain district of Assam where only one khadi production centre and four outlets (bhandars) are presently working. Following activities are practiced in the KVI institutions of Assam:

(a) Ghani oil
(b) Soap
(c) Village leather
(d) Pottery
(e) Bee-keeping
(f) Agarbatti (incense sticks)
(g) Silk khadi
(h) Honey etc.

The above activities are generally implemented by the district headquarters located mostly in state capital.

Marketing and production: Every KVI board works within a particular framework as directed by KVIC, Government of India. In the marketing wing of KVI the employees get a stipulated salary as per State Government rules. They have been employed only for selling the products but there is no fixed target of selling. Under such circumstances the work culture is deteriorated and KVIs shift their goal from 'no profit' to 'no loss'.

So far as the production is concerned, ghani oil (mustard oil) has got tremendous importance. Demand always exceeds its supply in case of ghani oil. Comparatively other products of khadi are in a precarious condition. This mustard oil is processed and produced in Dhekiajuli (28 kilometres far from Tezpur town) production centre with pure mustard purchased from the market. However, this khadi production centre was suffered from sickness till 2006 for manpower shortage. Presently it has been recovered and three employees are engaged in production. The shortage of manpower is an unique obstacle in Sonitpur district which is hindering its development. National flags, bedcovers and some silk khadi (endi, muga etc.) products are available in the four outlets. But most of the cloths are lying idle in the outlets for its high price and lack of strategic marketing. That is why the commission should reorganize its selling by reducing the price per unit ignoring its damages.

The large population of district is not aware to the pureness of khadi products for which most of them are consuming some piggyback and inferior goods. Therefore some consumer friendly strategies should be implemented in this sector. The sickness factor is not a new one in case of khadi production. It is worthwhile to mention that there was one pottery and terracotta industry located in Jamugurihat of Sonitpur district. But this small scale rural industry suffers from inadequate infrastructure for which it turns into a forest place.

Awareness camps: Proper implementation of government programmes in KVI sectors mostly depend on the district officer and other officials. Under Prime Ministers Employment Generation Programme (PMEGP), a fifteen day's Entrepreneurship Development Programme (EDP) have been launched. Rural unemployed youth who desire to work in village industries. Required financial assistance is allocated for the programme. Secondly, a block level Bee-Keeping project is to be initiated in KVI sector in Sonitpur district in association with DIC (District Industries and Commerce). The district authority informs that at least 200 unemployed youth will be trained within 2009-10. The prime motive of Awareness camp is to popularize PMEGP and to educate potential beneficiaries in rural, semi-rural and urban areas about the scheme. Preferences are given to the unemployed men and women with focus on special categories.

Extension of activities: In order to build khadi and village industries as one of the premium sector, there should be extension of its activities. As Khadi and Village Industries Commission (KVIC) is very concerned about adherence to standard norms of quality in its products, activities should be extended by taking into account of the fact.

Research and Development: Research and Development is a necessary precondition for making competitive and self-sustaining Khadi and Village Industries. Indian Institute of Technology (IITs), Indian Institute of Management (IIMs) and such type of bright institutions can be provided the task for research and development work.

Women empowerment through SHGs: The Self Help Groups (SHGs) in this regard have also an important role to play. A considerable women population of the state involved in SHGs producing diversified items. It reveals that under REGP, the SHGs can be an indispensable part of the economy if they are, also engaged in khadi production. The state of Assam is a hub of various ethnic identities. Each ethnic group has their unique potentiality of producing items for village industries. In that situation if all of them can be engaged in their production of consumer durables, the problem of communal crisis and identity assertion will be removed instantly.

Export Potentiality: As an industrial segment, the KVIC can be engaged in export of indigenous items. Once foreigners feel the pureness of KVI products, the processed items will be largely demanded by them. In such a situation the domestic capital formation and inclusive economic growth is inevitable.

KVI is one of the crucial segments of industrial structure of an economy which is evident from the current economic slowdown. 10 per cent of the annual budget is earmarked to the north-eastern region by Khadi and Village Industries Commission (KVIC) out of Rural Employment Generation Programme (REGP) as per directives of the Government of India.

The North-Eastern Region (NER) is facing an economic turbulence to the tune of Rs. 1,000 crores from recent economic turmoil which might have been more and more if the region was fully globalised. Under such circumstances, it can be mentioned that the khadi and village industries with indigenous technology and local manpower is untouched from such slowdown. Heavy concentration of rural areas and agricultural workers are essential ingredients of developing khadi and village industries.

Moreover, the Chief Minister of Assam, Mr. Tarun Gogoi states that economic development of the state can only be strengthened with rural development. Therefore, annual budget of the state have given more emphasis on the development of rural areas in every segment of infrastructure.

REFERENCES

Barua, Dr. B.K. (1969): "A Cultural History of Assam (Early period)" (Vol. I), Anmol Publication, New Delhi.

Chowdhury, P.C. (1966): "The History of Civilization of the People of Assam to the Twelfth Century A.D", Spectrum Publication, New Delhi.

Desai, V. (2003): "Management of a small-scale industry", Himalaya Publishing House, Delhi.

"North-Eastern Region Vision 2020" (Volume 1), Ministry of Development of North-Eastern Region and North-Eastern Council.

Paul, R.R. (2004): "History of economic thought", Kalyani Publishers, Delhi.

Roy, B.B. (1998): "Elements of History", Bina Library, Assam.

SECTION - IV
Entrepreneurial Development

16

Micro and Small Enterprises in North-Eastern Region

J. U. AHMED

Introduction

Micro and Small Enterprises (MSEs) are considered to be one of the principal driving forces in economic development. The importance of this sector is well recognized world over from its significant contribution in gratifying various socio-economic objectives, such as higher growth of employment, output, promotion of exports and fostering entrepreneurship. Micro, Small and Medium Enterprises (MSMEs) including khadi and village industries/rural enterprises constitute an important segment of Indian economy in terms of their contribution to country's industrial production, exports, employment and creation of an entrepreneurial base. The MSMEs sector contributes significantly to the manufacturing output, employment and export of the country. It is estimated that in terms of value, the sector accounts for about 45 per cent of the manufacturing output and 40 per cent of the total exports of the country. The sector is estimated to employ about 42 million persons in over 13 million units throughout the country. Further, this sector has consistently registered a higher growth rate than the rest of the industrial sector. There are over 6000 products ranging from traditional to high-tech items, which are being manufactured by the MSMEs in India. It is well known that the MSMEs provide the maximum opportunities for both self-employment and jobs after agriculture. Recognizing the contribution and prospects of the sector, the definitions and coverage of the MSE sector were broadened significantly under the Micro, Small and Medium Enterprises Development (MSMED) Act, 2006 which recognized the concept of 'enterprise' to include both manufacturing and service sector besides, defining the medium enterprises.

The North-Eastern Region (NER) of India has abundant of natural resources. These resources can be utilized for all-round economic development and employment generation in the region. The Ministry of MSME is actively promoting the development of Micro, Small and Medium Enterprises in the NER through the programmes and schemes implemented by the Ministry and its organizations. Pursuant to the government policy of allocating 10 per cent of the total funds for NER, under the Schemes/Programmes of Ministry, an outlay of Rs. 179 crore has been earmarked exclusively for the region. Khadi and Village Industries Commission (KVIC) have undertaken various programmes in north-east to ensure better implementation and monitoring of Khadi and Village Industries (KVI). The KVI programmes are being implemented through state KVI Boards, registered institutions, cooperative societies and entrepreneurs. Apart from this various schemes under implementation in the NER include Prime Minister's Employment Generation Programme (PMEGP); Scheme of Fund of Regeneration of Traditional Industries (SFURTI); schemes relating to KVI activities and schemes relating to promotion of coir and coir products. With this backdrop an attempt has been made in the proposed paper to examine the performance of MSEs in NER of India.

Literature Reviewed

The industrialization as a source of employment and capital accumulation has been recognized by various economists. There exist a number of studies dealing with different aspects of MSEs in India. Here is a glimpse of works done by various authors on the growth and performance of MSE sector.

Keynes (1936) propounded that entrepreneurs will offer the amount of employment which maximizes their output and profit. Here he stressed the productivity of labour as the determining factor of the level of employment. There is a positive relationship among productivity of labour, output and employment. The Village and Small Scale Industries Committee Report (1955), popularly known as

(Karve Committee) realizes the necessity of introducing better techniques in the village industry, so that they can keep pace with the progressively expanding economy and do not become unsuitable tomorrow. The promotion of small scale industries has been widely recognized as one of the most appropriate means of developing industry in developing countries, which are facing mounting pressure of population, an acute shortage in ingestible capital funds, and lack of entrepreneurial and managerial abilities (Bharti, 1978). The National Committee on Science and Technology Report on Khadi and Village Industries (1975) gave a gloomy picture of these industries as a source of employment in industrialization. The report shows that the compounded rates of growth of employment in these industries, as compared to growth of output, are very meagre. Prasad (1983) in his study found that the small scale industrial sector is an integral part of not only the industrial sector, but also of the country's economic structure as a whole.

The Small Scale Sector (SSI) has vast potential in terms of creating employment and output, promotion of export, expansion of base for indigenous entrepreneurship and dispersal of industries and entrepreneurship skills in both rural as well as backward areas. Desai (1983) also stated that rapid industrialization in India depends on the growth of small scale industries. Nayak Committee (1992) found that banks have insufficiently serviced the working capital needs of the small sector particularly that of cottage and tiny enterprises. There is a need for the setting up of specialized bank branches for small scale industries, the absence of which has led to serious bottlenecks. Abid Hussain Committee (1997) has suggested for proper institutional arrangements, policies and programmes for meeting long-term and short-term requirements of the small scale Industries. Mali (1998) in his study has observed that Small and Medium Enterprises (SMEs) and micro enterprises have to face increasing competition in the present scenario of globalization, they have to specifically improve themselves in the fields of management, marketing, product diversification, infrastructural development, technological upgradation.

The SSIs can play an important role in the development of hills areas as revealed by Hamid (1989) in the study of Jammu and

Kashmir. In his study he found that the state of Jammu and Kashmir is not ideally suited for developing large scale industries and as such the only remedy lies in the establishment of small scale and cottage industries, which are most suited to the socio-economic condition of the state. Pande (1983) explained few causes that attributed to the slow growth of SSIs in hill areas. The small industrial units in the village area and sub-urban localities suffer from a considerable degree of technological obsolescence, inadequacy of raw materials, shortage of marketing channels, unawareness of market situation in urban centres, poor credit facilities and the shortage of skilled labour and power supplies. Khanka (1998) in his study observed that the development of Small Scale Industries in Assam is at low level because of inadequate infrastructural facilities, problems of finance, marketing and insurgency. The study recommended for infrastructural facilities like transport, communication, power, energy etc.

Owing to the predominance of agricultural background of the region, Agarwal (1999) pointed out that the infrastructure for industrial development has not developed properly. Apart from lack of industrial tradition and managerial class, the state is handicapped by difficult terrain and disturbed socio-political conditions are also adversely affecting industrialization in the state. Thangmawizuala (1985) opinioned that the political disturbances especially the insurgency in Mizoram caused a great setback in the progress of industrial development in the state. He highlighted that the existing small and cottage industrial units could not make the desired progress due to the disturbances.

Dasgupta (1983) suggested that if labour intensive SSIs are established, they will provide some alternative economic opportunities to the people in the hill areas of the region as the improved cultivation with multiple cropping is difficult proposition in this area. According to Devi (1995) industrial development is a pre-condition for the economic development of an underdeveloped region. She is of the opinion that industrial development in general and development of small scale and cottage industries in particular is bound to play an active role in connection with the economic development of an underdeveloped state, like Manipur. Indian Institute of Entrepreneurship, Guwahati (2001) conducted a study on the performance of SSIs in Greater Guwahati area. The study revealed that large number of SSI units (30 %) in the study area did not avail any financial assistance from banks or any other financial institutions. State Bank of India is the major moneylender to the small sector followed by the United Bank of India, Assam Financial Corporation etc. All other financial institutions played more or less the same role i.e. providing loan to only 1 per cent to 3 per cent of units by each bank.

Cassar and Holmes (2003) investigated the determinants of capital structure and use of financing for small and medium enterprises in Australia. The study empirically examined the firm characteristics including: size, asset structure, profitability, growth and risk. The study suggested that asset structure, profitability and growth are important determinants of capital structure and financing of SMEs. Deb (2004) in a case study recommended that the financial institutions should minimize the procedural formalities in granting financial assistance to the modern small units as far as practicable. The instance of the financial institutions should be on viability of the project rather than on security offering capacity of the entrepreneurs. Misra and Panigrahy (2005) examined the working capital position and its management in selected paper manufacturing units with statistical and financial techniques. The paper established that there is a significant relationship between the working capital management and profitability of a firm. Kawadia, Dashmishra and Bargal (2005) attempted to examine the factors affecting employment productivity of small sector in Indian context and observed that industrial sector in general and small enterprises in particular are be to exposed to meet the International competitive environment. Subrahmanya (2005) examined implications of globalization and domestic economic liberalization in small-scale industries and analyses its growth performance in terms of units, employment, output and exports. He concluded with policy recommendations to ensure the sustenance and competitive growth of SSIs in India.

Saleh and Ndubisi (2006) examined the role of SMEs in different sectors as well as their major contribution to the economy of Malaysia. They found that the Malaysian SMEs still face many domestic and global challenges in achieving economies of scale and competing internationally. The challenges are the low level of technological capabilities and limited skilled human capital resources, a low level of technology and ICT penetration, low levels of research and development etc. Sophia and Baskaran (2007) studied on the capacity utilization and financial support in small sector. They found that even though the units get adequate credit to install a higher capacity, the cash flows have always limited to the working capital and consequently utilization as well.

Raj and Mahapatra (2009) studied on the growth and productivity performance of small manufacturing enterprises in India. He identified a few lacunas and found that the capacity utilization, manpower problem and other strategic issues etc. are the major deterrent for productive performance of this sector. Rai (2009) observed that the MSE sector has been accorded special status and importance in the Five-Year Plans since inception in view of the advantages it offers for better utilization of resources of capital and skill at the local level. Biswas and Chakraborty (2008) studied on the performance of MSMEs depending on their sources of technological know-how and estimated separate Cobb-Douglas production functions according to different sources of technology. The role of public sector R and D institutions has been found to be not so significant in bridging the technology gap. The study underscores the need for supplying better and effective technology to the MSMEs to help them tide over global competition.

The above studies have been found severely inadequate to explain the real phenomenon of industrialization in NER due to the reason that no major attention have been given by these studies to this particular aspect of MSEs. Moreover, because of its unique geographical location and its poor infrastructure, the policy recommendations that are applicable to other parts of the country may not necessarily be suitable for the region.

Recent Policy Reforms for SME Sector in India

In order to expand a dynamic MSEs sector in India, various measures and schemes have been launched from time to time. Some of the major policy reforms are highlighted below:

- A single comprehensive legislation for the promotion, development and enhancement of the competitiveness of the MSME sector i.e., Micro, Small and Medium Enterprises

Development (MSMED) Act, 2006 came into effect from October 2006.

- National Manufacturing Competitiveness Council (NMCC) was set up to energize and uphold the growth of the manufacturing industry. New promotional package for MSMEs, and focus on accelerating development of clusters.
- The revised strategy of lending and introduction of newer measures, such as the scheme to establish Small Enterprises Financial Centres (SEFC) for strategic alliance between branches of banks and SIDBI located in 388 clusters identified by Ministry of SSI.
- The SME fund of US $ 2.27 billion has been operationalized. The proposal for doubling the credit flow to MSME sector in next 5 years.
- Promotion and financial support for credit-cum-performance rating in MSME sector in India, to facilitate greater and easier flow of credit from the banking sector to SMEs.
- The National Commission for Enterprises in the Unorganized Sector (NCEUS) has been set up as an advisory body and a watchdog for the informal sector to bring about improvement in the productivity of these enterprises for generation of large scale employment opportunities on a sustainable basis, particularly in the rural areas.
- Facilitation of technology transfer through the Technology Bureau for Small Enterprises (TBSE).
- The Scheme of Fund for Regeneration of Traditional Industries (SFURTI) was introduced.
- Guarantee coverage under Credit Guarantee Fund for Small Enterprises (CGFSE) expanded substantially.
- Credit Linked Capital Subsidy Scheme for Technological Upgradation.
- In KVI, two new schemes have been launched namely Workshed Scheme for Khadi Artisans with a view to providing assistance for construction of workshed for khadi artisans for ensuring better work environment and the scheme for enhancing Productivity and Competitiveness of Khadi Industries and Artisans to assist 200 khadi institutions to make khadi industry competitive, market

driven and profit oriented through replacement of obsolete and old machinery and equipment.

Objectives of the Study

NER is bestowed with rich natural— forest and agricultural resources. Most of the state's wealth lies untapped yet, and these could provide a strong base for industrial development. Despite enormous latent potentialities for setting up of various resource-based industries, no significant progress could be achieved in the field of industrialization in the state. With a view to bring about sustained and balanced regional development of this region, the present paper aims to study the performance of MSEs in the region over the years.

The Position of MSE Sector at National Level

The MSE sector has maintained a higher rate of growth *vis-a-vis* the overall industrial sector as would be clear from the comparative growth rates of production for both the sectors during last six years as incorporated in the Table 16.1. The contribution of MSE to total industrial production was around 38.5 per cent and in Gross Domestic Product (GDP) was around 6 per cent during 2002-03 to 2007-08.

Table 16.1: Comparative Growth Rates and Contribution in GDP

Year	*Growth Rate of (in per cent)*		*Contribution of MSE (in per cent) at 1990-2000 prices in*	
	Overall Industrial Sector	*MSEs Sector*	*Total Industrial Production*	*Gross Domestic Product (GDP)*
2002-03	5.70	8.68	38.89	5.91
2003-04	6.90	9.64	38.74	5.79
2004-05	8.40	10.88	38.62	5.84
2005-06	8.10	12.32	38.56	5.83
2006-07	11.5	12.60	38.57	5.94
2007-08	8.00	13.00	nil	nil

Source: Govt. of India, Ministry of Micro, Small and Medium Enterprises, Annual Report 2008-09.

The MSME sector contributes significantly to the manufacturing output, employment and exports of the country. It is estimated that in terms of value, the sector accounts for about 45 per cent of the manufacturing output and 40 per cent of the total exports of the country. Table 16.2 presents the performance of MSEs in respect of number of units, amount invested, production, employment and exports in India. It is observed that the number of units of MSEs has been increased but percentage increase over previous year has remained the same i.e., 4.07 per cent during the period. The amount of investment in MSEs has also been increased from Rs. 1,62,319 crores in 2002-03 to Rs. 2,38,975 crores in 2007-08. The investment has recorded a significant growth over previous year. But the problems that experienced by these industries is that the capital base of these industries is usually very weak. The initial investment of these units mainly comes from their own fund or borrowed fund from unorganized sectors like friends, relatives and professional lenders. Much lesser proportion of required investment comes from organized sectors like banks, financial institutions and government channels. This apart small loans can be raised from government agencies but the procedure is so cumbersome that most of the entrepreneurs hesitate to avail these facilities due to their poor educational level.

The production of MSEs has been mounting which recorded an increase to Rs. 6,95,126 crores in 2007-08 from Rs. 3,15,850 crores in 2002-03. The number of persons employed in MSE sector in India has also been increasing. The sector has been doing well in export portico. Hence, it may be inferred that the MSE sector has been accorded special status and importance in the economy. This is because of the fact that a number of policy initiatives introduced over the years viz., MSMED Act, 2006, various programmes of KVIC, Skill Development Programmes (SDP), Entrepreneurship Development Programmes (EDP) etc. The enactment of the MSMED Act, 2006 is sure enough a reflection of the Government of India's commitment for the growth and the development of SMEs in India.

Table 16.2: MSEs Performance: Units, Investment, Production, Employment and Exports

Year	*Nos. of Units (in lakhs)*	*Fixed Invest-ment (Rs. in crores)*	*Production at 2001-02 prices (Rs. in crores)*	*Employment (nos. in lakhs)*	*Exports (Rs. in crores)*
2002-03	109.49	162317	315850	260.21	86013
	(4.07)	(5.16)	(11.54)	(4.36)	(20.73)
2003-04	113.95	170219	364547	271.42	97644
	(4.07)	(4.87)	(15.78)	(4.31)	(13.52)
2004-05	118.59	178699	429796	282.57	124417
	(4.07)	(4.98)	(17.90)	(4.11)	(27.42)
2005-06	123.42	188113	497886	299.85	150242
	(4.07)	(5.27)	(15.83)	(4.44)	(20.76)
2006-07	128.44	213219	585112	312.52	177600
	(4.07)	(8.67)	(17.53)	(4.23)	(24.54)
2007-08	133.68	238975	695126	322.28	NA
	(4.08)	(12.08)	(18.80)	(3.12)	

Note: (Figures in the parentheses indicate percentage growth over previous year).
Source: Govt. of India, Ministry of Micro, Small and Medium Enterprises, Annual Report, 2008-09.

Performance of MSE Sector in North-Eastern Region

The economy of North-east India has got its definite identity due to its peculiar physical, economic and socio-cultural characteristics. This region consists of eight states viz., Assam, Arunachal Pradesh, Manipur, Meghalaya, Mizoram, Nagaland, Tripura and Sikkim. The NER of India covers an area of 2.62 lakh sq. km. It accounts for 7.9 per cent of total geographical area of the country. With a total population of 39 million as per 2001 census, it accounts for 3.8 per cent of total population of India. Arunachal Pradesh lies to its north and Sikkim a little away in the north-east bordering China and Bhutan. Bangladesh and Myanmar lie to its south-west and east. The torrential Brahmaputra deposits its rich alluvial deposit along the banks of the plains of Assam. The tropical rain forest, rich in flora and fauna, spread their arms across Arunachal Pradesh into Assam. The western side of the north-east is connected to the eastern part of the Indian sub-continent by a narrow land corridor, sometimes referred to as the Siliguri Neck or Chicken's Neck. The eight states that comprise the region reflect ecological and cultural contrasts between the hills and the plains; there are also major elements of continuity. The available medieval and modern records indicate interdependence and interaction between the hills and plains. The north-east is one of the most bio-diverse regions in the world. The forest cover varies but average 65 per cent is government owned. The village communities, individuals and chiefs own the rest. The area can be divided into three geographical divisions viz., the Shillong Plateau, the North-eastern Hill Basin and the Brahmaputra Valley.

The region has plenty of natural resources and these resources can be utilized for all-round economic development and employment generation in the region. The Ministry of MSME is actively promoting the development of MSEs in the region through various plans and programmes implemented by the various organizations. The number of MSE units, fixed investment, production and employment in the north-east during 2004-08 has been incorporated in Table 16.3.

Table 16.3: Number of MSE Units, Fixed Investment, Production and Employment in NER

Year	Nos. of Units (in number)	Fixed Investment (Rs. in crores)	Production (Rs. in crores)	Employment (in number)
2004-05	356002	2749.9	7412.0	881052
2005-06	370903	2935.5	8822.3	922743
	(4.18)	(6.74)	(19.02)	(4.73)
2006-07	385890	3289.0	10368.0	981096
	(4.04)	(12.34)	(17.52)	(6.32)
2007-08	402209	3746.2	12318.3	1010210
	(4.22)	(14.20)	(18.81)	(2.96)

Note: (Figures in the parentheses indicate percentage growth over previous year).

Source: Govt. of India, Ministry of Micro, Small and Medium Enterprises, Annual Report, Various issues.

It is observed that the number of units of MSEs has been increased from 3.56 lakhs in 2004-05 to 4.02 lakhs in 2007-08. The percentage increase of units over previous year also experienced a higher face while compared with national growth scenario. The change in 2007-08 over 2006-07 was 4.22 per cent in the region as against 4.08 per cent at all-India level. In the same line, the investment in MSEs has also experienced a notable improvement, the figure being increased from Rs. 2,749.9 crores to Rs. 3,746.2 crores during the same period. During 2007-08, the region has experienced (14.2 %), a higher increase in percentage over previous year than the national level of 12.08 per cent in investment over previous year. This may be due to various measures and schemes that has introduced by the government particularly in NER. In the production front too, MSEs are performing better than any other region. This is reflective from the growth scenario of production in the region. Although the employment in MSEs sector has been increased during 2004-05 to 2007-08, the growth position in this particular variable is not impressive. The average number of employees in each unit is 2.51 in the region while the same is only 2.41 at national level as on March 2008.

The state-wise analysis of performance of MSEs indicate that Assam is holding the major chunk of MSEs activities in the region in terms of number of units, amount of investment, production scenario and employment front during the period under consideration. This may be due to immediate advantage of demonstration effect, geographical spread and locational reward of the state. Keeping in view the present raw-material potency, the states like Meghalaya, Arunachal Pradesh and Mizoram experienced a very low investment in MSEs sector. Interestingly, the isolated state Sikkim has a very negligible investment, the amount being only Rs.17 crores in 2007-08, and thereby the sector has offered employment opportunity to only 1,828 persons. Table 16.4 presents the state-wise performance of MSEs in the region.

Table 16.4: State-wise Performance of MSEs in NER

Sl. No.	Name of the State	No. of Units (in number)		Fixed Investment (Rs. in crores)		Production (Rs. in crores)		Employment (in number)	
		2004-05	2007-08	2004-05	2007-08	2004-05	2007-08	2004-05	2007-08
1.	Assam	219092	246980	1287.4	1733.1	4907.0	8155.1	487871	556896
2.	Meghalaya	25383	28851	164.5	224.1	481.0	799.8	75608	87397
3.	Tripura	27448	30772	329.3	423.6	461.0	765.4	62861	70774
4.	Mizoram	12529	14242	139.9	188.7	207.0	343.6	28622	32984
5.	Manipur	54101	60625	403.7	529.5	703.0	1168.5	153715	173663
6.	Nagaland	15823	18653	378.6	583.5	540.0	897.0	66466	81608
7.	Arunachal Pradesh	1411	1614	34.2	46.7	60.0	115.2	4330	5060
8.	Sikkim	415	472	12.6	17.0	44.0	73.7	1580	1828
Total		**356002**	**402209**	**2749.9**	**3746.2**	**7412.0**	**12318.3**	**881052**	**1010210**

Source: Govt. of India, Ministry of Micro, Small and Medium Enterprises, Annual Reports 2005-06 and 2008-09.

Hindrances of Micro and Small Enterprises

The troubles offsetting MSEs can broadly be divided into internal and external. The internal problems are those which are not influenced by external forces; mainly crop up from within the industry and can be controlled internally. The external problems on the other hand, are those which are the outcome of external factors and are beyond the control of a particular unit. The availability of power, communication and other infrastructural facilities etc. are examples of external problems while organizational structure, production, distribution, management, training etc. are internal problems. Most of the internal problems coupled with external problems put a major threat to the smooth functioning of the MSE units. The internal problems of MSEs are given below:

- Most of the MSEs belong to individual proprietorship form of organization. The owners come with personal egos and ideas, proprietarily attitudes and ineffective delegation.
- To a large extent the development of the MSEs units depends on the attitude, audacity and spirit of the owners which in turn influenced by personal and family requirements.
- There is a lack of expertise, professionalism and planning and the dealings are informal. The emphasis is on short-term gain even at the cost of quality.
- There is no logical reasoning, proper career plan and strong motivation. Pay scales are generally lower, goodwill and job security is absent.
- In many cases, business ideas and exposures are not up to date and adequate, rules and regulations are not complied, product and market knowledge are not up to the mark and business remains confined to the local level.

The major external problems that hinders the development of MSEs in the region are mostly related to:

- Financial support and investment promotion.
- Consultancy and counselling services.
- Quality control, market promotion, testing, scientific research and development facilities.
- Entrepreneurship development, training and skill formation.

- Technology development and applications.
- Infrastructure development.
- Establishment of linkages between various industries and other sectors of the economy.

Despite these problems MSEs continue to survive due to the efforts of the owners but remain limited in their progress mainly because of the non-application of right corporate approach and team-work.

9. The Intrinsic Problems of MSEs in North-Eastern Region

The NER of India comprising the seven states is quite different from the rest of the country due to their socio-economic, geographical and cultural diversities. Similarly, the problems faced by the industrial sector in this area are also different from their counterparts in the other parts of the country. The MSE sector in this region suffers from a number of innate constraints like geographical, financial, social, political, infrastructural and entrepreneurial. Although the rate of growth in terms of number of units registered in this region has been higher than all-India growth rate, the status of MSEs can be expressed as unhealthy in terms of size, bank finance, market access, entrepreneurial excellence, etc. The development of MSE in this region is lagging far behind as compared to the other regions especially western and southern part of the country. Despite the vast potential for different types of resource based industries; the pace of industrialization is too slow due to the unique geographical location, poor availability of funds, inadequate infrastructure, apprehensive investment climate, remoteness of market and lack of entrepreneurial skill, etc. There has been a significant growth of MSEs in the country; a disconcerting feature is that the growth is uneven and biased towards relatively advanced states than in the backward areas.

The NER is mostly hilly terrain. Due to the steep slopes of the hills transport and communication especially railways, roadways and even airways are not properly developed. These areas also suffer from lack of sufficient plain areas to be used for industrial purposes. The ethnic feeling which is very strong especially in Mizoram and Nagaland and Arunachal Pradesh retards the industrial growth. Because of the ethnic reason, the political economy does not permit free movements of potential investors, skilled manpower from other part of the country. There is a tendency among the tribal people to get rich quickly. This mentality adversely affects their courage to take risk in setting up industrial units. Moreover, the investment environment in this region is considered to be insecure due to growing insurgency and terrorism problems prevailing in the entire north-eastern region. Frequent racial clash, extortion of money by the insurgent groups etc. create an insecure investment climate which discourages the national and multinational companies in investing in the region and ultimately goes against the interest of industrial development in the region. Though industrialization is necessary to accelerate the economic growth of the region, it brings lots of problems in its wake especially in tribal areas where people belong to pre-industrial society. The rehabilitation resulting on dislocation, psychosomatic and sociological alteration, assimilation in the new set up etc. is some of the few quandaries that are created by industrialization of the tribal areas.

The SSI units which are run by an individual or a few partners usually suffer from some innate deficiencies like poor capital base, lack of proper technical know-how, weak bargaining power, poor marketing capacity of products etc. Given the poor performance of the primary sector of this region in accelerating economic growth, it is necessary to establish linkages among different sectors of the economy to boost the overall progress of the region. Though the geographic location, unique hilly landscape combined with infrastructural bottlenecks and other constraints rule out the viability of major industries in the region; the linkages can only be established by the development of MSEs in the region to create income opportunities and employment generation.

The diversification of society, emergence of elites, rich class and the growing number of government servants are creating demand for luxurious and modern sophisticated factory made goods, motor vehicles, cosmetics etc. to maintain their high standard of living, thus the demonstration effect fail to generate sufficient demand for indigenously produced goods. The rich people prefer to spend money in construction of multi-storied buildings which yield easy money in the form of rent. Somehow, they are reluctant to invest in industrial units which yield low profits, take long gestation periods and involve high risk.

Besides, the various policy reforms and industrial development programmes announced by the government lack inefficiency in management. Moreover, there is no proper coordination among various agencies in proper implementation of the programmes. The poor accountability and lack of vigilance on the part of administration leads to under-utilization and misappropriation particularly in financial areas. Subsequently, the region cannot optimally reap the fruits of various plans and policies announced by the government from time to time.

Measures for Tackling the Problems

Having analyzed various lacunas of growth and development of MSEs in the region, it may be observed that MSEs have been committed towards improving their performance. However, the following suggestions may be offered for betterment of MSEs sector:

1. There is a need to manage the evolution process towards the market economy and within this process enterprises need advice on how to behave and how to adapt to the new economic order keeping in view the existing resource availability in the region.
2. The SMEs promotion should be considered as a government task and many measures are taken to promote SMEs. This should pave the way towards a second generation of enterprise policy. Its implementation clearly embodies major challenges as well as tangible promises for the future.
3. The improvement of management training for SMEs managers is much needed in the changing industrial profile. There is a general recognition that SME managers, especially in small firms in the start-up phase, have to carry an enormous burden, as they have to perform various functions simultaneously.
4. The reduction of administrative burden for SMEs is the need of the day. The SMEs have special difficulties in complying with too many regulations and procedures, especially in the start-up phase. SME managers have little time for this, and cannot afford consultants and lawyers to help them with advice and administrative requirements. Measures are taken in some countries to develop so-called 'one-stop-shopping'—physical or virtual, with the help of information technology—

where all administrative requirements are concentrated in one place, in order for SME managers to save time, and to diminish the waste of time with such procedures.

5. Intuitional financing with suitable mechanism for SME is a must. This is an important and sensitive issue, as many SMEs have continuous cash-flow problems. As practice shows, large banks are much more ready to give loan for larger enterprises as a small one. Often SMEs have to pay 2-6 per cent more interest rate for bank credits than larger firms.
6. It is necessary to stimulate industrial research and development (R and D) activities in SMEs. Many SMEs perform little or no R and D, partly because they have no tradition of it, and partly because they cannot afford it. The measures to stimulate industrial R and D in SMEs have to be created, especially if the SME is a supplier to a larger firm.
7. The appropriate strategy for providing consultancy to existing training institutes in course design and curriculum development including trainers training programmes have to be introduced. In this context, specialized/tailor-made training courses for specific target groups may be recommended.
8. The degree of economic growth is highly related with the generation and consumption of electric power. The growth of industry in a particular region depends upon adequate and uninterrupted power supply. The power shortage, power shutdown and power cuts could paralyze industrial activity. The positive steps must be taken to supply adequate power to small sector and for enhancing the electrification.
9. The demand and the availability of local resources should be analyzed properly. The training institutes, extensions of basic infrastructural facilities, promotion of entrepreneurship spirit among the educated youth, maintenance of peace and harmony etc. are some of the prerequisites for creating an industrial atmosphere in the region. A gradual approach is necessary, apart from the government, the capitalist class and the educated youth must come forward with a new vision and energy to break the vicious circle of non-industrialization and to exploit the innate potential of industrialization in the region.

REFERENCES

Agarwal, A.K. 1999. *Industry of Mizoram,* in Banerjee, A. and Kar, B. (ed.), Economic Planning and Development of North-Eastern States. Kanishka Publishers, New Delhi, pp. 232-240.

Bharti, R.K. 1978. *Industrial Estate in Developing Economies,* National Publishing House, New Delhi.

Biswas, I. and Chakrabarty, M. 2008, *Can Indian Micro Small and Medium Enterprises (MSME) Sustain Globalization with the Present Technology Mix? A Disaggregated Study According to Sources of Technological Know-How,* October 15, Productivity, 49 (2-3): 202-213.

Cassar, G. and Holmes, Scott. 2003, *Capital Structure and Financing of SMEs: Australian Evidence,* Accounting and Finance, 43 (2) , 123–147, July.

Dasgupta, P.K. 1983. *Social Dimension of Planning with Reference to North-East India,* Omsons Publications, Delhi.

Deb, R.B. 2004. *Employment Generation in Small Units: A Case Study,* Yojana (48):41 May.

Desai, V. 2006. *Small Scale Industries and Entrepreneurship,* Himalaya Publishing House, Mumbai, p. 288.

Desai, Vasant, 1983. *Problems and Prospects of Small Scale Industries in India,* Himalaya Publishing House, Bombay.

Devi, S.A. 1995. *Development of Small Scale and Household Industries in Manipur during Plan Period* (Unpublished Ph.D Thesis), School of Social Science, Manipur University.

Hamid, S.A. 1989. *Management and Development in Small Scale Industries,* Anmol Publications, New Delhi.

http://www.bankingindiaupdate.com/nayak.html

Indian Institute of Entrepreneurship, Guwahati, 2001. *Small Scale Industries in Assam—A Study in Greater Guwahati Area.*

Kawadia, G., Dashmisra, M. and Bargal, H., 2005. *Growth Trends and Performance of Small Scale Industries in India.* The ICFAI Journal of Industrial Economics, November, II(4):20-29.

Keynes, J.M. 1936. *The General Theory of Employment, Interest and Money,* Harcourt Brace and Co., New York.

Khanka, S.S. 1998. *Development of Small Scale Industries in Assam,* Yojana, 42(9): 48-54, September.

Mali, D.D. 1998. *Development of Micro, Small and Medium Enterprises of India: Current Scenario and Challenges,* SEDME (Small Enterprises Development, Management and Extension), Journal, Vol. 25, No. 4, December.

Misra, D.P. and Panigrahy, D., 2005. *Working Capital Management and Its Impact on Profitability: A study on Selected Paper Manufacturing Units.* AURA, Journal ISM 2(3):59.

National Committee on Science and Technology, 1975. Report on the Science and Technology Panel for Khadi and Village Industries, Government of India.

Pande, G.C. 1983. *Field Report on Socio-economic Achievements and Emerging Issues in Hill Development*, Seminar on Development of Hill Areas. Himalaya Publishing House, Bombay.

Prasad, L. 1983. *Industrialization—Concept and Issues*, S. Chand and Co., New Delhi.

Rai, D. 2009. *Development Policies for Micro, Small and Medium Enterprises (MSMEs) in India*, SME Times, 27 January, http://smetimes.tradeindia.com/smetimes/in-depth/2009/Jan/27/development-policies-for-micro-small-and-medium-enterprises.html

Raj, S.N. R, and Mahapatra M.K. 2009. *Growth and Productivity Performance of Small Manufacturing Enterprises (SMEs): Insights from Major States in India*, Journal of Indian Business Research, Emerald Group Publishing Limited, 1(1): 39– 56.

Report of the Expert Committee on Small Enterprises, Ministry of Industry: 1997. Department of SSI, A. and R.I. (Abid Hussain Committee). Government of India. New Delhi.

Report of the Village and Small Scale Industries (Second Five Year Plan) Committee 1955, Commonly known as the Karve Committee Report, Government of India.

Reserve Bank of India. 2005-06, Handbook of Statistics on the Indian Economy,

Saleh, A.S. and Ndubisi, N.O. 2006. *An Evaluation of SMEs Development in Malaysia*, International Review of Business Research Papers, 2(1):1-14.

Sophia, S. and Baskaran, A., 2007. *A Study on Financial Support to SSI and Capacity Utilization*, Productivity, 47(4):394-398.

Subrahmanya, M.H.B. 2005. *Small-scale industries in India in the Globalization Era: Performance and Prospects*, International Journal of Management and Enterprise Development, Inderscience Publishers, 2(1): 122-139.

Thangmawizula, H. 1985. *Economy of Mizoram, Seminar on 'Tribal Economy of NER'*, Spectrum Publications, Guwahati.

17

Entrepreneurial Development for KVI in Arunachal Pradesh

DEEPALI MANDAL

The main principle of Gandhian approach is to set up a system of village self-sufficiency. In this regard, the hypothesis of M.K. Gandhi was establishment of 'Gram Swaraj' in the countryside which means the complete independence of the Indian villages. The ultimate goal of Gandhian planning was to make Indian villages fully independent. Mahatma Gandhi often used to say that the real India was to be found in the villages, not in the cities and towns. This sector has not only continued to play a vital role in fulfilment of socio-economic objectives but also offers an excellent opportunity for industrial self-employment.

It was Mahatma Gandhi, who pioneered the revival of the age-old self-sufficiency (*Gram Swavalamban*) and leased a new life and extinct glory to the concept of Swadeshi. According to Gandhi, the law of Swadeshi was the *swardharma* of the *Gita* interpreted in terms of one's physical environment. Gandhi advocated Khadi as the necessary and most important corollary of the principle of *Swadeshi* in its application to society, he warned that "it is the greatest delusion to suppose that the duty of Swadeshi begins and ends with merely spinning some yarn and wearing Khadi made from it. In Swadeshi there is no for ill-will. It is a doctrine of selfless service and has its roots in the purest *ahimsa*, love". (*R. Chowdhury, Gandhi's Ethical Ideas, 2007*).

The aim and objective of the Khadi and Village Industries (KVI) in the state is to promote the industrial activities in the state and thereby to provide employment opportunities to the rural and urban and to improve the economic conditions of the people. About 94 per cent population of Arunachal Pradesh lives in the rural belt making agriculture the main occupation. The world is moving towards natural and eco-friendly products. More and more people are becoming conscious of responsibility towards the environment and ecology and products like plastic, etc. are highly looked down upon and greater demand is being generated for bio-degradable and eco-friendly products. The KVI Sector produces a wide range of exclusive products which are having distinct characteristics. Most of the projects of KVIC are local resource based and eco-friendly and which is very much suitable for a place like Arunachal Pradesh.

Khadi Industries have played a pioneering role in restoring the lost glory of the time tested for self-employment model, the model of just distribution of wealth, the model that generates maximum number of employment, the model that employs local resources and local talent to produce for masses. As we know, the advent of the British in India saw an emergence of a new politico-economic policy, which aimed at annihilating the traditional industry and handicrafts to find an outlet for its own products in the Indian market. The shear discrimination and oppressive policy totally led to destruction of the Indian handicrafts *vis-a-vis* the village self-sufficiency. It was Mahatma Gandhi, who pioneered the revival of the age-old self-sufficiency (*Gram Swavalamban*) and leased a new life and extinct glory to the concept of Swadeshi. Initially, Khadi and village industry was entirely a non-governmental effort under the inspired guidance of Gandhi. In 1923, he founded the All India Khadi Board, an integral part of the Indian National Congress. In 1925, he formed an autonomous organization called All India Spinner Association (AISA). In 1935 for promotion of other village industries he set up All India Khadi and Village Industries Association (AIVIA). To Gandhi, Khadi and Village Industries are absolutely interdependent and so later the AISA and AIVIA were merged into a single entity under the banner of Akhil Bharat Sarva Seva Sangh. After Independence, the Government of India set up the All India Khadi and Village Industries Board in 1953. This Board, aimed to function in close cooperation with the State

Governments and the Akhil Bharat Sarva Seva Sangh plagued with procedural handicaps. It was then decided in 1955 to replace this Board by a statutory body. Accordingly, the Khadi and Village Industries Commission (KVIC) came into being in 1957. The broad objectives of the KVIC are (i) The social objective of providing employment, (ii) The economic objective of producing saleable articles and (iii) The wider objective of creating self-reliance amongst the people and building up a strong community spirit.

Rural industrialization is important not as a means of generating employment opportunities in the rural areas with low capital cost and raising the real income of the people, but because it contributes to the development of agriculture and urban industries. Without rural industrialization, it would be considerably more difficult to solve the problem of agricultural unemployment and widespread underemployment. Rural industrialization promotes rural industry.

According to Khadi and Village Industries Commission, "rural industry or village industry is the one which is located in the rural area and produces any good or renders any service with or without use of power and in which the fixed capital investment per head of an artisan or a worker does not exceed rupees 50,000." (Dr.N.K.Trikha, 2005). The definition of village industry has been recently modified by the government so as to enlarge its scope. Accordingly, any industry located in rural areas, village or town with a population of 20,000 and below and an investment of Rs.10 million in plant and machinery, is classified as a village industry.

Rural industry embraces different kinds of village and small industries. All the village industries have been grouped into seven major categories as follows:

(i) Mineral based industry
(ii) Forest based industry
(iii) Agro based industry
(iv) Polymer and Chemical based industry
(v) Engineering and non-Conventional industry
(vi) Textile industry (excluding khadi) and
(vii) Service industry.

Need for Rural Industrialization

Developing industries in the rural areas is essential because:

1. Rural industries are labour intensive.
2. By providing employment, these industries have also high potential for income generation in the rural areas.
3. These industries encourage dispersal of economic activities in the rural areas and thus, promote balanced regional development.
4. Rural industries also help protect and promote art and creativity i.e., the age-old rich heritage of the country. Rural industries being environment-friendly lead to development without destruction.

Programmes: The Government has taken a number of policy initiatives through various Central Ministries for over-all promotion of village and small scale industries. Some of the important policies are:

1. Progressive allocations made in the Five Year Plans.
2. Policy of reservation.
3. Price preference (up to 15 %) and purchase preference policy for marketing small scale industrial products.
4. Technical assistance through industrial extension service centres.
5. Provision of built up factory accommodation in industrial estates.
6. Supply of machines under the hire purchase system.
7. Subsidy on power consumption.
8. Provision of raw material.
9. Policy of priority credit, and
10. Entrepreneurship Development Programmes conducted by various National Institutes and support to state level Institutes.

The Centre and State Governments in India have sponsored various employment generation and poverty alleviation programmes for development of rural industries. Some of them are as follows:

1. Prime Minister's Rozgar Yojana (PMRY): The PMRY was launched on 2nd October, 1993 with the objective of providing employment opportunities to educated unemployed youth through setting up of small-scale enterprises in rural and urban areas. The loans under the scheme are available to all educated unemployed youth between 18-35 years (18-45 years for women) who have passed 8th standard examination for undertaking all economically viable activities including agriculture and allied activities. This scheme also provides for preference to weaker sections and women. The PMRY has been allocated Rs. 196.65 crores in 2005-06 budget. It has a Tenth Plan target of setting up 11 lakh micro enterprises providing employment to 16.5. lakh persons.

2. Swarnjayanti Gram Swarozgar Yojana (SGSY): SGSY which was initiated on April 1, 1999, is a credit-cum-subsidy programme. It aims at establishing a large number of micro enterprises in rural areas. The beneficiary families may be individuals or groups (SHGs). In order to give an impetus to the group, a revolving fund of Rs. 25,000 is provided from banks. In addition, for individual, subsidy is also provided at 30 per cent of the project cost subject to Rs. 7,500. In respect of SCs/STs and disabled persons subsidy is 50 per cent of the project cost subject to a maximum of Rs. 10,000. For groups of swarozgaris the subsidy is 50 per cent of the scheme cost, subject to per capita subsidy of Rs.10,000 or a total of Rs. 1,25,000 whichever is less. Within the target group, special safeguards have been provided to vulnerable sections by way of reserving 50 per cent benefits for Scheduled Castes/Scheduled Tribes, 40 per cent for women and 30 per cent for disabled persons. It is envisaged that 50 per cent of the groups formed in each block should be exclusively for women.

Today, in the country, two lakh SHGs are linked with banks under this scheme. The number will be increased to 2.5 lakh in 2005-06. The Swarnjayanti Gram Swarozgar Yojana (SGSY) has been allocated Rs. 862.24 crores from the total central plan outlay for 2005-06.

3. Rural Employment Generation Programme (REGP): The Government through Khadi and Village Industries Commission is implementing this programme for the promotion and development of Agro and Rural industries. The revised target for the Tenth Plan under the REGP is to generate 25 lakhs additional employment opportunity and Rs. 369.95 crore has been provided for the rural employment generation programme in 2005-06 budget in the country.

Under this scheme, the KVIC provides margin money assistance at the rate of 25 per cent of the project cost up to Rs.10 lakhs and for projects above Rs. 10 lakhs and upto Rs. 25 lakhs, rate of margin money is 25 per cent of Rs. 10 lakhs plus 10 per cent on remaining cost of the project. In the case of SC/ ST/OBC/women/ physically handicapped and other special category, the margin money grant is 30 per cent of the project cost up to Rs. 10 lakhs and for projects above Rs. 10 lakhs and up to Rs. 25 lakhs, it is 30 per cent of Rs. 10 lakhs plus 10 per cent of the remaining cost of the project. Under this scheme, the beneficiary's contribution is 10 per cent of the project cost. In the case of SC/ST and other weaker sections, beneficiary's contribution is 5 per cent of the project cost.

4. District Rural Industrial Project (DRIP): The National Bank for Agricultural and Rural Development is implementing this programme. The main objective of the project is to generate sustainable employment opportunities through coordinated efforts in financing rural non-farm enterprises, creation of essential infrastructure and also enabling promotional agencies to take up entrepreneurial development, technology upgradation, raw material supply, marketing assistance and other common services with an area covering the entire district. The emphasis in the project is on provision of timely and adequate credit support.

The State Khadi and Village Industries Boards have come into existence in response to advice of the All India Khadi and Village Industries Board which was required by the Government Resolution of January 14, 1953 to work "in close cooperation with the State Government". Today there are 33 States and Union Territories Khadi and Village Industries Boards in the country.

The Arunachal Pradesh Khadi and Village Industries Board (APKVIB) was created by a state Act. The Board was initially under the administrative control of Department of Industries lately on bifurcation of this department and on creation of Department of Textile and Handicrafts it was placed under latter's administrative control. This Board like any other State Boards was positioned to promote the KVI sector and to act as a replica of KVIC at the state level. The Board is a promotional body with no income of its own as it does not undertake any commercial operation but generally channelizes and monitors utilization of central sector developmental funds provided by KVIC. The broad objectives are similar to that of the KVIC within the jurisdiction of the state of Arunachal Pradesh. However, the state government has to bear its establishment and administrative expenses. The APKVIB Act was amended in 1998 and also framed its Rules and Regulations in this year. The Board got its first developmental fund from the KVIC in year 1991-92.

The tribal communities were extremely self-reliant; they constructed their own inter village path, build their own cane bridge, devised their own indigenous equipments to husk or grind rice and millets, weaving their own cloths, ornaments and jewels, hats, cooking vessels, weapons. This shows the exceptional similarities of Gandhian concept of self-reliance in the Tribal Communities of the state. However, there was hardly any development. The economy and the society at the dawn of independence were primitive. But, now the days are fast moving far from culture of self-sufficiency in this tribal soil. Thus, in the context of changing scenario, the study aims at making a study that the KVI sector is relevant in the tribal soil of Arunachal Pradesh. In view of this, the paper attempts to address the objectives: (i) To investigate the development of Khadi and Village Industries and Employment Scenario, (ii) To find out the major problems faced by Khadi and Village Industries, and (iii) To find the probable solutions of the problems in the state.

Development of Khadi and Village Industries and Employment Scenario

The nodal agency for implementation of KVI programmes in the state is APKVIB. The Arunachal Pradesh Seva Sangh runs HRD Programme in the MDTC including Khadi spinning and weaving. The KVIC's state office headed by Assistant Director with 9 other supporting staff has been implementing REGP and other Programme. The APKVIB is in a shocking position. It devoids the attention of the authority. The Chairman is appointed casually. There is no regular or full time CEO. The post of vice-chairman is non-functional and creates unnecessary strains on hard earn resources. State government's funding is abysmally meagre with no long term plan on anvil. Indifference of the state authorities coupled with lack of institutional in-built capacity has resulted *inter alia* a low treatment by KVIC in sharing developmental funds. The Board has ended up by distributing KVIC funds without further follow-up/monitoring. The KAVIRC observes, 'although these Boards were supposed to be replicas of the KVIC at the state level, but in reality they have not gone beyond the disbursement of KVIC funds. The Boards have even not efficiently and properly performed their primary functions' (Report of KAVIRC, 1987). 'Organizational weakness, lack of trained manpower and technical expertise, inadequate support from the State Government are some of the reasons for inability of the Board in making any significant impact' (Majumdar, 2000). The number of units of KVI established in different years is shown in Table 17.1.

Table 17.1: No. of Units of KVI Established in Different Years

Year	*No. of units*
1999–2000	9
2000–01	60
2001–02	23
2002–03	16
2003–04	14
2004–05	20
2005–06	19
2006–07	30
Total	191

Source: The Arunachal Pradesh Khadi and Village Industries Board.

The year-wise employment generation, total investment and per capita investment are shown in Table 17.2.

Table 17.2: Year-wise Employment generation

(Rs. in Lac. and employment in No.)

Year	*Employment*	*Total investment*	*PCI*
1991 - 92	107	26.70	0.250
1992 - 93	98	24.62	0.251
1993 - 95	222	55.48	0.250
1995 - 97	160	132.79	0.830
1999 - 2000	100	41.52	0.415
2000 - 01	378	187.21	0.495
2001 - 02	168	95.79	0.570
2002 - 03	190	103.83	0.546
2003 - 04	78	67.78	0.869
2004 - 05	137	99.64	0.727

Source: The Arunachal Pradesh Khadi and Village Industries Board.

Per Capita Investment (PCI) low and almost fixed then sudden high in 1995-97. The PCI has been near stabilized from 1999-2000 to 2002-03. Then sudden jump and again in 2004-05 fall considerably. Again the year-wise employment generations in different industries are shown in Table 17.3.

Table 17.3: Industry-wise Employment Generation

Year	*Khadi*	*Mineral based*	*Agro based*	*Chemical based*	*Engineering and NCE*	*Textile*	*Forest based*	*Service industry*	*Total*
1991-92	10	-	2	-	33	42	20	-	107
1992-93	10	-	23	-	24	36	2	3	98
1993-95	2	16	52	8	37	18	89	-	222
1995-96	-	-	19	38	46	18	39	-	160
1997-99	-	-	-	-	-	-	-	-	Nil
1999-2000	-	22	16	-	34	-	22	6	100
2000-01	-	-	79	-	98	66	57	78	378
2001-02	-	24	48	-	46	-	32	18	168
2002-03	-	36	14	-	78	18	20	24	190
2003-04	-	-	-	-	38	26	14	-	78
Total	22	98	253	46	434	224	295	129	1,501

Source: The Arunachal Pradesh Khadi and Village Industries Board.

With the impact of globalization and development of education the number of job-seeker is increasing drastically. The Khadi and Village Industries in the state are playing a significant role in employment generation.

Problems

The KVI are not commercially viable due to (i) lack of interest of weavers as minimum wages prevailing in the states are much higher than wages payable to Khadi Spinners and Weavers as per Khadi cost chart provision, (ii) lack of raw materials, (iii) lack of working capital or timely finance, (iv) lack of marketing facilities, (v) lack of capacity utilization, (vi) lack of technical know-how, (vii) devoid of organizational strength,(viii) competition on Khadi (hand spun and hand woven) from power loom(machine spun and machine woven) and handloom(machine spun and hand woven), (ix) lack of entrepreneurial knowledge, (x) lack of power, (xi) lack of transport facilities, etc. Let us discuss some major constraints.

Market: The KVI sector is not accessible to the modern means of marketing. In modern market economy, the buyer and seller are able to get in touch with one another so that the exchange of goods and services for money takes place between them. This can also be done through E-mail, internet, telephone, courier, speed post and ordinary mails. It is undisputedly accepted that success of an industry depends on market of its products. It has no well organized market outside this state and even inside the state. It has no world-wide Website and no advertisements through electronic or print media. Only entrepreneurs are given opportunities to participate to various exhibitions etc. which are also due to intrinsic reasons not availed to full extent.

Inner-line System: Inner-line System that was introduced in 1873 still exists even in the present changed scenario. This restricts the free movement of Non-Arunachalees to the state. A Non-Arunachalee who wants to cross beyond the Inner-line has to get the IL Pass issued for a limited period with certain conditionality as it is viewed that the territory is located at strategic-point from the standpoint of defense. Besides, the Government of India feels it necessary to protect the tribal and their land and forest, who has a vivid socio-economic and cultural dimension, from the Non-Arunachalees' hunger of grabbing.

Globalization refers to a process of increasing economic integration and growing economic interdependence between the contemporary world economies. It is associated not only with increasing cross-border movement of goods, services, capital, IT, and people but also with an organization of economic activities which crosses national boundary. To get the good effect of globalization in the state it needs first cross-state flows among the states of India. In fact the Inner-line system posing as a major hindrances for free flow industrial environment.

The N.E. Region is isolated, landlocked which shares only 2 per cent of its border with the rest of the country and rest with Bhutan, Bangladesh, Myanmar and the Tibetan region of China. For most of this international border has been artificially created. The result has been the elimination of the region's trade, commerce and other linkages, which existed in the pre-independence days. These N.E. states are very close to the dynamic South-East and East Asian economics. It is imperative to develop a coherent policy linking this area. (Dr. G. Sachdeva, JNU).

Entrepreneurial lack: In the N.E. Region, the unemployment problem has become a paradox because the unemployment in the region is growing, not because there is lack of opportunities, but because the unemployed youths have failed to take advantage of the opportunities available. It is an accepted fact that the availability of entrepreneurship is the most important determinant in the process of industrialization. The government in its efforts to create entrepreneurship provides for various monetary and non-monetary incentives like the development of an infrastructure, assistance in marketing and procuring raw-materials, providing finance or granting subsidies on investment. Various state and central organizations have accordingly been created to cater to the needs of entrepreneurs.

It can be argued that that lack of entrepreneurial skill of the local people and their deficient interest to invest and innovate has contributed in preventing the evolution of modern economic system in the state. One example of their lacking interest in setting up enterprises is that those tribal boys/girls who go for craft training do not want to have their own business but like to join as craft teachers in government organizations (Krishna,2000). The mindset of the tribal is not to establish their own enterprise but to venture either in politics, contract business, or government services to earn "*easy money*". This mindset can be termed as **psychological barrier** which has emerged very strongly in the present socio-economic context of the state. Some tribal people within a very short period of time have experienced income and wealth inequalities to a high degree. Very few of them have been found to become very rich overnight and enjoy luxurious life and prefer conspicuous consumption which has been adversely affecting the rest of the society. The income inequalities in the tribal society are very strong. Some are very rich and some are stark poor. The presence of high degree of corruption at all level and existence of underground economy is also a deterrent to states economy (Mandal, 2006).

License issuing system: The outsiders who want to venture business in the state are to obtain license in the name of some Arunachalees who get rent from the concern businessman for the license. These trading people earn money and mostly siphon off in their respective home because they don't get the right to buy property for independent business. This status largely refrain the private investors in coming and opening up ventures in A.P. Institutional credit for trade and industries are available to the local people but they lack entrepreneurial skills and show hardly any interest in industrial activities. Therefore, like IL permit, the **License issuing system of the government has discouraged** the opening up of KVI units in the state.

Lack of dignity of labour: The contemporary Arunachalee, mostly, oblivious of their age-old pride of dignity of labour and even for petty household works they depend on migrated labour. This has quietly uprooting the habit of doing productive works on self-help basis and making them dependent on others. This is contrary to the entrepreneurial trait.

Power: Power is one of the major infrastructures for the growth of industrial activities of any size. 'Arunachal has a huge potential for the development of hydroelectric power because of its many rivers. The state has the potential to supply a third of total hydroelectric requirement of the country. The per capita consumption of electricity in Arunachal was 86.9 kWh in 2001-02 against the all-India average of 335 kWh' (APHDR, 2005, page, 45).

In addition to water resource, the state has oil, natural gas and coal resources that can be used in the production of electricity. The Government of India has taken initiative for large scale production of hydropower. Such initiative will also have the spin-off benefits like employment avenues, increase in consumption of industrial products, roads, schools, banks, health care, postal facilities, and training centres etc. In 1971-72 only 37 villages were electrified. By March, 2001 this has rose to 2506 out of 3649 villages. The state having untapped estimated hydropower potential of 49,000MW, may emerge as powerhouse of India when this potential is fully harnessed (**Source:** Dept. of Power, GoAP).

Transportation: The service of transportation is a prerequisite for economic development. The road density in the state is very low. In 2001, the road density was 17.36 km per 100 sq. km of area as against the national average of 82 km per 100 sq. km. The main reasons for this low density are: the difficult topography and undulating terrain, the late start of development process, and the high cost of construction in the inaccessible and remote areas (APHDR, 2005, p. 44). The states does not have lateral roads connecting districts, since roads run vertically connecting places in Assam with districts or sub-divisions in A.P. This has not only resulted in high transportation costs but also affected by disturbed law and order situation and insurgency problem of Assam. The state at all has no railways except 1.26 km metre gauge railway line laid in 1989 connecting Bhalukpong with Indian railway map. This is a major handicap.

Banking Scenario: KVI comes under the priority sector *vide* RBI's circular No.RPCD.PLNFS.BC.84/06.0612/93-94 (Source RBI). The REGP is only scheme in common to be offered as rural industrialization tool. Under this major assistance has to come from bank as loan. In 2000-01, there were only 99 bank offices with an average of 9.07 offices per 1,00,000 populations and availability of finance is not widespread in Arunachal yet. The credit-deposit ratio is only 17.25 per cent, which is lowest among the N.E. states and is considerably lower than the national level (58.53%) (APHDR, 2005). There are vast areas where either there is no any bank or is a single man branch which is obviously not equipped to go beyond the normal banking transactions.

Vocational Training / Education: The state government has a network of 88 craft centres, earlier called Cottage Industries Training and Production Centres, (CITPC). Lack of modern tools-equipments, poor physical infrastructure, shortage of competent training instructors, outmoded curriculum and training methods, neglect of skill upgradation, low stipend offered to trainees etc. are some of the reasons for the suboptimal performance of the craft centres (Majumdar, 2000).

The dropout rates in Arunachal at the primary and upper primary level in 2003 were 20 per cent and 36 per cent respectively (APHDR, 2005). After primary school, vocational streams should be available to train the boys and girls in the local context so that they find education is relevant and employment oriented. A. P. is below the National level of female literacy (NHDR, 2001). This is a case of Gender disparity contrasting women empowerment.

Probable Solutions

The following may be few suggestions to consider in order strengthening the KVI in the state.

1. The state KVIB needs to be strengthened in different ways. It is in awful condition. The sector needs in rejuvenate in totality. A carefully drawn holistic plan is the only panacea.
2. The sector needs advertisement for its product through all modern media. Initially, the free web-space provided by the KVIC in their website (www.kvic.org.in) for the state KVIBs should be filled with information.
3. The state government and the KVIC should implement the good recommendations made in the Anindo Majumdar Report, 2000.
4. Priority to develop border trades with Bhutan, China and Myanmar to be given.
5. A comprehensive techno-economic survey of the entire territory of A.P. should be done to find out potential area of activities under this sector.
6. Modernizing the government run craft centres is needworthy. Incorporation of innovative training streams on the basis of potentiality study. Setting up of inter-face with existing good technical and managerial institutes like SFRI, NERIST, IIE may be considered.

7. Complete financial support and its proper utilization in any probable unit should be shouldered by the government. KVIC at its special dispensation should do it. Identification of non-REGP villages and devising alternative scheme for these localities will be generous step in this direction.
8. Implementation and execution of KVI schemes and programmes should be left to APKVIB, the local KVIC may perform mainly the supervisory and liaisoning role with GOI, KVIC head office etc.
9. The flow of relevant information relating to VSI (Village and Small Industries) should be regularly circulated to keep the entrepreneurial world abreast with the recent trends. The Department of Industries may launch a periodical bulletin.
10. The bank and FI should play more constructive role in lending credit support to good proposals. The A. P. Industrial Development and Financial Corporation needs to be revived. The monitoring machinery needs to be strengthened including detection of sick industrial units and draw up a nursing plan for their rehabilitation.
11. Tourism/eco-tourism may be encouraged which will have ripple effect on the VSI. Nearing to the Eco-tourist spot, Gramodyog Darshan Park may be established to showcase the treasure trove.
12. The state should strive hard to be self-sufficient in raw material, technical know-how, machines/tools and a well knitted marketing network.
13. A single item can be identified which could be synonymous with the name of the state. Escort services are given to V.I. unit in graduating it to a SSI unit.
14. The existence of IL System appears to be irrelevant in present global scenario and therefore authority may contemplate twice on its continuation.
15. Sustainability of any project depends upon fulfilment of certain basic requirements. Systematic approach, training to entrepreneurs, technology, Quality Control and marketing support etc. if all these will be taken care adequately, the KVIC can play an exemplary role in the process of Socio-Economic Development in Arunachal Pradesh.

Conclusions

The KVIC's funding policy need flexibility to the context of the state socio-economic situations. The state government may display needed wisdom to reciprocate with KVIC to augment the efforts. The APKVIB needs a complete overhauling. The door be kept opened so that the autonomy that granted by the provision of Act is realized unfettered for the benefit of the people. But again it should be under the scanner of social audit. The Chairman of APKVIB should not be a political man so that he cannot use its benefit for realizing the political mileage. It will be more befitting to the occasion if the Development Commissioner or Commissioner of Industries is made ex-officio chairman. A full time Chief Executive Officer is appointed for a sufficiently long tenure to work under direct control of chairman. This key post has to be hold by an officer having proven track record of integrity, adequately qualified in the field of rural development and an aptitude for working in the unglamorous social sector. The Board should have a separate budget in the plan and non-plan document and should be released in form of statutory grants on time and not to depend on lump-sum grant in aids. Adequately reasonable service conditions will attract good professionals to serve in the Board.

Employment is the surest way to enable the vast numbers of people living below the poverty level to raise them above it. KVI is capable of offering employment opportunities at the place of residence to a large section of population. This has the capacity to correct regional imbalances by initiating industrial activities on dispersed basis in the most neglected, backward inaccessible areas like most of the areas of North-East States where perhaps large scale sector is unable to penetrate. KVI is a key to rural development and rural prosperity.

NOTES AND REFERENCES

Arunachal Pradesh Human Development Report, 2005, Deptt. of Planning, GoAP.

Compilations of statistics/Reports of A. P. Khadi and V. I. Board, Itanagar.

Human Development Report, 2005 of UNDP.

Information from various records of Department of Industries, GoAP.

Kamalakannan, K. (2008): "Rural Industrialistion and Poverty Alleviation", *Kurukshetra*, A Journal of Rural Development, Ministry of Rural Development, May, Vol. 54, No. 52, New Delhi.

Majumdar (2000), *The Khadi and V.I. Sector in Arunachal Pradesh*, published by KVIC, Govt. of India, Report under their Fellowship Programme.

Mandal, R. K. (2005), "Arunachal Economy: Socio-Economic Transformation. Champion Publisher and Distributor, Itanagar, pp. 90-91.

Mandal, R.K. (2006), "Constraint of Economic Development in Arunachal Pradesh with special reference to Globalization and Inner Line System", *Artha Beekshan*,Vol.15, No.3, Kolkata.

National Human Development Report, 2001.

Publication of NIRD on Rural Industrialization 1999, NE Regional Centre, Guwahati.

Report of High Power Committee on KVI, 1994 under the Chairmanship of Lt P.V. Narasimha Rao, then Prime Minister of India.

Report of the Khadi and V. I. Review Committee, under the Chairmanship of M. Ramkrishnayya, Ex-Chairman, NABARD and Ex-Dy. Governor, RBI, year 1987.

Sachdeva, G. *Introduction to the North East*, NE Yellow Pages, 2005-06.

Samiran Das, Amal Prava Das (1986), A biography translated by Hiranmoyee Devi, Publisher H. Devi.

Various issues of *Jagriti*, a monthly Journal of KVIC.

18

Entrepreneurial Problems of Village Industries in Manipur

O. DEEPAK KUMAR SINGH AND RAJMANI SINGH

Introduction

Rural Industrialization is a means to stimulate rural economic growth and overall development of the rural masses. It has the potentialities of increasing agricultural production, increasing the capabilities of individual production, inducing the development of agro based and village industries, which in turn generate a large employment in rural areas. Village industries have become an indispensible tool to rural development specially the North East India where more than 70 per cent of the population live in rural areas.

Village industry is one of the areas where large number of entrepreneurs are groomed and nourished. More particularly a large number of women entrepreneurs are also coming out in this field. Manipur is one of the industrially and economically backward states in the north-east region of India. A high literacy rate of 70.50 per cent as compared to 65.38 per cent in census 2001 of India has bring no good result in generating employment opportunity in the state. Approximately, 27.65 per cent of the total population is still unemployed as per the report on 31st October, 2008 as against the 12 per cent for the north-east India. The mounting problem of unemployment has brought into focus the importance of small scale, agro and village industries as well as development of entrepreneurship in the related fields where low capital investment and little training are involved.

Manipur has 57,171 Micro Small Enterprise (MSE) units with a fixed capital investment of Rs. 428 crores and an average production of Rs. 984 crores as compared to 3,85,890 MSE units with a fixed capital investment of Rs. 3,289 crores and an average production of Rs.10,368 crores of North-East India. MSE has been successful in generating employment opportunities in the state with an average of 1,62,667 persons as compared to 9,81,096 persons in the north-east India (MSME, Annual Report, 2007-08).

The traditional sector of industries in the sate falls within the purview of organizations such as Khadi and Village Industries Commission (KVIC). The KVIC include artisans in tiny industrial units and defines it as any industry located in a village or town inhabited by a population not exceeding 10,000 which produces goods and renders services with or without the use of power in which the fixed capital per head does not exceed Rs. 15,000.

Objectives of the Study

Following objectives were established for the purpose of this study:

1. To study the profile of present economic activities undertaken in the various Village industries.
2. To study the basic entrepreneurial problem faced by the village industries.
3. To suggest the remedial measures to resolve the entrepreneurial problems faced by the village industries in Manipur.

Research Methodology

Both primary and secondary data are used for the purpose of this study. Primary data was collected through interview schedule and descriptive research design is being used in carrying out the study. 90 respondents were visited and interview schedule was administered personally. 36 entrepreneurs were visited from Imphal East District while 54 were interviewed from Imphal West District. The interview schedule comprised of questions pertaining to the objectives of research study. Out of the 36 entrepreneurs from Imphal East District, 9 are women and out of 54 entrepreneurs from Imphal West District 21 are women thus; all together there are 30 women entrepreneurs covered in the present study. Most of the respondent's age range from 25 - 40 years. The collected data was tabulated and analyzed for drawing the inferences. The analysis was based on the total numbers of response made by the 90 respondents. Secondary data includes various publication, research work and annual report of government and other body.

Village Industries in Manipur

Manipur continues to remain as one of the industrially backward state in the country, in spite of its rich natural resources. None of the medium and large scale industries in the state are considered to be worthwhile except some traditional industries like Khadi and Village Industries, handlooms and handicrafts and some food processing industries etc. The main reasons behind the undeveloped industrial scenario in the state are its difficult terrain, inadequate infrastructural facilities, varying climatic condition and also lack of entrepreneurial skills and experiences.

The new industrial policy of 1996 of the state give emphasis to generate employment opportunities through industrial development based on locally available raw materials and manpower.

The Khadi and Village Industries are taking an important role in providing employment to people in rural and semi-urban areas at low investment per job and also utilize local skill resources and provide part-time as well as full-time job to rural artisans and women. Khadi and Village Industries Commission, Manipur has been playing a pivotal role in the development of village industries in the rural areas in coordination with other agencies engaged in rural development. KVIC has successfully assisted in 219 units with an employment to 1,943 artisans from the year 2002-03 to 2007-08 through the scheme of Rural Employment Generation Programme (REGP) in the two Districts of Imphal East and Imphal West. During the year 2003-04, a sum of Rs. 15 lakhs under plan and Rs. 56 lakhs under non-plan were provided as grants-in-aid to meet the establishment charges of the Khadi and Village Industries Board.

Table 18.1: Khadi and Village Industries in Manipur

Districts	*No. of units*	*Percentage of total*
Bishenpur	18	05.73
Chandel	37	11.78
Churachandpur	04	01.27
Imphal East	62	19.75
Imphal West	157	50.00
Senapati	21	06.69
Tamenglong	09	02.87
Thoubal	05	01.59
Ukhrul	01	00.32
Total	314	100.00

Source: State KVIC, Manipur.

The village industries assisted by the KVIC in the state are distributed un-equivalently. 50 per cent of the units are from Imphal West while only 1.59 per cent is from Thoubal District. Among the hilly districts, Chandel has a maximum of 11.78 per cent while Ukhrul district has 0.32 per cent.

Table 18.2 shows the KVI units in Imphal East and Imphal West districts of Manipur. A maximum number of 51 forest based units were established in the two districts in the six consecutive years followed by mineral based industries with an aggregate of 41 units. Food processing and agro based industries stood to be 33 and 30 respectively and polymer and chemical emerged to be the least by a total number of 5.

On the other hand Handloom and Handicraft industry is considered to be the largest cottage industry in the state. Most of the handloom weavers in the state are self-employed artisans and has been a major source of employment generation and income generation in the state. As per the handloom census conducted by the Ministry of Textile in 1995-96, Manipur has more than 2.77 lakhs looms as against the national statistics of 34.86 lakh. The state has more than 3.40 lakh persons engaged in the field of handloom weaving and allied activities, against the national total of 65.5 lakh, which is 5.2 per cent of the national total.

Table 18.2 : Khadi and Village Industrial Units in Imphal East and Imphal West Districts of Manipur (Assisted by KVIC, Manipur)

Industries Types	*2002-03*	*2003-04*	*2004-05*	*2005-06*	*2006-07*	*2007-08*	*Total*
Food Processing	3	3	14	0	0	13	33
Agro Based Industry	1	0	1	6	22	0	30
Forest Based Industry	2	13	4	13	13	6	51
Textile Industry	6	2	10	7	4	2	31
Mineral Based Industry	7	5	7	9	7	6	41
Rural Engineering	1	4	5	3	2	1	16
Service Industry	4	1	2	3	2	0	12
Polymer and Chemical	0	0	2	0	2	1	5
Total	24	28	45	41	52	29	219

Source: KVIC, Manipur.

Entrepreneurial Performances

As a means to develop the entrepreneurial talents under the Rural Employment Generation Programme (REGP), EDP programme has been imparted successfully; the number of training provided has been increased from 96 in 2004-05 to 143 in 2005-06. Workshop and People Education Programme has been performed continuously but Awareness Programme and Bankers Meet are held once in the year 2005-06 when it was 2 and 3 respectively in the year 2004-05.

Table 18.3: Activities under Rural Employment Generation Programme

Sl. No.	*Particulars*	*2004-05*	*2005-06*
1.	EDP Imparted	96	143
2.	Awareness Programme	2	1
3.	Workshop	4	5
4.	Bankers meeting	3	1
5.	People Education Programme	7	5
6.	Exhibition	3	—

Source: Programme and Activities, KVIC, state office, Manipur.

Problems Faced by the Entrepreneur

Industrial development has been acting as a means to uplift the socio and economic problems of a nation, but in the state like Manipur, the pace of industrial development is very slow which can be subsequently considered as a consequence of many and varied entrepreneurial problems faced by them. Some of the problems are due to its topographic features, but many other problems are also influencing the activities of the entrepreneurship. Some of the problems which can be considered are Social Problems, Marketing Problems, Problems in Availing of Government Assistance, Financial Problems, Production Problems, Managerial Problems and other problems which are very milled but indirectly affect the entrepreneurial behaviour.

100 per cent of the respondents are facing the social problems in some or other ways, 83.33 per cent have financial problems, and 63.33 per cent have problems in getting Government Assistance. Marketing and Production problems have been respectively 46.66 per cent and 36.66 per cent. 40 per cent of the respondents are facing managerial problems while 10 per cent react against the other problems like seeking for job which are more secure and stability, adopting entrepreneurship in village industry is the final option to most of the entrepreneur, because of not getting good and lucrative job.

Table 18.4: Problems Faced by the Entrepreneurs

Problems	*No. of Response*	*Percentage (%)*
Social Problems	90	100.00
Marketing Problems	42	46.66
Availing Government Assistance	57	63.33
Financial Problems	75	83.33
Production Problems	33	36.66
Managerial Problems	36	40.00
Other Problems	9	10.00

Source: Personal Field Survey, Data indicate multiple responses.
(No. of Respondents = 90)

Social Problems

The socio-economic situation has becoming more worsening day after day due to many social problems like bandhs, general strike, law and order situation, militants outfit and act of terrorism, which severely affect the progress of entrepreneurship. All the 90 respondents of the survey have reacted against the ill effect and the consequence of law and order situation. The militant outfit and different unlawful organizations have been a big troublesome to the different entrepreneur operated in Manipur. Expansion and development of business have to keep in consideration with the mercy of different outfit.

Table 18.5: Social Problems of Entrepreneur

Problems	*No. of Response*	*Percentage*
Law and Order Situation	75	83.33
Work Culture of the Society	6	06.66
Economic Backwardness	21	23.33
Lack of Confidence	6	06.66
Lack of Education and Information	15	16.66

Source: Personal Field Survey, Data indicate multiple responses. (No. of Respondents = 90)

Earlier the Manipuri societies have a bad work culture, most of youth seek for Government Job, but nowadays the time has changed and they are working to get self-employment. As per the report of PIB, Government of Manipur (Based on 61st Round of NSS), the percentage of person below poverty line in the year 2004-05 is 17.30 while it was 28.54 and 33.78 per cent in 1999-2000 and 1993-94 respectively. The statistics revealed that there is tremendous development in the rate of persons in below poverty line, but they have less means to establish their own venture due to lack of education and information. Simply it is also true that establishment of own venture in the field of village industry need skilled and experience which may be either acquired from past job or family business, therefore it is important to have enough skill and experience, apart from modern education and information of current trend for both domestic and global.

Marketing Problems

Most of the production in village and cottage industry in the state means for local sales, except some enterprises that are participating in National and International Trade Fair. Due to the lack of marketing knowledge, many entrepreneurs cannot cover a wide market area. The products of handicraft have a good demand all-over the country but cannot met all the demand due to improper strategy of marketing. The number of handicraft artisans in the state in the year 2004-05 cross 4.01 lakhs. Some local entrepreneur have expressed about the differentiation in pricing of their products with those which have a good image in various trade fairs. Most of the handloom products have local demand only and it needs to be more diversifying, keeping in view the choice of the people around the country. There are always problems of lack of proper publicity/advertisement of their products/services on account of limited availability of finance by looking for cheaper alternatives.

Table 18.6: Marketing Problems of Entrepreneur

Problems	*No. of Response*	*Percentage*
Lack of Marketing knowledge	21	50.00
Marketing Competition	3	07.14
Difficulties due to Middlemen	3	07.14
Inadequate Sales Promotion	12	28.57
Unavailability of Sales Outlet	15	35.71
Others	6	14.28

Source: Personal Field Survey, Data indicate multiple responses. (No. of Respondents = 42)

Problems in Availing Government Assistance

Government of India is putting its maximum effort for the development of Micro, Small and Medium Enterprises in the country. The Khadi and Village Industries Commission was established with a view to create employment opportunities in the rural areas. It promotes and extends financial support for implementation of Khadi programme in the form of free loan and grant under capital expenditure and working capital.

But in practice selected entrepreneur have expressed their view regarding the difficulties in obtaining various government assistance. During the survey 63.33 per cent of the respondents were found to be facing one problem or the other pertaining to government assistance. Paper formalities and complicated procedure like preparation of project report has been a big troublesome to innocent rural entrepreneur and on the other hand they also expressed about the lack of awareness regarding the various programmes and schemes taken up by the Government of India.

Table 18.7: Problems in Availing Assistance

Problems	*No. of Response*	*Percentage*
Tedious and Complicated Formalities	33	57.89
Lack of Awareness	9	15.78
Corruption	21	36.82
Time Consuming	9	15.78
Others	3	05.26

Source: Personal Field Survey, Data indicate multiple responses. (No. of Respondents = 57)

Some of the respondents have due consent regarding the selection of beneficiaries. Sometimes, the innocent rural entrepreneur felt that if the official procedure of selecting beneficiaries are affected by the influence of politicians, bureaucrats or other outfits. Officials of government departments are also facing the same problems of pressures from different directions. Some of the respondents do not know where the office of KVIC is actually located, but they have already heard about the activities of this body.

As per the response given by one of the officials of KVIC, the project report prepared by the entrepreneur do not fulfill the right criteria; need to be modifying again and again.

Financial Problems

Finance is considered as the life blood of a business. One of the reasons for declining the line of business activities is the mismanagement of fund. Lack of adequate finance at the time of starting the enterprises is one of the crucial problems faced by them. Out of the 30 respondents, 20 expressed the problems in getting loans and subsidies. In spite of not able to keep collateral securities, rural entrepreneur are not aware about the channel for applying and getting the benefit. Lack of working capital also hampers the activities of the business. They have expressed the view that self finance and loan from unorganized sector should be more timely and fruitful but it bears high rate of interest and more risky.

Table 18.8: Financial Problems of Entrepreneur

Problems	*No. of Response*	*Percentage*
Getting Loan and Subsidies	60	80.00
Tight Repayment Schedule	12	16.00
Poor Financial Management	18	24.00
Inability to Provide Collateral Securities and Margin Money	12	16.00

Source: Personal Field Survey, Data indicate multiple responses. (No. of Respondents = 75)

Production Problems

Production in an enterprise is the result of the coordination of many activities like availability of raw materials, working area, technical support, power supply etc. Out of the 90 respondents, 33 have one or more problems regarding their production activities. 114 village industry units based on agro, forest and food are operated in Imphal East and West District of the State, which rely on locally available raw materials, but now a days these locally available materials have become scarcer due to the deterioration of nature and deforestation. The entrepreneurs have to install their workshed with no proper amenities. They always face problems in acquiring the advance technology due to limited knowledge and supportive service to assist them.

Table 18.9: Production Problems to Entrepreneur

Problems	*No. of Response*	*Percentage*
Unavailability of Raw Material	12	36.36
Inadequate Working Area	15	45.45
Inadequate Technical Support	6	18.18
Irregular Power Supply	33	100.00
Others	12	36.30

Source: Personal Field Survey, Data indicate multiple responses. (No. of Respondents = 33)

Managerial Problems

Some entrepreneurs are well versed with the entrepreneurial talents and already attended many entrepreneurship development programmes. Most of the respondents did not have basic knowledge of general management and labour administration. There are many governmental and non-governmental agency that arrange entrepreneurship development programme like Institute of Cooperative Management (ICM), All Manipur Entrepreneurship Association (AMEA), Khadi and Village Industries Commission (KVIC), Small Industries Service Institute etc., they also impart technical and non-technical skills to labour and entrepreneurs at different levels. It is revealed from the interviews that one of the results of failure in the business of village industries is lack of managerial knowledge, even if they have good skills in their work.

Table 18.10: Managerial Problems to Entrepreneur

Problems	*No. of Response*	*Percentage*
Lack of Managerial Knowledge	24	66.66
Improper Record Keeping	24	66.66
Unavailability of Skilled Labour	3	08.33
Unclear Objectives	6	16.66
Others	3	08.33

Source: Personal Field Survey, Data indicate multiple responses. (No. of Respondents = 36)

Other Problems

Even though there is tremendous potential in the village industries, the indigenous methods, experience and design of this region could not compete with the national and international products. Workshed are not separated from their houses, they used to install their machinery around some corner in the courtyard or parlour. Due to limitation in financial resources the machinery are not standardized and outdated. Lack of technical knowledge, production know-how, present market trend, etc. has been one of the reasons that hamper the performance of entrepreneur. On the other hand the entrepreneurs like to take less risk and prefer a stable and secured job.

Table 18.11: Other Problems to Entrepreneur

Problems	*No. of Response*	*Percentage (%)*
Improper Transportation	3	33.33
No Proper Workshed	6	66.66
Inadequate Machinery	9	100.00
Less Technical Support	6	66.66
Preference for stability and Security	0	—

Source: Personal Field Survey, Data indicate multiple responses. (No. of Respondents = 9)

Suggestive Measures

As regard the different problems faced by the various entrepreneurs following suggestions would like to be forwarded as a measure to resolve its difficulties.

- The relationship of banker with the entrepreneur seems to be not excellent, therefore the Government of Manipur as well as the different supportive agencies should arrange conglomeration meet for a better relation.
- It is also the responsibility of the state government to uplift the socio-economic condition of the state, since the law and order situation is a main factor in hampering the entrepreneurship activities.

- Entrepreneurship must be the first priority option to the educated youth of the state otherwise the pace of the economic development will remain very slow.
- The foremost step in the development of village industries is to establish customer loyalty with personal contact and satisfy them with their credibility and quality of the products.
- Apart from skill acquired from past experience and elders of their family, it will be very important to understand the latest and sophisticated technique from some other advance enterprises, which can be gathered from training, EDP and exposition to other firm.
- Advertisement and sales promotion has been always lagging behind from other entrepreneurial activities. Even though the products of village industries are very good people are not aware about it, particularly those who are outside the state. Therefore, initiative should be taken up to cover all the products of village industries under one common brand.
- System of packing and bottling are not standardized and cannot compete with the various MNCs and big enterprises. So, the government should assist the entrepreneurs with the right technology for packing and bottling.
- Right identification of beneficiaries for grant of subsidy and loan is the foremost and crucial activities, since it is the main reason to promote aspirant entrepreneur and on the same way wrong identification also deride prospective entrepreneur. Therefore, the government and development agencies decision should be free from bias.
- Workshed and plot should be especially reserved for deserving village entrepreneur with uninterrupted power supply. Since the state is at the grim of shortage of power supply, it is suggested that government should initiate to implement prospective mini and micro hydel power project for uninterrupted power supply of the state.

Conclusions

The present study was a brief attempt to analyze the entrepreneurial problems of village industries in the Imphal East and West District of Manipur. From the above analysis we have come to conclude that the operation of village industries are entangled with different problems.

The present socio-economic and political environment seems to be becoming more severe. Therefore, it is very important to make an earnest attempt to resolve the economic problems in the state through the employment of educated youths of different backgrounds in the village industries, because they will prove to be more innovative and aspirant.

The development of village industries will be a revival of degrading Gandhian ideology in this modern age of hypocrisy. It will be the awakening of true philosophy of no mass production but production by the mass.

It will be a crucial decision of the government of the state to add more extra curriculum activities in the syllabus of school and university that orient into development of skills and entrepreneurial knowledge to the young students. They should be properly influenced to adopt entrepreneurship activities, instead of looking for some meagre salaried job of limited income because, it is an alternative means to increase net domestic income of the state.

Finally but not the least, the entrepreneur need to diversify their products looking forward into the present global trend and orient to compete with international firm.

REFERENCES

Census Report on Handloom, 1996-97, Directorate of Commerce and Industries, Government of Manipur.

Basic Statistics of North Eastern Region 2006, Evaluation and Monitoring Sector North Eastern Council, Secretariat, Government of India, Nongrim Hill.

Sharma, DD and Dhameja SK, "Women and Rural Entrepreneurship" Abhishek Publications (2007), Chandigarh.

Prasain, G.P., *Entrepreneurship and Small Scale Industries*, Akansha Publishing House (2006), New Delhi.

Sreedevi, R., *Village Industries in Kerala - Problems and Prospects*, Mahatma Gandhi University (1992), Kerala (Thesis Unpublished).

Annual Report, Ministry of Agro and Rural Industries, Government of India (2005-06).

Annual Report (2006-07), Ministry of Small Scale Industries, Government of India.

Khadi and Village Industries, *Activities and Programmes*, 2006-07, KVIC, Manipur.

Datta Ray, Gurudas Das, *Dimensions of Rural Development in North-East India*, Akansha Publishing House (2004), New Delhi.

KVIC 1956—2006 Golden Jubilee, Directorate of Publicity, KVIC (2006), Mumbai.

19

Women Entrepreneurship in Small and Cottage Industry of Nepal: A Tool of Poverty Alleviation

VED RAJ ACHARYA

Background

Industrial development is the key to rapid economic progress of a country. Industrialization not only provides opportunity for employment and produces other amenities of life, but it also helps accelerate the development of other sectors of the economy. A nation's move upwards for a rural economy to an efficient one with higher levels of material well-being mainly through industrialization. Industry provides employment, relieves population pressure on land, raises living standard of the people, develops technological and managerial skills, and enables export development and import substitution.

Industrialization is not merely a means to enhance production, nor is it merely the introduction of new technology: it is a change process affecting social and economic backwardness of a developing country like Nepal can only be developed by gearing up of industries (Thapa, 1993).

In Nepalese context, due to low disposable income among the people, inadequate infrastructure and scattered market situation in many of developing countries like Nepal, the prospects for establishing big enterprises are limited. Therefore, the importance of small enterprise development is profound. Similarly, lesser growth of agriculture and higher rate of population also require small enterprise development to generate employment and income of the majority of people especially in rural areas where till now economic activities invariably are limited (Bista and Shrestha, 2000). Cottage industries are the oldest industries of Nepal. These are operated mainly by family members either as a part-time job or as a full-time job. In most cases, outside labourers either are not employed in it and the productive work brings largely on the skill of the craftsman. Since cottage industries in rural areas are greatly associated with agriculture, these are conducted mainly as a seasonal job.

Small scale industries, on the other hand, are operated mainly with the help of outside labourers ranging in most cases from 10 to 25 heads. These industries are generally operated as a full-time occupation in both rural and urban areas. Cloth weaving, blanket weaving, wood carving, furniture making, curio goods making, oil processing, dyeing and printing, etc. are some of the most important small scale industries of Nepal (Shrestha, 1998). Nepal is predominantly rural and subsistence agriculture economy. Hence, the role of cottage and small industries is of utmost importance (Kansakar, 1996). In this regard, the famous economist mentioned his view in his famous book *Asian Drama*, "Crafts and small-scale enterprises have deep and well-established roots in South Asia's indigenous economic development."

Economy and Poverty in Nepal

The World Bank Report 2000/2001 states that "Poverty is more than inadequate income or human development; it is also vulnerability and lack of voice, power and representation." Thus, the poverty is the situation of inadequate income, illiteracy, malnutrition, lack of social services like health care, sanitation and lack of social and political status.

The level of living of the people of Nepal is influenced by several factors viz., the stock of resources and their distribution pattern, the size and the growth rate of population, the initiation of the efforts on modernization, and interest and commitments of the people to solve their problem. In many respects, unless the urges for bringing change will not occur in the mind of the beneficiaries of such changes, society cannot be changed. Poverty is resulted with several elements and interrelationship between poverty and other factors, which are very intricate and demand for a comprehensive policy to overcome the problems arising out of them (Timilsina, 2000).

Total population of Nepal in 2001 was 23.15 million and is growing at 2.1 per cent per annum. It is projected that the total population will reach to 32.7 million by 2015 (UNDP HDR, 2000).

Nepalese people are rural in character because majority of people are living in rural areas. Though the proportion of population living in rural areas is declining in Nepal over time, it is still more than 85 per cent in 2001. Similarly, majority of people were living in hill areas of Nepal until 1991 but the proportion living in Tarai has surpassed hill since 1991. The proportion of population living in hill and mountain areas of Nepal is declining over time, while on the other hand it is increasing in Tarai (Shakya, 2004).

Nepal's economy and society have seen significant changes and improvements over the last two decades. The economy has diversified. The share of agriculture has decreased from 62 per cent of the economy 25 years ago to less than 40 per cent now, while the share of industry has increased from 13 per cent in the 1970s to 20 per cent. Gross School enrollment has increased from 78 per cent in 1980 to 113 per cent today, and longevity from 48 years in 1980 to 59 years. Acceleration of per capita economic growth to 2.5 per cent since the mid-1980s, compared to a growth of less than 1 per cent before then, has helped to underpin these changes. It shows that the economy has become more integrated, as the share of trade in goods and non-factor services has nearly doubled over the past decade to about 50 per cent of GDP, the second highest ratio in South Asia (MoS, 2004).

Despite these improvements, as its per capita income indicates, Nepal still has a highly underdeveloped, predominantly agrarian economy, with agriculture accounting for around 40 per cent of GDP and 76 per cent of employment, manufacturing accounts for a mere 9 per cent of GDP. Even after the progress of recent decades in developing physical infrastructure and human capital, Nepal is the least developed of South Asian countries in these areas.

The Nepal Living Standards Survey, 2003-04 estimated that 31 per cent of Nepalese were living below the poverty line. There is significant disparity in the incidence of poverty, and its spatial dimensions are marked. First, poverty is predominantly rural, rural poverty rates are nearly twice those of urban areas, and more than 90 per cent of the poor live in rural areas. As data shows, 4 per cent of people living in the urban Kathmandu valley are poor, in contrast to 56 per cent living in the mountains. The eastern region has much less poverty than the mountain or hill regions or the mid-western region generally. Not coincidentally, especially poor regions are those where transport infrastructure is poor, resulting in inadequate development of markets and commerce and poor government services.

The evidences suggest that poverty in Nepal is correlated with such factors as family size, dependency ratio, and size of landholdings and use of irrigation in agriculture, level of education of the head of the household, in addition to distance from markets and degree of commercialization. Typically a poor rural family has a large family size with a high dependency ratio, low landholdings with mostly non-irrigated land, is relatively less educated, lives farther from markets, and depends on its own production or wage labour. Poor households also depend on labour remittances, but these come from family members working in Nepal, as opposed to other better-off households, whose remittances come from earnings outside the country.

Situation of Women Entrepreneurs in Nepal

Women and development have become in the last two decades an important space within the development literature. Now a days, it seems the role of extensive documentation on the impact of development on Third World Women. Rapid industrialization and the introduction of modern technology have been the basic tools for bringing about development. Behind these two causes, on the context of traditional economies, have generated bad impact to destabilize the situation. In this process, women have had a particularly raw deal. Inherent contradictions in policies led to the displacement of women without their incorporation into the new economy. The position of women in the handicrafts industry is a case in point, where their marginalization has accompanied the well-intentioned efforts of policy-makers (Deshmukh, 1989).

In Nepalese context , women entrepreneurship, in a formalized sense, is a relatively new phenomenon in Nepal. Although certain ethnic communities in the country, especially the Newars and Tibeto-Burman Highland Groups such as the Sherpas, Gurungs, Thakalis are known to have long tradition of women being involved in small business enterprises (CEDA, 1981). But for the past 3 decades the concept of women entrepreneurship has progressively gained some achievements with perception of their importance in Nepalese society. It is almost proved that women have unique talents which could be harnessed for development creating employment opportunities for others. They can contribute in the national economy with remarkable quantities.

Gender equality and economic development go hand in hand. Since the early 1980s, the policy-makers and planners have become acutely aware of the economic significance of women's productive activities and the nature of their contribution to income generation. It has been firmly established that women in Nepal are vital and productive contributors to the national economy but their access to knowledge, skills, resources, opportunities and power still remain rather low (Shtrishakti, 1995).

Although women constitute a little over one half of Nepal's population, they rank lower than men in almost every social indicator in the country. Due in part to their lower education levels women also earn less than men. The proportion of men currently employed in the formal non-agricultural or "modern" occupational sector is much higher (21%) than that of women (6%). Women continue to be confined primarily to unpaid family labour. Nearly 60 per cent of currently employed women fall in this category, compared to 21 per cent of men (The World Bank and DFID, 2006).

In the present context, women's participation in the modernizing sectors of the economy is increasing. And, manufacturing of commodities such as carpets is shifting to the factory place from the household. Trade and services sector businesses are also getting formalized. Women are slowing coming out to join these expanding modern sectors, particularly in manufacturing, trade and commerce in urban areas. After agriculture, it is these sectors that employ the largest share of women. Tourism and related sectors have expanded the employment opportunities for women to some extent (Acharya, 2000).

Over the past thirty years women's participation in economic activities has also moved beyond agriculture into the local market economy. In search for wage employment, women are moving into small business and self-employment ventures thereby creating many formal and informal opportunities for work. Women are increasingly migrating to urban areas for employment in a range of cottage industries, such as carpet weaving, textiles and handicrafts, and service sector as well.

By 1970s, entrepreneurship had been an unknown territory for women in Nepal. Some women, who were courageous and career conscious they joined the jobs as teacher in schools, clerks in the government offices and banks. But, 1980s proved to be an important decade in the history of women entrepreneurship, as a few enterprising women stepped into the world of entrepreneurship. Establishment of women focused entrepreneurship organizations, such as, Women Entrepreneurs' Association of Nepal (WEAN) and creation of Women Entrepreneurship Development Committee (WEDC) under the umbrella of the Federation of Nepalese Chamber of Commerce and Industry (FNCCI), which is apex body in the field of business and industries were the important milestones for women entrepreneurship development in Nepal. WEAN focused its programmes for creation and development of women entrepreneurs through various skill upgrading and entrepreneurship trainings integrated with product development, marketing and micro-credit programmes. Such trainings were conducted in close cooperation with various government and non-government organizations such as Cottage and Small Industries Development Board (CSIDB), Small Business Promotion Project (SBPP) (now called IEDI). Similarly, WEDC constructed on development of women units in the district chamber of commerce and to support fully for the upliftment of the existing women entrepreneurship organizations through various programmes. Establishment of Mahaguthi, Sana-Hastakala and Association for Craft Producers (CAP) and WEAN co-operative further helped to market the handicraft and agro products, in which women have been traditionally good. Women saw the new avenue in the field of economic empowerment through entrepreneurship apart from working as service holders and working in wage earning jobs, Government organizations, Non-governmental Organizations (NGOs), and international non-governmental organizations (Shrestha, 2001).

As per the Census, 2001 women constitute almost 43 per cent of the labour force, 48 per cent in agriculture, and 34 per cent in the non-agriculture sector. This increase is accounted for by three factors; increase in actual participation defined as economic, redefinition of the activities themselves, and more detailed and specific description activities in the census manual and training. All these factors are positive from the perspective of women's empowerment (Acharya, 2003).

The development of major export industries, such as carpet, garments, and wooden goods, has opened new avenues of formal employment for women. The proportion of women in the non-agricultural workforce has increased to 34 per cent. However, here also women are concentrated at low paying and less productive, low capital intensive jobs (NLFS, 1999). Most of the labour regulations are sidetracked by employing women at piece rates (GDS/FES, 1997, GEFONT, 2003). Overall women earn about 4/5th of what men earn in agriculture, but 3/4th outside of agriculture as daily wages.

Table 19.1: Selected Indicators on Economic Activity and Workforce 2001

Indicators/Years	*1981*	*1991*	*2001*
Male	83.1	68.1	71.7
Female	46.2	45.2	55.3
Female % total economically active	34.6	40.4	43.4
Female % in agriculture	36.4	45	48.1
Female % in non-agriculture jobs	14.3	20.2	34.4
Female/Male Wage Ratio			
Agriculture	-	-	5/4
Non-agriculture jobs	-	-	4/3
Female % total working force (usually Economically active+home-makers)	50.8	53.6	52.5
Female % among full time home-makers	99.7	90.8	94.9

Source: Population Census 2001.

A substantial proportion of women are confined to household work due to social and reproductive reasons. Even if the home-making activities, such as household maintenance and childcare, do not fall within the production boundary defined by the system of National Accounts (UN, 1993). Currently, such activities nevertheless are necessary for human reproduction and no economy can survive without them.

As to the access of women to economic assets and property, there is no ground to believe that women's access to land and other economic resources have increased in the last 20-25 years as their legal rights over property and inheritance has not changed much during this period. Even the recently promulgated amendment to the law on property rights of women does not change her access to parental property substantially. The law however, does provide easier access to property for her in household. As per the census 2001, about 11 per cent of the households reported some land in female legal ownership (Table 19.2).

Similarly, only 5.5 per cent of the households had some house in women's name. Only 7.2 per cent households reported female livestock ownership does in spite multiple credit-institutions targeting and funding this activity for women. In spite of various credit programmes, women's access to institutional credit remains marginal, both at individual and household enterprise levels irrespective of ecological regions, urban/rural areas and ethnicity/caste (Acharya, 2002). Only 0.8 per cent of the households had all three — house, land, and livestock in female ownership. Almost 83 per cent of the household had no property, whatsoever, under women's legal ownership. Women get only half the earned income of what men get, in terms of purchasing power parity (purchasing power parity dollar is a more realistic measure of purchasing power of income converted into US $ at market rates. It compares the basket of goods the two currencies can bye in their respective areas).

Female-headed households, which constituted about 15 per cent of the total households, owned smaller landholdings than the male-headed ones. Compared to male heads, female heads of the households were educationally much more disadvantaged.

Table 19.2: Selected Indicators on Income and Property, 2001

Per capita Purchasing Power Party ratio PPP$	
Male	1752
Female	880
Female/Male Ratio	0.5
Female Ownership of Property in Percent to total	
House	5.5
Land	10.8
Livestock	7.2
House, land and livestock	0.8
None	82.9
Operational Landholdings (hectares)	
Male-Headed Households	0.78
Female-Headed Households	0.58
Population Illiterate	
Male Heads	36.2
Female Heads	64
With Graduate and above education	
Male Heads	9.2
Female Heads	4.5

Source: Acharya, 2003.

Features of Women Entrepreneurship in Nepal

- Enterprises are started at later stage of life,
- enterprises are established at micro level,
- starting of enterprises without adequate technical training,
- small number of employees,
- not able to take big risk,
- tendency for proprietorship, and
- Multiple burdens (Shrestha, 2001).

Type of Enterprises Women are Involved in:

- Agro-based enterprises,
- handicraft,
- service business, and
- Trading (Shrestha, 2001).

In this context, the feminine enterprises are not found successful. There was clear contradiction in the qualities that were seen necessary for a successful entrepreneur with the Table below:

Feminine Entrepreneurs	Successful Entrepreneurs
1. Modest goal on profit.	1. Aggressive goals on profit.
2. Primary interest in personal satisfaction.	2. Interest in continued growth.
3. Small and good preferred.	3. Big and profit generation.
4. Low capital in finance.	4. High capital relies on equity.
5. Products, which need personalized service.	5. Look at certain niches.
6. Enters agreements in the small market.	6. Seeks larger markets.
7. System seems to remain informal, decentralized and small.	7. System formalized and centralized.
8. Personal approaches and non-monetary.	8. Monetary and non-personalized rewards, merits.
9. Weak in management.	9. Strong in management.
10. Operational control remains weak, unsystematic, record-keeping not strong.	10. Operational control strong and centralized, systematic and record-keeping is one of the first things emphasized upon.
11. Small size, family personnel, little expertise when hiring staff.	11. Staff grows rapidly, impersonal advice.
12. Friendly, motherly, sisterly, team oriented and informal.	12. Impersonal, formal, almost autocratic in the beginning becomes more delegate.
13. Not very assertive, sense of power is not kept, decision making is more intuitive and emotional.	13. Decision making is intuitive but rational.

(Tuladhar, 1998).

As the above table shows, women had basic management skills gained by home and family management experience. But the enterprises demand a different kind of management – a systematic, record-keeping and non-personalized management.

Problems of Women Entrepreneurs

- Lack of access to land and property and control over financial assets or resources.
- Lack of inheritance rights to land and property.
- Limited government resource allocation for women's programmes.
- Lack of appropriate business training and adequate level of education.
- Lack of access to bank loan and credit.
- Lack of social support and triple roles and responsibilities.
- Lack of information dissemination about the appropriate technologies.
- Lack of mobility.
- Low level of confidence.
- Low value attached to women's work.

Recommendations

- Various skill developments training for women and women entrepreneurs should be conducted by the government, NGOs and INGOs.
- Government should mobilize INGOs and NGOs to provide necessary training on product design, marketing costing, pricing and book-keeping.
- Government resources allocation should be adequately increased for conducting various women development programme.
- Government should legalize equal inheritance rights of land and property to women.
- Access to bank loan and credit should be improved by the government for women and women entrepreneurs.
- Women and women entrepreneurs should be active in quickly collecting their long-term credit on sales.

- Proper channels should be developed for information dissemination about appropriate business technology.
- Women entrepreneurs should be aware of government policy regarding their business.
- Women entrepreneurs should improve their mobility.

Conclusion

Governmental efforts towards women entrepreneurs are not adequate. The activities and initiations taken by women for self-development are not advanced and in accordance with the need of the day. Thus, the efforts of government and initiation by women themselves are needed to be broadening.

REFERENCES

Acharya, Meena (2000). *Labour Market Development and Poverty with Focus on Opportunities for Women in Nepal*. Kathmandu: Tanka Prasad Acharya Memorial Foundation and FES.

Acharya, Meena, (2003). *Efforts at Promotion of Women in Nepal*. Kathmandu: Tanka Prasad Acharya Memorial Foundation and FES.

Bista, Nirmal K. and Shrestha Binod K. (2000). Entrepreneurship and Enterprise Development on SMEs in Nepal: Challenges and Opportunities, *Economic Journal of Development Issues*, Vol. 1, No. 2 (July-December 2000). Kathmandu: The Department of Economics, Patan Multiple Campus, Tribhuvan University.

Centre of Economic Development and Administration (CEDA) (1981). *The Rural Women of Nepal: An Aggregate Analysis*, A summary of Eight Villages Studies, Kathmandu: CEDA.

Deshmukh, Joy P. (1989). *Women in Development in South Asia*, (ed.) V. Kauesalingam, New Delhi: Committee on Studies for Cooperation in Development in South Asia.

GDS/ FES (1997). *Women in Garment Industries*, Kathmandu: GDS/FES.

GEFONT (2003). *Search for Alternatives*, Kathmandu: GEFONT.

Kanskar, Vidya Bir Singh (1996). Role of Rural Development Projects in the Growth of Cottage and Small Industries in Nepal, *Social Economy and National Development*, (eds.) Madan K. Dahal and Horst Mund. Kathmandu: NEFAS and FES.

Ministry of Supplies, Government of Nepal (2004). *Nepal: Trade and Competitiveness Study*. Kathmandu: Ministry of Supplies.

Shakya, Dhanendra Veer (2004). Population Characteristics of Nepal, 1971-2001, *Nepal Population Journal*, Vol. 2, No. 10, July 2004, Kathmandu: Population Association of Nepal.

Shrestha, SH (1998). *Economic Geography of Nepal*. Kathmandu: Educational Enterprises Pvt. Ltd.

Shrestha, Shyam Badan (2001). *Women Entrepreneurship Development in SMEs, Small and Medium Enterprises Development in Nepal*, (eds.) Bishwa Maskey and Narayan Manandhar. Kathmandu: Centre for Development and Governence and FNCCI.

Shtri Shakti (1995). *Women, Development Democracy: A Study of the Socio-economic Change in the Status of Women in Nepal (1981- 1993)*, Prepared for USAID, DANIDA, CCO.

Thapa, Ajit Narayan S. (1993). Industrial Development in Nepal: Issues and Perspectives, Future of Nepalese Economy (ed.) Madan K. Dahal. Kathmandu: *Nepal Foundation for Advanced Studies* (NEFAS) and Friedrich Ebert Stiftung (FES).

The World Bank and DFID (2006). *Unequal Citizens*. Kathmandu: The World Bank and DFID.

Timilsina, P.P. (2000). Poverty in Nepal : Some Issues and Perspectives, *Economic Journal of Development Issues*, Vol. 1, No. 2 (July-December 2000). Kathmandu: The Department of Economics, Patan Multiple Campus, Tribhuvan University.

Tuladhar, Jyoti (1998). *Poverty Alleviation through Women Entrepreneurship Development*: Social Aspects, Paper presented in SAARC Level Seminar-cum-Exhibition on Poverty Alleviation through Women Entrepreneurship Development, Kathmandu, Nepal 5-7 Sept. 1998 organised by Federation of Nepal Cottage and Small Industries.

UNDP (2000). *Human Development Report 2000*, New York: UNDP.

20

Entrepreneurial Efficiency for Production of Bio-diesel in Rural Energy Needs

S. SURESH KUMAR AND M. MURALIDHAR

Introduction

With the increasing concerns of finding sustainable alternative renewable sources of energy for rural energy needs, bio-diesel seems to be one of the good options for alternative source of energy in future. Arunachal Pradesh being hilly terrain, having vast wasted and barren lands has scope of cultivation of bio-diesel which will not only meet the rural energy needs of this region but also improve the economic development of particular region. Besides contributing to the clean environment it also provides freedom to rural areas to access power and agricultural purposes. Cultivation and consumption of bio-diesel derived from oil bearing trees prevent soil erosion and global warming. Hence bio-diesel standout as the most preferred alternative fuel for rural energy needs as well as sustainable growth.

Rural Energy Resources

- firewood
- manure
- solar energy
- biogas
- biofuels

Firewood: These are the natural resources of energy which are freely available abundantly in forest areas where local population can easily access to convert these into useful work like cooking of food etc. But more use of these resources leads to depletion of forest covers as well as negative environmental effects.

Manure: It is directly available from the domestic animals waste and contributes more smoke while utilizing these resources. Using of manure is being discouraged because it consumes most valuable manure which could be used in agriculture.

Solar Energy: This energy is directly available from the sun through radiation.

Biogas: Biogas is produced from shrubs, farm waste, animal and human wastes. It is mostly used for domestic consumption in rural areas. Decomposition of organic matter yields gas, which has higher thermal efficiency in comparison to kerosene, dung cake and charcoal.

Biofuels: Biofuels are renewable liquid fuels coming from biological raw materials specially grown for biofuel production including from jatropha and pongamia.

Bio-diesel

Bio-diesel is a substitute for, or an additive to, diesel fuel that is derived from the oils and fats of plants, like Sunflower, Canola or Jatropha.It is an alternative fuel that can be used in diesel engines and provides power similar to conventional diesel fuel. Bio-diesel is a renewable domestically produced liquid fuel that can help reduce the countries dependence on foreign oil imports.

Advantages of Bio-diesel

- Bio-diesel is the most valuable form of renewable energy that can be used directly in any existing, unmodified diesel engine.
- Bio-diesel fuel can be produced from oilseed plants such as rape seeds, sunflower, jatropha and pongamia.
- Bio-diesel is environmental friendly and ideal for heavily polluted cities.
- Bio-diesel is as biodegradable as salt.
- Bio-diesel produces 80 per cent less carbon dioxide and 100 per cent less sulphur dioxide emissions. It provides a 90 per cent reduction in cancer risks.
- Bio-diesel can be used alone or mixed in any ratio with mineral oil diesel fuel. The preferred ratio if mixture ranges between 5 and 20 per cent (B5 - B20).
- Bio-diesel extends the life of diesel engines.

- Bio-diesel is cheaper then mineral oil diesel.
- Bio-diesel is conserving natural resources.

Bio-diesel plantation in Arunachal Pradesh

Arunachal Pradesh has lot of degraded forest lands where climatic, topographic and geographic condition is suitable for cultivation of bio-diesel plant. Some of the advantages are listed below for the cultivation of jatropha plant:

- Sufficient degraded lands
- Less input compared with other commercial crops
- Less gestation period i.e. one year
- Easy to cultivate
- Financial support from various financial institutions.

As such there is good prospect of jatropha cultivation in Arunchal Pradesh in the degraded forest land, abandoned lands which are not suitable for cultivation of commercial crops.

Bio-diesel Extraction

The process of converting vegetable oil into bio-diesel fuel is called Transesterification. Chemically, Transesterification means taking a triglyceride molecule, or a complex fatty acid, neutralizing the free fatty acids, removing the glycerine, and creating an alcohol ester. This is accomplished by mixing methanol with sodium hydroxide to make sodium methoxide. This liquid is then mixed into the vegetable oil. After the mixture has settled, Glycerine is left on the bottom and methyl esters, or bio-diesel is left on top and is washed and filtered. The final product Bio-diesel fuel, when used directly in a Diesel Engine will burn up to 75 per cent cleaner than mineral oil Diesel fuel.

The technology is mature and proven. Presently, the indigenously designed bio-fuel plant for 250 lt./day is in operation. We have to design and develop bio-fuel plants of 3 to 10 tonnes per day capacity for installation in different parts of the country. Effective marketing chain needs to be planned for enabling farmers to reap the benefits directly. Biofuel mission will provide technological and employment generation focuses for the rural sector. Use of eleven million hectares of wasteland for Jatropha cultivation can lead to generation of minimum twelve million jobs.

Table 20.1: Properties of Bio-diesel

Sl.No.	*Parameter*	*Bio-diesel*	*BIS Specifications IS 15607:2005*
1	Cetane No	58-62	51(min)
2	Flash point°	>120	120(min)
3	Viscosity@40°C cst	4.5-4.8	2.5-6
4	Calorific Value Kcal/Kg	9600	
5	Density@15°C kg/m^3	874	860-900(max)
6	Boiling Point	>290	
7	Melting Point	12	
8	Pour Point	16	

Application in Rural Areas

- Agriculture
- Power Generation

Biofuel makes an attractive choice to meet the local energy requirements as operating stationary engine for pumping water to agriculture fields and stationary power generation to provide lighting to rural households.

Role of RGP and NERIST in Rural Energy Needs

RGP and NERIST play an important role by organizing workshops, skill orientation programme and conducting regional seminars for the development of rural community which in turn developing the rural areas.

Conclusion

Despite of being rich in natural resources, development of this region has lagged behind rest of the country which is mainly due to lack of infrastructure, poor communication facilities and geographical isolation. Further, inadequate exploitation of natural resources like mineral resources, hydro power potentials, lack of development of industries have contributed significant hurdle for the development in this region. Hence biofuel is the best option for upliftment of rural community and also employment generation especially in rural areas.

REFERENCES

Bio-diesel Revolution, *Science Reporter*, Jan. 2006, pp. 14-15.

Facts and figures of Bio-diesel, Bio-diesel technologies of India, available www.biodieseltechnologiesindia.com

H. Hazarika, P. Rethy, *Prospect of growing Bio-diesel plants in Arunachal Pradesh.*

M. Muralidhar, *Role of biofuels and hydro power in rural energy needs of North-East India.*

Suresh Kumar D. Devarasiddappa, Biofuel-Engine Applications.

Vern Hofmann (2003) *Bio-diesel fuel.* AE-1240, Feb. 2003.

❑❑❑

Index

❑❑❑